The Phantom of the Psyche

Freeing Ourself from Inner Passivity

Peter Michaelson

Library of Congress Catalog Card Number: 2001-130069

Publisher's Cataloging-in-Publication Data

Michaelson, Peter

The Phantom of the Psyche: Freeing Ourself from Inner Passivity

Bibliography: p

1. Self-Actualization (psychology) 2. Personal Growth 3. Applied Psychology 4. Self- Esteem

Author's Note

The names and identifying details in the case histories in this book have been changed to protect confidentiality. Anyone with a history of emotional disorders should consult a mental-health professional before doing the exercises in this book.

To Madeline, Michael, and Nicholas

Also by the Author:

Psyched Up: The Deep Knowledge that Liberates the Self

Why We Suffer: A Western Way to Understand and Let Go of Unhappiness

Democracy's Little Self-Help Book

Freedom from Self-Sabotage: How to Stop Being Our Own Worst Enemy

Secret Attachments: Exposing the Roots of Addictions and Compulsions

See Your Way to Self-Esteem: Healing the Psyche through Depth Psychology

Books by Sandra Michaelson _(1944-1999)__:_

LoveSmart: Transforming the Emotional Patterns that Sabotage Relationships

Is Anyone Listening? Repairing Broken Lines in Couples Communication

The Emotional Catering Service: The Quest for Emotional Independence

To order, visit Amazon.com or the author's website, WhyWeSuffer.com.

Table of Contents

Introduction

The phantom in The Phantom of the Opera is a heavenly singer, tormented by deformity, loneliness, and self-rejection, who prefers the pits of the opera house to the pleasures of the company. This phantom doesn't have a friend in the world, except perhaps for the talented, beautiful Christine, who falls under his spell.

The phantom of the psyche, or what I call inner passivity, also dwells in dark places and hesitates to step out upon the stage of life. We have to go looking for it and persuade or drag it into the open. While this inner phantom is not an evil presence, it is not much of a friend either.

Most people have only a vague sense of this phantom's existence, and most psychologists and mental-health professionals don't address it at all. Only the toxic symptoms of its existence are readily visible. These symptoms include fear, anxiety, distrust, apathy, self-doubt, and loneliness, as well as lack of belief in ourselves and difficulty in regulating our behaviors.

Inner passivity is much more than just our difficulty in standing up for our rights when someone is trying to take advantage of us. It is complex and mysterious, much more elaborate than the conventional meaning of the word passivity. It is everywhere, hiding out in our unconscious mind beneath our anger, disappointment, weariness, lack of fulfillment, and depression.

Inner passivity is front and center in feelings of being helpless, ineffective, and indecisive. It is deeply enmeshed in our feelings of being confused and unworthy, and it is a major contributor to anxiety, procrastination, and failure, as well as to addictive and compulsive behaviors.

When Chapter 1 begins, the inner phantom is no longer described as a character but rather as the psychological characteristic of inner passivity. The phantom drops out of sight, somewhat in the manner of the operatic phantom who, at the climax of the opera, disappears behind his cloak, leaving only a half-mask behind. This book is an exposé of a fundamental psychic element, presented to readers through a combination of metaphoric language, the best information from psychology, my experience as a practicing psychotherapist, and my knowledge as a former science writer. My references to passivity throughout this book are understood to stand for inner passivity.

Chapter 1 of this book is entirely devoted to defining inner passivity and indicating its extent. The rest of this book establishes the case for its existence, shows its consequences, explains why it developed as a fundamental component of our psyche, describes how it can be dislodged, and considers what we might expect of ourselves once free of it.

The Phantom of the Psyche is also my attempt to persuade people to become more respectful of our unconscious side and to make a hero or heroine's effort to penetrate into those mysterious and mythic dimensions of our inner life. Many of us hate any mention of these unconscious realms and are determined to live as if this part of us doesn't exist. Doing this, however, we run the risk of being reactive, easily offended, distrustful, and burdened by dreary, life-effacing negativity. We would almost certainly limit ourselves and risk living out our fate rather than our destiny.

A nasty fall on the ice precipitated a breakthrough in my understanding of inner passivity. While skating in January 2000, I suddenly lost my balance and came crashing down on my back. Instinctively, my hands shot out to break the fall, and I injured my wrists. I hurried home and soaked my forearms in a bucket of ice water—but my wrists soon were severely swollen.

The next day I could barely pull a tissue out of the box. Friends came by to help me prepare dinner and feed my cats. The following day my wrists had recovered enough strength so that I could manage my household. Nevertheless, I shuffled around for several days feeling as if I had aged twenty years.

Yet my fall proved to be a blessing: a caravan of dreams— passivity dreams—visited me nightly for ten days following that accident. In these dreams I was repeatedly entangled in various predicaments involving feelings of being ineffective, and I found myself being indecisive and rendered helpless. Invariably, I "flubbed up" some undertaking or stood by on the sidelines passively observing someone else muddle along.

These dreams uncovered deeper reaches of my psyche and unearthed golden nuggets of insight. For fifteen years I had been intrigued with inner passivity and have read widely to find evidence of it. I also wrote about it in my previous books, though with more limited understanding of this elusive psychic element. My accident and its aftermath opened up a new level of awareness. I began to understand more fully the nature of my inner passivity and to see it more clearly as a universal aspect in the psyches of us all. It is an emotional identification that, for the most part, is unconscious. It is often painful and it always limits how we know and experience ourselves.

In the months following my accident, I redirected my psychotherapy practice to focus more on the influence of this passivity. I began to show my clients where passivity resides in their psyche and how they can free themselves from it. Often they made comments to the effect of, "This is the hardest thing to see; I can't quite get a feeling for it." Soon they did begin to see it in themselves. We penetrated into the mystery of this emotional quirk, humbled and thrilled by new revelations of the depth of our being. Some frustration and grief tempered our satisfaction; as is always the case with inner work, we encountered mazes of dead ends, tangles of deadwood, and choruses of defeat. Yet while psychological growth often moves at a glacier's pace, if at all, here we were, darting quickly through and around our psychic debris, blowing up old defenses, exposing inner lies, recognizing and befriending resistance, and seeing positive results at a comparative lightning speed.

Throughout this book I frequently use the word *ourself*. This word is not often seen in modern usage—the collective *ourselves* is employed instead. Webster's Third New International Dictionary defines *ourself* to mean, "the self that each one of us separately possesses" and "the individual self that each one of us separately is." Many of us experience ourselves as detached, dispersed, and divided. We either take ourselves for granted or else have an antagonistic relationship with ourselves. I use *ourself* in this text to foster recognition of our unique being, to advocate the unification of our conflicting parts, and to promote mastery of our inner self.

My use of the word refers to our psychological center, the inner point of integration or crystallization through which we experience connection, peace, and harmony with our being. The word also suggests the presence of the steward, or potential steward, of our existence, and includes a sense of being our own best friend and supporter. When attuned to ourself, we feel, think, and speak as if we are our own wise advocate. This benevolent sense of self emerges from our inner life, drawn to us and distilled within us as we explore our unconscious issues, eliminate our passivity, and bring together the disparate aspects of our psyche. This is the process of becoming crystallized and self-actualized.

I also refer at times to our true or authentic Self. For the most part, I maintain a secular, psychological stance throughout this book. I have found, though, that the deeper we work on ourselves, the more likely we are to encounter a sense of the divine. We certainly shift in the direction of becoming the better angel of our nature. In any case, my main intention is to show how awareness of inner passivity is a royal road to an improved, more harmonious relationship with others and with our self.

I hadn't expected to write another book. My wife of twenty years and fellow psychotherapist, Sandra Michaelson, died in 1999 of breast cancer. Working together, we each had authored three psychology books— a total of six titles—over a 12-year period. We had labored long hours on each other's books, and now, with her passing, I didn't believe I could go on writing without her help. However, by the late summer of 2000, as my success with clients mounted as a result of my deepening awareness, I couldn't ignore the click of my mouse, the call of my muse.

Whenever I got stuck in the writing process, I went back to Sandra's most recent notes for encouragement and guidance. In the year before she died, as preparation for her next book, she had composed material on the quest for our authentic self, and that writing helped me appreciate more fully the benefits of depth psychology.

Peter Michaelson
Santa Fe, New Mexico
March 2002

Chapter 1
The Prevalence of Passivity

Each of us is under the influence of inner passivity. The presence in the psyche of this emotional element limits the flow of our creativity, hinders our self-expression, and impedes the development of intimacy with others. It interferes with our attempts to connect with and to express our higher values of courage, integrity, compassion, and love.

In these pages we plunge into the depths of our psyche to discover our inner passivity and other startling truths about human nature, particularly knowledge concerning the manner in which we all hold on to negative emotions and create our own misery and defeat.

The passivity I am referring to is much more than the experience of being weak, shy, and timid. This book goes far beyond a discussion of wimps and weaklings. Neither is it about the introverted personality type—an extrovert can be just as passive in the sense I am discussing in this book.

Inner passivity is almost invisible in the psyche and can be best approached and identified through its symptoms. Like subliminal advertising or carbon monoxide, it influences us strongly even as we are oblivious to its presence. It is a subtle phenomenon and a complicated psychic condition that is a problem for both men and women.

This passivity produces an inner determination to replay and recycle unresolved feelings that go back to our childhood. In various situations in the present we feel refused, deprived, controlled, overwhelmed, helpless, and discounted. In childhood we interpreted some of the actions of our parents and siblings through these same feelings. Now as adults, we color the evidence in a given experience, creating the impression that we are indeed being unduly deprived, refused, overwhelmed, and made helpless and ineffective, when in fact the problem is our own inner determination to feel this way.

Our inner passivity plays tricks on us and presents us with challenging conundrums. In one aspect of passivity, for instance, what we most desperately feel we want is often what we are emotionally attached to not getting. We will hurt ourselves and others, sometimes tragically, trying to get what we are attached to not having. Or we will urgently feel the need for a sense of control and power, and act out inappropriately, in order to cover up our readiness to experience some situation in a passive manner.

We have enormous resistance to seeing this phantom component within ourself. Inwardly it is very offensive to consider the implications of it. We either ignore altogether the suggestion of our passivity, conveniently forgetting that it was ever proposed, or we become indignant or angry at the insinuation that inner passivity is a psychological screening system (or RDF—Reality Distortion Field—as one teenage client of mine called it) through which we experience others, the world, and ourself. We prefer to be accused of being cruel, controlling, rejecting, selfish, greedy, or angry rather than being passive.

Passivity takes conventional thinking, or common sense, and throws it for a loop.

Four important attributes of passivity, elaborated upon throughout this book, are listed here to illustrate its nature and influence. These themes reveal the dramatic mental and emotional shift (a true paradigm shift) that absorption of this knowledge and the transformation it implies demand of us.

1. Passivity, not aggression, is the root cause of anger and violence. Unhealthy, reactive aggression is a symptom of passivity, a means through which passivity is covered up, denied, or defended against. Passivity triggers anger when we overreact to an alleged provocation to "prove" (as a defense) that we are not passive—that we will not be pushed around and disrespected. So inappropriate aggression is both a symptom of passivity and a defense against realization of it. Our hostility covers up a deep inner resonance with the feeling of being weak, helpless, overwhelmed, and somehow victimized, feelings that linger in our psyche from childhood. We much prefer to attribute our anger to external provocations such as injustice or oppression, or to blame it on our problem of anger management, rather than see the roots of it in our passivity. (Terrorists, for instance, have a great deal of inner passivity, as I explain in Chapter 4.)

2. Influences such as television and other compelling visual and electronic technologies do not cause passivity. Rather, it is our passivity that causes us to come so much under the influence of inactive forms of entertainment, as well as advertising and propaganda. Under the influence of mass entertainment, we embrace a second-hand experience of life. Visual technologies combined with

cunningly crafted marketing and advertising impair our creativity, undermine our imaginative powers, and make our passivity more of a problem for us. What we are seeing and finding ugly in the couch-potato set is the stranglehold of our own passivity.

3. Addictions to certain substances are, at a deeper level, addictions to passivity. The addiction is not so much to tobacco, alcohol, or drugs as it is to the experience of passivity, meaning the feeling of being under the influence of a craving or desire that feels more powerful than one's ability to resist it—even more powerful than one's own self. Although certain characteristics of our genes and biochemistry can make us more prone to addictions, having an addiction is nonetheless primarily the acting out of an emotional weakness. It is very important to avoid believing that we are victims of our genes or biochemistry, for this belief will render us even more helpless and passive.

When we shake off passivity, we acquire healthy self-regulation. Compulsive behaviors involving overeating, gambling, exercising, shopping, sexual conquest, and maximal cleanliness are also the result of unresolved negative emotions that can be related to inner passivity. Our emotional issues, including our secret affinity for the passive experience, along with our self-aggression and our egotism, generate and maintain negativity within us. We pay a price for our unresolved negativity, often through the lack of both behavioral and emotional self-regulation. To eliminate our negativity, we have to understand its origins and take responsibility for it rather than deny it and try to cover it up.

4. Passivity can hinder us from connecting with our inner resources, such as courage, integrity, purpose, and

perseverance. We lack trust and belief in ourself and fail to support ourself at critical times. We limit ourself and remain fearful and self-preoccupied, unable to access our higher capacities of creativity, self-regulation, trust, humility, compassion, and understanding. Because of the insight gained in the process of overcoming passivity, we act more appropriately and true to our humanity rather than defensive, willful, and inflexible. The absence of inner passivity provides access to our own authority, where we discover that our truth is aligned with universal goodwill.

The best way to access our inner passivity and to see it in action is to examine, as this book does, some of the thousands of symptoms and reactions we have to it. The book also investigates the inner operation and mechanisms of passivity to make it more visible and more accessible for the purposes of dislodging and eliminating it, thus strengthening ourself. Whatever is undiscovered or unresolved in our psyche determines how we will experience ourselves, and we are compelled to act out the hidden dynamics that have not been fully realized and incorporated into our conscious intelligence, even when doing so is self-defeating and painful.

The experience of passivity is imprinted on our psyche through our protracted childhood helplessness. It takes on a life of its own, contributing to our limited and often painful impression of who and what we are. We experience passivity in thousands of different ways, and anyone who wants to eliminate it has to see and understand his or her own unique formulation of it.

Passivity can be present and entrenched in people who outwardly appear to be the strongest and most capable. A person who is powerful in one context can be passive in another. A formidable political leader or the CEO of a large corporation, for instance, who has his colleagues spellbound by his power, may be passive with his wife or children or mother, a condition that is hidden from the public and even from the individual's own awareness. A career climber may run roughshod over his competitors not so much because he is ambitious but because he experiences himself passively when he is not being ruthless and aggressive. So a symptom of passivity can be the appearance of an inappropriate or unbalanced power, in reality a pseudo-power, the exercise of which is a reaction to underlying passivity. This kind of "power" serves as a defense against realization of one's passivity, and invariably it is inappropriate, if not egotistical and offensive, rather than wisely dispensed. In such cases, the individual's unconscious defensive mechanism is saying, for instance, "I'm not passive—look at the power I have and look at all the people who respect me for it."

Similarly, a person who is unable to achieve happiness in relationships may associate the feeling of falling in love or surrendering to another in sexual union, or in the give-and-take of everyday interactions, with submission and passivity. Thus, in defense, this person resists or avoids such experiences, withdraws and holds resentment, or becomes angry and critical. Though this person may be desperate for intimacy, invariably he or she sabotages it. We fear intimacy because it feels too much like being absorbed and taken over by our partner. But in reality surrender as expressed in a healthy relationship is a letting go of our passivity and ego, and a sign of trust in life, our partner, and ourself.

Our reactions to passivity are usually self-defeating, some more so than others. For instance, an overweight person finishing off a bag of cookies may say, as he musters up the feeling that he is acting through his own power and volition, "No one is going to tell me what I can and can't eat. I'll eat what I want, when I want." Thus, he feels powerful, but at the heart of the matter is his passivity, made visible through his submission to his craving for food and the self-destructive consequences of overeating.

Through passivity, we do not act; rather we react. Through passivity, we feel nothing when it is appropriate to feel something, or we feel a strong negative emotion when the situation we are encountering doesn't call for such a reaction. A passive reaction can also consist of doing something that is inappropriate while not recognizing what is appropriate.

Passivity is often experienced as a sense of inertia, as having no power, being stuck, unable to move forward in one's life or powerless to make something positive happen. It is the condition of accepting one's fate rather than believing in and creating one's destiny. As one person put it, "It is the feeling that things happen to me rather than me choosing." It is also the condition of believing in oneself and one's destiny but not being able to fulfill it. Another person told me, "Sometimes I feel I'm all dressed up, ready to go, but my shoes are tied together."

Here's a partial slate of variations or flavors of the passive experience: We feel under the influence of something or someone, overwhelmed, helpless, taken advantage of, beaten down, conned, violated, lied to, persecuted, intimidated, trapped, forced to submit, manipulated, pushed around, dominated, consumed, inhibited, restrained, held up, made to endure inappropriate behavior, imposed upon, made to look bad, forced to pick up the burden or do it all oneself, and required to see or do things according to someone else's needs or demands.

Often, we are not conscious of either our passivity or our reactions to it. For instance, a man's reaction to his passivity could be anger or fear, but he might not consciously register his anger until someone comments, "And what are you so angry about?" Meanwhile, it is understood that an emotionally strong person can be restricted or imposed upon (to take words from the above list) by some person or situation and yet not be triggered by inner passivity. This individual may graciously comply or submit, for purposes of strategy or necessity, to the controls being imposed, and yet does not get triggered emotionally by the feeling of being controlled.

The following experiences are also variations of passivity: expecting loss, feeling deprived or refused, missing out, never having enough, feeling dissatisfied and drained; feeling ignored, neglected, and excluded; feeling gypped or ripped off; and feeling disqualified, discounted, and dismissed. The more extensive our inner passivity, the more painfully we resonate with these feelings.

Finally, deep in our psyche are the ultimate, most painful manifestations of inner passivity: feelings of being rejected, abandoned, betrayed, negated, hated, and annihilated. It is through these feelings in particular that we feel one of the main symptoms of inner passivity, namely the great pain of being lost to ourself.

Through our passivity we retain and circulate these negative emotions in our experience of life and ourselves. We resonate like a tuning fork with them. One client who was beginning to understand his deep affinity for his unresolved emotions said, "It's like I have a little Bermuda Triangle in my soul."

Passivity is often represented in dreams by the experience of being chased by tormentors or pursued by an evil presence. It is also represented when the dreamer, identifying with another person, observes that person being inept, clumsy, overwhelmed, or ineffective. The dreamer may feel he or she is in an awkward or confined position from which it is impossible to feel motivated or to succeed. As a teenager, I played golf with my parents, and later in life I often had dreams of trying to tee off in a cramped, confined space where I was unable to swing the club properly, or where, on the course, I was hitting one bad shot after another.

My own passivity has been painful and self-defeating, and I share more of my encounters with it throughout this book. Because of the inner work I've done, my passivity is less a problem than it used to be; however, despite my training and vigilance, I certainly do not catch and become aware of all the ways in which my passivity continues to be experienced and played out.

At this point, it is important to say that readers may have emotional reactions to this exposé of inner passivity. A reader's inner resistance, for instance, may tempt him or her to put this book down and not look into it ever again. While consciously we want inner liberation, we oppose it with tremendous unconscious resistance. When a powerful form of liberation is presented to us, we have a reactionary impulse and tend to revert to our old form, even as we may fervently wish on a conscious level to overcome the limiting influences acting upon us.

Another common reaction to the revelation of passivity is to find oneself becoming grumpy, on edge, and belligerent, and being tempted to express that aggression and negativity to others. This reaction represents pseudo-aggression, about which I write more in Chapter 4. Pseudo-aggression, an impulse that makes us feel as if we are being the opposite of passive, is an unconscious attempt to cover up our passivity. It is inappropriate and can be quite self-defeating. Another reaction is to feel passive to the awareness of our passivity. Here we feel overwhelmed by the sense of it and convinced it is more than we are able to deal with.

The experience of passivity is often very subtle. It is present when we don't eat properly, don't exercise, and procrastinate about going to the doctor when we know we should. It is also represented in the feeling that we are not deserving of anything good. It can be an aspect of the feeling that we won't ever get what we want or that we are a disappointment to ourself, as well as the feeling of being defensive, on guard, and needing protection or validation. For instance, people who feel the need to have handguns in their homes may be expressing underlying passivity. This is especially so if they frequently produce imaginary scenarios in which they see themselves using these weapons against others in fantasies of being threatened, overwhelmed, or brutalized.

Passivity can cause us to live under different doctrines or emotional contracts, whether secular or religious, because we don't know who we are without living under or through some such definition or imposition. Passivity is often validated and encouraged by traditional religions. Aligning oneself with the will of God is not a passive act, but history has shown that being submissive to the guidance of allegedly religious men and women certainly risks falling afoul of our best interests. Passivity blocks us from recognizing those who will help us and those who will use us, and thus we may routinely misplace our trust.

We can also be passive to an inner doctrine, as is someone who believes he or she will die young, or who wants to believe he is unattractive or unintelligent, or who believes he is hopelessly stuck with a "fatal flaw." Another example involves the condition of compulsive goodness, based on the fear of being anything but "good." This form of passivity puts the individual in a place where his freedom is curtailed, and he is locked into a limited behavioral mode that he accepts as his lot and role in life. Another variation is to have an unconscious contract with one's parents, where the adult son or daughter continues to be "the good little boy or girl" in exchange for continued approval and support from dysfunctional parents.

We can be passive to our own mind, to our intellect. Obsessive thinking, when our mind runs rampant, is a result of passivity. When we allow our mind to run the show, it produces a constant stream of thoughts— memories, speculations, and considerations—that are unbidden. They have a life of their own and stream through our consciousness in random and chaotic fashion. Often these thoughts consist of self-preoccupation—erotic and fanciful daydreams, security worries, self- condemnation or self- aggrandizement, and speculations on future prospects, revenge, and recrimination.

Our passivity is reflected not just in obsessive thinking but also in the everyday random thinking common to everyone. We do not choose this random thinking—it happens to us because, in identifying with the mind and thus with ourselves in a limited way, we give enormous power to the mind. One client struggling with issues of passivity told me, "My mind is like a sleazy salesman. Every time he talks, I get sucked into what he's saying." Another client, a man deeply mired in passivity, said "I'm always trying 'to power' into situations with my mind, thinking I can solve anything. But I end up going back and forth—I don't really get clarity. I see now that I've been creating a false sense of power."

The opposite of obsessive thinking can also be a problem of passivity. Under intense inner pressure, some individuals will actually stop thinking. They "space out" or "shut down," blocking out the inner turmoil by adopting, as one client called it, "a reptilian mode." A client who was beginning to see this form of passivity in himself called it "brain fog," or the escapist lifestyle, where "we sit around, hang out, watch TV, go to sleep, feel nothing, get drunk on weekends, and become oblivious." Still another client said, "It's like being on autopilot, which, incidentally, I can do for days at a time." True power includes the ability to pacify the mind and to be present to oneself in the here-and-now.

In more serious cases of inner passivity, the result is depersonalization, in which an individual feels confused, out of touch with himself and things around him, to the point that his thinking is impaired and he feels he is losing control of himself and his mind. This can also include bouts of dissociation, a more serious condition still that involves time lapses of which a person has no memory.

Our mind is not us and we are not our mind. Yet most people identify with their mind, or body, or personality, or ego, or a combination of these. This identification limits us, creates suffering, and gives our passivity a wide-open playing field on which to cavort. Our mind or body or personality can only produce for us a second-hand experience of who we are. The deeper, fuller experience is beyond words and thoughts, an inner journey into our psyche and into our heart for deep illumination.

Ultimately, passivity is a denial or negation of ourself, as it is a limitation of our freedom. In the clutches of passivity, it feels as if nothing or no one is present within ourself to speak for us, to represent our interests, and to support our decisions on our own behalf. We can't truly believe in ourselves. We don't have the connection to be our own advocate or our own best friend. Instead, we are often at the mercy of a harsh inner critic or judge that appears to be able to tear us apart at will (see Chapter 3).

Passivity causes us to be absent to ourselves. We find ourselves in some inner "no-man's land" where our own self is neglected or taken for granted. Even as we have this neglectful relationship with ourself, we can be self-absorbed, feeling that, "No one understands me—no one sees or cares about who I am." Without our self-absorption, it feels as if we are nothing. So we try to support ourself or care about ourself through narcissism, while underneath we resonate with the feeling of having no value. We register our pain through this limited, false self. So the extent of our inner passivity reflects the degree to which we are not in touch with our true strength, our true being. We are not believing in ourself and supporting our existence, the way a kind, wise parent would be present and loving to his or her child.

The knowledge I am presenting here may seem daunting to some readers. In fact, it can be easily assimilated and can begin immediately to benefit us. The path of freedom involves seeing our passivity and feeling how we experience life and ourself through it. As we begin to see our passivity, we move it to the side and begin to navigate around it. Over time, it vaporizes and its influence wanes.

An example of seeing and understanding inner passivity involves how we handle the experience of someone cutting in front of us, say, while we're driving on the highway or in a supermarket checkout line. We might have an emotional reaction (anxiety, fear, withdrawal, denial, or anger). If inner passivity is *not* a factor, we would be able to say calmly and firmly to the offending person words to this effect: "You cut in front of me. Please move aside so I can have my place in line." Or wisely picking our battles, we might decide to say nothing at all, doing so out of the strength of *not* getting triggered.

If we do speak up and the person, either politely or rudely, refuses to comply, we would not feel humiliated or defeated by letting him go ahead and waiting behind him or going to another checkout. It would be hard to avoid some annoyance, of course, but the healthier we are the more we rise to the emotional challenge. We can still feel good about representing ourself assertively. If we were truly enlightened, we might laugh to ourself, or even aloud, as we waited in line or walked off to another cashier.

Because of their inner passivity, some people feel the need to react with anger or aggression in this kind of situation. They feel pushed around, discounted, or disrespected. They take it personally. As I said, an angry or aggressive reaction is usually a sign of passivity. The anger or aggression is our unconscious attempt to cover up or defend against the underlying passivity. (I refer to this defense in different contexts throughout the book because it can be challenging to understand.) Our unconscious defense contends: "I am not into feeling passive. Look, my behavior proves I'm aggressive!" But rather than empowering us, acting on the impulse to be aggressive or angry leaves us with a significant emotional and physical disturbance. Our negativity is also more likely to induce a negative reaction in the other person. Because our negative emotion is so intense, it can feel for hours afterwards that we have engaged in a brawl. We can also feel guilt, shame, or fear with respect to our angry outburst. Again, this is a typical self-defeating symptom of a passivity-based reaction.

If on the other hand passivity is present in our psyche and we do or say nothing to the checkout-line interloper, we can also feel bad about ourself for many hours afterward. Inwardly we are assailed with accusations of our passivity, and we gamely defend ourself with various rationalizations and contentions (e.g., "I wasn't going to make a scene in public"). Sometimes we are not aware of the existence of this inner dialogue or even that it is going on (we are just enveloped in it), though all the while it is draining us of creative and positive energy.

If passivity is less present, we may choose, as mentioned, not to do or say anything to the rude interloper, and to let this person go ahead without protest. Again, under this condition, we process the situation internally until it is reduced to the level of nuisance. Here we avoid using rationalizations or excuses that cover up our passivity. The healthy internal process is the equivalent of being able to push a delete or exit key to emerge emotionally neutral from such a situation. If, however, the encroaching shopping cart happens to be overflowing and the other checkout lines are backed up, the individual with a minimum of passivity will likely decide to make a statement in support of his position in line. If the interloper refuses to step aside at this point, the healthy response is still to take the situation as a test of one's ability to remain centered and nonreactive.

In another example, a woman is approached by an old acquaintance at a party. He "hangs around" her for the next hour, making pleasant conversation and apparently enjoying himself. She, however, is becoming increasingly uncomfortable with his presence and wishes he would excuse himself and wander away. Finally, she decides to leave the party just to get away from him. Later, she is angry with him for "spoiling" the evening and also upset at herself for not having shooed him away. The real problem is that she began to experience his presence at the party through her passivity. She acted out her readiness to experience herself through that familiar feeling. If she were aware of this phantom element in herself, she would be in a stronger position to override her passivity and take action that would free herself from her predicament. If passivity were not present in this situation, she might excuse herself or else find that the man's presence doesn't bother her.

Passivity's Widespread Nature

The following are more examples and aspects of how passivity is experienced and acted out. These examples indicate the widespread nature of this self-defeating emotional attachment.

1 - Depression, panic attacks, and phobias often are symptoms of underlying passivity, where the individual is caught in an emotional tangle from which he feels unable to extricate himself. Problems with procrastination, fatigue, and lack of motivation can cover up passivity, as does evasion and avoiding direct answers.

2 - Many of us have fears and anxiety about being unable to take care of ourselves physically or financially as we get older. Through passivity, we are preoccupied about the future because we are ready to live through the feeling that we won't be able to take care of ourselves or be supported by others and by life. It feels that we need someone else to protect us, guide us, and make decisions for us.

3 - Passivity can accentuate the fear of dying. Through passivity, the unconscious wish is to feel: "I am too weak and feeble to survive my own death in any form. Nothing will be left of me. I will be completely annihilated." Even for a dying person who believes in God and an afterlife, the presence of passivity can create various irrational fears.

4 - In passivity, we often make statements to others or to ourselves to the effect of, "There's nothing I can do about it;" "Oh, I don't know;" "Who knows;" "Well, anyway;" "If only things had been different;" "Whatever;" "What difference does it make;" "It's up to you;" and "This isn't going to work." Deep and frequent sighs are another indicator, as is repeated use of the expression, "Everything is fine." Even the common statement on the telephone, "Okay, I'll let you go now," assumes to represent power but has a passive underbelly.

5 - Body language and facial expression such as rolling one's eyes, looking goofy, stumbling or moving awkwardly, shrugging, raised shoulders, and locked knees when standing also are indicators.

6 - Daydreams and fantasies of being reduced to poverty and being at the mercy of others and of life, of being homeless and abandoned, are indicators, too. Included

are fears of being diminished, vanquished, and annihilated.

7 - Under the influence of passivity, members of an audience can be held spellbound by a dynamic speaker, while the truth of what he or she says or represents is secondary. Truth is associated with the emotional impact such a speaker has on us: we believe what's said because he or she said it so convincingly.

8 – Conversely, it can feel that one has to withhold oneself in order to avoid being overpowered or "swallowed up" by some other person. Teenagers can react negatively to parents as they try to break away from parental influence and establish their own sense of autonomy. The feeling of having to give up one's reality to accommodate someone else and is often associated with guilt and shame. Initially, this feeling can be experienced with a parent, while later in life it is transferred onto others. Such a person may often avoid others, feeling that he or she needs separation in order to feel whole or complete.

8 – A related indicator is an individual's feeling that he can't avoid being unhappy if his partner or a family member is unhappy. Or vice-versa—if others are happy, now he can be happy. It's the feeling of having no choice but to be under the influence of the mood or energy of others, rather than choosing and maintaining the quality of one's own mood or experience. It's also the feeling of slipping into a bad mood, whether others are present or not, without the hope of regulating oneself or the notion that it is possible to do so.

9 - Common to passivity is the experience of becoming emotionally distraught, or "puffed up," fearful or angry, simply to state one's needs. With passivity, it is difficult to

say something to the effect, "Sorry, I can't do it now. I have things I have to do." It also feels that if we make a simple request or express a need, the other person will object. There is a tendency to avoid confrontation or, conversely, to be inappropriately harsh or demanding when confronting someone. Another symptom is to avoid asking for help or for money one is due.

10 - Railing and complaining about people, events, or a situation over which one has no control or influence is a sign of passivity. Complaining is the defense, covering up how much we are secretly "into" the feeling of being helplessly enmeshed and hopelessly at the mercy of what we are complaining about.

11 - Indoctrination of our children to a subscribed mentality, particularly any dogma, reflects an unconscious compulsion to condition them to submit passively to what we acquiesced to as children. Or the reverse applies: also to the detriment of the child, a passive parent abdicates his responsibility to set boundaries, impose reprimands, and offer moral or spiritual guidance.

12 - Men often resist the development of the soft, intuitive, compassionate (feminine) side of their nature because they associate it with passivity. Normally the development of feminine qualities is a plus for men. Men who criticize or attack gay men are projecting and thus denying, not necessarily homosexual inclinations, but their own passivity, which unconsciously they associate with weakness, humiliation, and femininity.

13 - Acting out of habit is passivity based. We claim that a bad habit is hard to break, that it enslaves us. But the inability to break a harmful habit is founded in passivity,

as is the pattern of forgetting inner resolutions or failing to complete projects.

14 - Tuning out or spacing out, absent-mindedness, or incessant daydreaming also indicates the influence of passivity. The practice, for instance, of retreating into the living room to read journals or newspapers and shutting others out, or reacting to their overtures with an absent-minded "Uh huh," is a prime example, as well as a daily occurrence in many homes. One client said of her father when he did this, "I am amazed at how deep he went into that place."

15 - The chronic need for excitement or stimulation—whether as a gambler, sports fanatic, daredevil, or "party-goer"—can be the consequence of a "dead-zone" within oneself that blocks access to life's little pleasures, a zone created in part by inner passivity.

Typically, a passive person will be passive in one context and aggressive or controlling in another. This is commonly observed with parents, one of whom may be passive to the other or passive, say, at work, but strict and rigid with his or her children. At times we can be passive to someone else's passivity. A woman who was struggling to regulate her food intake described it this way: "When I was a teenager, I could fight with my father. We could even scream at each other, and I could argue with the best of them. I could do this because I didn't have to take care of my father's feelings. My anger didn't wound him. But then my mother, who was very passive, would say to me, 'Oh dear, please just don't get into it with him—it's just too hard on my nerves.' So, even though I was angry with my father about something, I would just go limp and have to swallow whatever crap he dished out. I couldn't go against my mother because it would hurt her too much."

As this woman began to regulate her food, she noticed that she began to get angry with her husband for his cigarette smoking. "Now, like I did with my mother, I become passive to his passivity," she said. "In other words, I feel my passivity when I see him caught in his."

It's common for us to displace our passivity from one experience of it to another. We have to be alert to all the subtle ways it sneaks in. If we see it, we can stop it.

As mentioned earlier, we can also react passively—feeling overwhelmed or defeated—by the realization of our inner passivity. My clients sometimes "space out" in my office, and conveniently stop hearing what I'm saying— particularly when the analysis is deepest—as they feel the challenge of encountering the inner reaches of their psyche.

Another interpretation of passivity, from the Taoist spiritual tradition, helps us to understand the passivity about which I am writing. The way of the Tao encourages passivity, but here the meaning is different. Taoists refer to a conscious, healthy form of passivity, a witnessing awareness from which any impulse to action or inaction is observed and tested for appropriateness. Taoists teach the desirability of choosing to be at a state of rest or non-action, because action, drive, and intensity are seen by them as the product of ego and based on the need to feel significant, worthwhile, and powerful. Indeed, much of the action and industriousness we see in the world is counter-productive or even destructive, intended for ego-satisfaction, control of others, and mastery of the environment. Such action represents various expressions of self-interest and self-aggrandizement.

The concept of Taoist passivity helps us understand the roots of action, how some action originates in subversive intention and motivation. From the Taoist perspective, the use of power and action are appropriate when they emerge from the center of peace and silence within oneself to address a true need. The passive option, when consciously employed, is often the way of greatest wisdom and power. For instance, the pacifist, the one who refuses to go to war, will often be stronger emotionally and more integrated psychologically than many of the recruits who let others decide their fate. The Chinese master Sun Tzu said that good warriors cause others to come to them and do not go to others, while in conflict the summit of virtue is the defeat of the enemy without a fight.

Taoists teach the desirability of surrendering to the Tao, the divine way of things, to show implicit faith and trust in existence. Westerners are not adept at surrendering, however, because in attempting to do so we feel too vulnerable, too passive.

Another perspective on passivity and our inner nature is provided by Sufis, the followers of an esoteric Islamic tradition more than 1,000 years old. Sufis say that all of us are under the influence of a false self, or Commanding Self, that induces us to react to people and situations with a mixture of primitive emotionality and irrelevant associations. We are subservient to this off- center part of ourself and react to it in thoughtless impulse. This Commanding Self masquerades as our personality as it strives to maintain itself and its power over us. In Sufi teaching, the intention is not to destroy the Commanding Self but to observe it and to ask oneself: "Does it command me or do I command it?" Freedom from the Commanding Self involves the growing awareness of its existence and influence and the ability to be alert to one's experience in the present moment.

In depth psychology, the Commanding Self is the inner critic (self-aggression or superego). This aggressive part of us, the hidden master of our personality, is enabled by inner passivity. It is inner passivity that grants license to the inner critic to rule our inner life.

We cannot overcome our passivity through acts of will. Roberto Assagioli, founder of the healing system known as psychosynthesis, wrote in his book, *The Act of Will*, that this quality of will, meaning a positive force enabling us to act consistently on behalf of our higher purpose, is an inner power that can be developed through awareness and practice.[i] When I did some inner work in the psychosynthesis format more than twenty years ago, I found it to be fascinating and helpful, though limited in penetrating into the unconscious. To dislodge passivity, penetration into its deeply endemic patterning is essential. This involves unraveling its web of subversive influence, exposing the defenses that cover it up, recognizing our emotional attachment to it, and overcoming our resistance to dealing with it.

The condition of inner freedom, "the opposite of passivity," is represented in a person who knows what is right and healthy and creates for himself what is appropriate and wise. Many passive individuals reading this will say, with sincerity, "That applies to me—that's exactly what I do!" The tendency is to project our self-image onto any positive model.

We find in overcoming passivity that we become more creative, more expressive, and more in harmony with ourself and with others. This emotionally independent person does not rely on external circumstances to feel good about himself. He does not need to be validated or praised, nor does he fear rejection.

This person is able to assert his or her rights and feelings without alienating others. He takes responsibility for his faults and mistakes, and is not afraid of knowledge—in fact he welcomes it—that challenges his preconceptions. He has the capacity to sustain committed relationships with others, and does not use the weaknesses of others to feel disappointed, neglected, or judged. Kind people are attracted into his life, and he treats them with honor and respect, giving and caring with no hidden motives. He has no need to change or reform them, nor does he feel a need to please them or be what they want him to be.

An inner gratitude for what he has grows and deepens. He takes life as it comes in the present moment, while being prepared for possible future challenges. Life, as he understands it, is not like a parent giving to him only when he is good. Life does not consider him special because he has struggled for happiness or enlightenment. He wants only to know the truth and to open his heart.

What we do for ourself in this way we do for each other. On a global scale, the world's economic, political, and social order will change dramatically for the better when humanity comes into an awareness of inner passivity and works to overcome it. Unconscious passivity, as I illustrate it in this book, is an impediment to reform, peace, prosperity, and good order, for the individual, the family, and the local and global communities.

Chapter 2
Passivity in Action

Frank, a client in his mid-forties, had never fulfilled the promise indicated by his early success in high school and college. "My life is like an unfilled work-sheet," he said. "I haven't created a body of work, and my efforts have been scattered. I've invented technological devices that I never got patented, and I've created lovely art and paintings without pursuing a career there. So much of what I started I haven't finished." He was now working as a handyman in a rural area.

I had seen Frank for only a half-dozen or so sessions at this point, and he had begun with my help to consider inner passivity as one of the major elements behind his lack of achievement and his dissatisfaction with himself. One night he had two dreams. In the first, he was in a huge classroom where the professor had begun to lecture. He thought to himself, "Oh Jeez, now he's going to start lecturing." Frank realized that he had no pencil and paper with which to make notes. He looked around at the other students and saw that they had their writing materials and were already taking notes. "I'm not prepared," he thought to himself. "And look, I'm the only one not doing what I'm supposed to be doing."

I asked Frank if he felt the dream and the feeling he had of not being prepared corresponded to circumstances in his life.

"It is a common feeling," he replied. "I haven't made the kind of money I was capable of. I didn't finish things or make wise decisions. And I procrastinate. It's almost a guilty feeling—that I haven't done my part. I don't get to things. I'm juggling too many things in my head, trying to do a lot, and then not acting on anything. Like I don't have a real theme or focus in my life. It's the feeling of being bogged down with little things and overwhelmed by choices."

In his second dream, Frank was on a beach at one of the Great Lakes where six-foot-high swells were rolling onto shore. Friends in the water floated on surfboards and rode the swells. Frank was talking to someone on the beach, all the while watching his friends having fun in the surf. He just continued talking to this person and never did get in the water to join them.

He said in discussing the dream, "It was seeing something desirable, and within reach, but just not getting to it. I guess, again, it's this passivity you're talking about." He sighed in frustration. "But what is it anyway? That word passivity just sits here on my forehead. It's just a word, if you don't mind my saying so. Where is it and what is it?"

I nodded in sympathy. "I understand your difficulty grasping the concept. It's elusive for us all. The sense of it comes into better focus as you consider it in conjunction with experiences and incidents in your life. It does take a bit of time to see and understand it."

"Well, maybe it has something to do with how I felt about what happened this past week. The post office informed me that they wouldn't be bringing my mail to my current mailbox. I will have to walk further, another couple of hundred yards or so, to a new place where they're going to leave it. I was quite incensed—we pay a lot for stamps and now we get less service. I made some phone calls to the postmaster to protest. I couldn't get through to him, but I did leave a curt message about my feelings."

"How upsetting was this?'

"I was very annoyed for a couple of days. Then I seemed to be able to let it go."

"This is an example of what we're talking about. It looks as if you're experiencing the situation through the sense that something undesirable is being imposed on you and that you have to submit to these bureaucratic decisions."

"Well, something is being imposed on me. This is an inconvenience. Why shouldn't I be upset?"

"It's true that it's an inconvenience. But these nuisances are typical of what we all deal with at times. We need to process these experiences successfully if we want to minimize negative feelings. As you said, you spent a couple of days feeling 'very annoyed.' That adds up to a lot of unpleasantness, what I would call unnecessary suffering. If passivity were absent in a situation such as this, you might say, 'Darn it all,' and let the annoyance go within a few minutes. You might also call the Post Office to see if you could convince the people there to reconsider. Meanwhile, whatever the outcome, there would be no reaction within you that produced suffering. That suffering is not something you need to experience. Under healthy circumstances, you would simply not take on suffering for something as minor as this. If we're going to suffer, let it be for something really significant."

"Okay, maybe so, but what about this—I'm feeling some sadness. It has to do with what I said earlier, about all the
41

unfinished things I've left behind, about feeling as if my life is going to be wasted."

"Say more about the sadness."

"It's just that, a weepy, sad feeling, as if all of who I am and what I've accomplished is basically a waste. Now, at my age, I'm helpless to do anything about it. I get this feeling especially in the morning, just before I get up. It's the sense that I'm at the mercy of fate."

"Frank, this is just another way the passivity is sneaking in on you. You're playing with the idea that your life is over, that you're all washed up, and that you can't hope to turn this situation around. Let me tell you, if you dislodge this passivity, you might feel a whole new creativity come sweeping in. You could have more energy, and you'll get up in the morning with some zest to face the day. You won't leave projects or business unfinished. Your whole interest will be in your creative fulfillment and self-expression, and you will find a lot of pleasure in the experience of carrying it out."

It is difficult for me to describe exactly how Frank (and the other individuals who contributed to this book's examples) gained some measure of freedom from the influence of inner passivity. Insight is the most valuable ingredient in our struggle for inner freedom, and genuine insight requires knowledge of the universal principles of unconscious functioning. With awareness of our specific psychic ingredients, we apply that psychological knowledge to understand the substructure of our actions, thoughts, beliefs, and emotions. Throughout the book I give my readers a taste of what I teach and how I facilitate. I do my best to map out the terrain of the deep unconscious and to explain how knowledge becomes insight and then inner freedom. That process is ultimately mysterious, sacred, and unique to each individual.

Passivity lurks in the wings behind numerous emotional and behavioral derivatives. It has a genius for disguising itself. As I've said, each individual has to find his own expressions of it (there likely are many) if he wants to clear it from his system.

Varieties of Passivity

At this point, it is important to give more examples of how, in an individual psyche, different varieties of passivity are at play. Even psychotherapists find it challenging to recognize and separate the various conflicts that are at work, interacting within the psyche of any one individual. Without separation and distinction, the mix of emotions becomes an undifferentiated jumble, making clarity and resolution impossible.

Jerry, a client in his fifties, was renegotiating child support with his ex-wife and her lawyer. The process had been dragging on for several months, during which Jerry had become increasingly moody and depressed, "completely beside myself," as he put it. He had also begun to feel resentful and angry toward his current girlfriend, especially concerning her financial dependence on him and his sense that she was always wanting more from him. Jerry had four intersecting conflicts or issues that were being stirred up in this situation. He was feeling passive toward his ex-wife and her lawyer, inwardly playing up the feeling of their power over him. Emotionally, even as he pledged to fight them to the bitter end, he gave them enormous power, referring to them in several instances as "feminist ball-breakers." As he gritted his teeth and clenched his fists, vowing they would never get the best of him, he secretly indulged in feeling oppressed and even defeated, and this indulgence generated much anger.

Jerry was also feeling financially stressed, and indeed his income in the past few years had remained stagnant while his debt and expenses had grown significantly. In a manner that was both conscious and unconscious, he played with the feeling or prospect that his ex-wife and her lawyer would manage to extract more money from him, leaving him feeling drained, depleted, and broke. He became frantic about the state of his health. He was concerned he wouldn't have the energy or ability to go on earning income at his present rate, and he became more belligerent toward his girlfriend whenever she approached him for money.

Jerry was also feeling angry at himself. He had made a financial arrangement years ago with his ex-wife that he now felt had been too generous. He became highly critical of himself for having made that contract with her. "I just caved in," he said. "I couldn't wait to get out of that relationship. She got everything she wanted." Jerry was criticizing himself for having been passive and for agreeing to all her financial requests. Even as he berated himself, the criticism spilled out toward his girlfriend and he became more disapproving of her.

Finally, Jerry also took it very personally that his ex-wife and her lawyer "don't care about me as a person." All they wanted, he said, was his money. In his view, they had no respect or concern for him and his difficulties, or for what he had done in the past to support his ex-wife and their children. Jerry was transferring onto this situation his emotional memories of his relationship with his father, who he felt had never cared about him nor recognized him as a distinct and worthy person. He was entangled in his attachment to the feeling of not being appreciated or valued, of being unloved. Deep in his psyche, he still experienced himself through this negative feeling. He needed to understand how determined he was unconsciously to continue to experience himself through this feeling. The feeling created pain and anger in him, and also prompted him to feel less caring and affectionate toward his girlfriend.

To extricate oneself from an emotional morass such as Jerry's, one needs to see these distinct issues and deal with them separately. Otherwise, the psyche remains uncharted territory, leaving the individual awash in misdirection, chaos, and confusion.

The following example reveals passivity in a powerful mix with self-criticism and its more painful cousin, self-condemnation. A young college student, Janice, was having obsessive thoughts about some of her teachers.

"Is this all confidential?" she asked me. "It is so important that they don't know about this obsessing. I would be so ashamed."

"If I use aspects of this case in my writing," I replied, "I will use an alias and change extraneous facts so that no one would suspect the information refers to you. Now tell me, are you harsh and condemning with yourself for having these thoughts?"

"Very much so. I go to great lengths so that no one will find out because I'm so ashamed to act and think this way, but I still feel driven to obsess about the whole thing. I know it is self-defeating behavior, but I'm so deep inside the problem that I can't see it from any other point of view other than being right in the middle of my own mind. It all seems justified in my mind, though I'm aware that this obsessing is getting me nowhere and ultimately brings me no happiness. Yet I feel completely powerless to change it. Yes, I could cut off correspondence with this one teacher, but I would just find someone else to obsess over. That has happened over and over in my life. So that is not necessarily the answer. Besides, I really like this teacher—she is a mentor and a friend. I feel like, in a way, I have to act like I'm someone else when I write to her, because I'm so afraid that she'll find me out.

"I constantly obsess about her when I am here and she is fifty miles away. But whenever I go to see her, I actually feel ill driving up her street because all the feelings go away when I see her in real life. I become disgusted with myself for having those feelings in the first place—which as I said are not sexual. Even as I'm driving away from her place, I start obsessing again and want to turn back and go to her house again. It is almost like she's not really the person I'm obsessing about—that person is someone I create in my mind out of what this teacher writes to me in our email exchanges. We write emails pretty much every day, but when I see her in person once or twice a month, it feels like I don't even know her."

"Two emotional issues are involved here," I said. "You have created an obsession through which you can experience yourself in a condemning manner. Do you understand? That's where some of the shame you feel comes from. Unconsciously, you are determined to experience this condemnation of yourself. With your emotional attachment to this feeling, you then create some inappropriate or questionable behavior or situation—

such as this obsession with your teacher—through which you can generate the feeling of self-condemnation. So the self-condemnation is there from the start, in search of an inappropriate behavior, or even something you imagine doing but don't act on, and you feel that this behavior or imagined behavior merits the condemnation and shame you apply to it, or to yourself. Some individuals generate this self-loathing or self-condemnation through eating disorders, addictions, sabotage in relationships, or in general non-acceptance of their body, their personality, or themselves. You are able to generate it through this obsessive fixating on teachers.

"Your fear that you might be found out is your defense. The defense operates on this basis: 'I am not looking for the feeling of self-condemnation. Look at how anxious or fearful I am that they might find out about my weird obsession. I want it to be a secret.' However, in truth, you are looking for the feeling of self-condemnation, but your psyche does all it can to cover up this attachment. "In addition, you also experience passivity in another way, in the feeling of being, as you said, completely helpless as these feelings converge and then helpless to change your behavior. As a result of this passivity, you are unable to connect with your inner power. The emotional need to experience yourself through this old passivity, which we have identified as an element in your parents' psychic lives, is too compelling. This need also contributes to the shame you feel.

"You can break free of this emotional morass by becoming conscious of these attachments while you pass through the 'working-out' process. You need to see your secret willingness to experience yourself through self-condemnation and passivity. As you expose these attachments, your intelligence and your whole being will be empowered. You will see what you are dealing with. You will recognize it as if it were an old software program that has to be replaced by an updated program. The new program represents who you truly want to be, a program for living and for experiencing yourself, and you now begin to create it out of the power of your growing awareness.

"All of this does take some time. Be patient. Observe yourself carefully, and you will see how you gravitate toward self-condemnation. Learn how your defenses work, in order to see how you use these defenses to cover up your collusion with inner passivity. Grow in this inner awareness, and you will be able to fulfill your destiny."

Boomerangs and Other Devices

Passivity is also evident in the way we communicate with each other. Verbal boomerangs are one indication of foul play in communication, and a person who feels vulnerable, trapped, cornered, caught, panicked, or helpless employs them. The use of boomerangs represents an unconscious willingness to sabotage communication. We use them when we're afraid of the truth about ourselves because we feel it would expose us to criticism or ridicule, or because we feel honest dialogue would threaten our illusions and self-image. We also use boomerangs to defend an event or situation about which we are uncertain. In a paper on the subject, Nordic Winch writes that boomerangs "appear to be a [verbal] weapon aimed at the opponent, but they come back on the user. They rely heavily on the listener, the targeted victim of boomerangs, to fall for these verbal 'tie-ups' by also feeling trapped, caught, and helpless to the one with whom he is speaking."[ii]

Coming under the influence of a boomerang is the feeling of being hog-tied by one's own passivity. One person said, "It feels as if you're in a poker game where someone keeps throwing out wild cards." Negative feelings are evoked when communication between two people breaks away from mutual respect. The language and demeanor employed deteriorate into a power play of interruption and interrogation where one person, representing the parent, assumes a dominant position, while the other person, reverting emotionally to the feeling and pattern of his childhood passivity, feels himself to be "on trial" and held accountable.

Here are a few of Winch's examples of boomerangs:[iii]

1 - Finding contradictions. In a discussion, one party says, "But yesterday you said something different . . . " The aim is not to clarify but to attack, to get an "edge up" on the other person, to cast doubt on his word or his worth, in order to compensate for a feeling of being intimidated or under his influence. The person at whom the accusation of contradiction is aimed now gets into trouble by defending himself about what exactly he did or did not say, rather than seeing and addressing the intention behind the words. Both parties can slip into passivity as their verbal exchange falls deeper into confusion and obfuscation.

2 - Misuse of authority for contradiction. "The Bible says . . . Mother says . . . My therapist says . . . The twelve-step program says . . . " In resorting to such comments, our intention is to detract from the other person's sense of authority, in order to identify with his feeling deflated, uncertain, and passive about himself. We also use this

boomerang because we will feel deflated, uncertain, and passive about ourself if we let his statement stand. The feeling is that we are not entitled to represent our own authority.

3 - The witness. This type of boomerang is similar to the previous one. Use of the witness ("My husband agrees that this is unfair") is employed to verify and justify a defensive position or point of view to which one is clinging tenuously. Backup is needed because the individual, on his own, feels himself on shaky ground. Others are also enlisted to support one's position for the purpose of avoiding deeper realization or truth.

A variation on this boomerang is to claim, "I'm not the only one who thinks this way, or who acts this way, or who makes mistakes."

4 - Changing the subject—a diversionary tactic. When Robert's wife asks how much money his business made in the past week, he tells her how hard he worked and how poorly others in the region did. To reply directly is, for him, to confess to poor earnings and failure. So he changes the subject and invites debate on how hard he worked.

A little boy spills milk on the floor. "I don't do it all the time," he cries out. The matter of spilled milk is changed to the frequency with which it happens. He is contending it would be unfair to scold him.

5 - Going literal—avoiding the sense intended. Wanting to let his roommate know that they needed to plan ahead for the use of the computer they shared, Ralph told a story about a canoe trip. "You've got to keep paddling, guiding, working with the current of events," Ralph said, "or you

will be at the mercy of white water and rocks and waterfalls."

His roommate replied, "I'm an expert. My father taught me all about white water when I was a kid. I could show you a thing or two about how to use a paddle."

"I never said I was better than you at canoeing."

"You're the guy who brought it up."

The roommate feels pestered and criticized by Ralph. By replying to the literal content of Ralph's story, he deflects Ralph's effort at effective communication and does nothing to resolve the problem of how he feels with Ralph.

Non-verbal cues can also be instruments of control or prompting to induce passivity. A look, a cough, a yawn, a clearing of the throat is often used to influence the behavior of others. One person's sudden restlessness may cut short the words of another. Withdrawing gives the message that the person doesn't want to talk. A limp, haggard body posture can depict resignation and defeat.

Joan, a real-estate agent in her forties, felt intimidated and thwarted in her relationship with her husband, who frequently resorted to verbal boomerangs to throw her off-stride.

She described her passivity in this way: "I feel lectured to. It's the feeling of being too close to someone in a bad way, like feeling his hot breath on me or slipping into his body."

At one point she said, "I wish I had the skill to talk to him better. I don't know what to say to him." Joan was pleading guilty to being inept at dealing with her husband's verbal land mines, and having pleaded guilty to this "crime" she now felt bad about herself for this shortcoming. But the deeper issue involved her tendency to be passive: she felt herself to be under his influence and at the mercy of his controlling stratagems. By pleading guilty to being verbally inept, she covers up her passivity and thereby blocks out awareness of the roots of her difficulty.

I saw a verbal boomerang used in an article on the value of educational software in *The Wall Street Journal*. The article stated that children who were tested after using the *Reader Rabbit* software program had a fifty percent drop in creativity. A vice-president at the Learning Company defended *Reader Rabbit*, saying: "I wouldn't say it's better than a teacher or a parent, but it's very effective and engaging. It does enhance learning. *Would you rather have them playing Doom?* [Emphasis added]."[iv]

That italicized question has nothing to do with the issue of whether *Reader Rabbit* impairs the creativity of children. In asking such a question, the company official reveals to the trained listener that he feels trapped and cornered. Nonetheless, the comment does appear to make a point, and if the person being spoken to is also passive he or she may not be able to challenge the obvious obfuscation.

Laziness is another symptom of passivity. It is typical for a person to claim that he is lazy and to feel guilty for allegedly being lazy, rather than to understand that his behavior springs out of his passivity. By pleading guilty to laziness, he thereby gives it the headlines and overlooks the underlying passivity stuck away in the classified section. So he is using laziness as his cover story, and, in doing so, he feels guilty for allegedly being lazy. He is making an inner bargain to suffer with guilt for alleged laziness in order to cover up (remain unconscious of) his passivity.

The defense goes something like this: "Hey, I'm not passively stuck in the mud, going nowhere in my life. Passivity is not the reason for my unwillingness to motivate myself and feel energy and purpose. The real reason I'm going nowhere is that I'm lazy. And look, I'm willing to feel guilty for being lazy." Here the individual blames himself, but the blame is for a symptom (or, in some cases, an alleged symptom) of the passivity. Often times the person is not truly lazy. He is simply stuck, lacking in motivation and purpose, as a condition of his passivity. To my mind, the designation of laziness can't be separated from passivity.

One writer, a self-confessed incurable lazybones and "spectacular non-go-getter," wrote a tribute to laziness titled, "Who speaks for the lazy?—Skirting success is harder than it looks."[v] He said in his article that over the last twenty-five years he often earned annually only eight or ten thousand dollars after taxes. Behind his lack of success, he stated, was a corresponding lack of energy, drive, and commitment. Other symptoms he acknowledged were lassitude, aloofness, and low-grade depression. Nowhere, of course, does he mention passivity, because his whole article is an unconscious defense against recognition of it.

Just as laziness can be a symptom of passivity, so can the opposite behavior—the efforts of a frantically ambitious workaholic. The workaholic is driven to his work by the passivity he feels about himself and his life when he is inactive or attempting to be in a place of rest. His typical defense is as follows, "Of course I'm not passive. Look at how hard I work. Look at how aggressively I pursue advancement and success."

Passivity can be expressed very subtly. A client sitting in my office asked quite matter-of-factly, "Is it all right if I use your restroom?" When he returned, I told him his manner of asking about the restroom was an example of his difficulty experiencing his own authority.

He thought about it for a moment and said, "I was only trying to be polite."

"That is a rationalization, a defense," I replied. "Can you think of another way to say it?"

Immediately he said, "Excuse me, I have to use the restroom."

"Much better."

"You know what, that feels good, as if I'm in charge of my own life."

A client in his forties continued to be plagued by memories of an incident that occurred when he was seven years old. He had made friends with a "really cute girl" his age, and one Halloween night they went out together trick-or-treating. Walking along a path in the darkness, they were jumped by three older boys who grabbed their candy, pushed them to the ground, and ran off laughing.

"Why does this memory still pop into my head?" this man asked. "It wasn't all that serious a matter, and no one was physically hurt."

"Did it feel at the time that you didn't protect your friend?" I asked. "Did anyone imply that you hadn't protected her?"

"Yes, it did feel that I should have been able to stop that from happening. She never said that to me, but I recall that someone did, maybe my mother or father."

"And what is the feeling for you now when the memory comes up?"

"It's unpleasant. Sometimes I fantasize that I stop the boys by punching them and sending them running off in fear of me."

"This recurring memory serves an unconscious purpose," I said. "Remember what I've been saying: we are emotionally attached to the feeling of our passivity. Difficult as that is to unde stand and accept, we secretly go looking for that passive feeling whenever or wherever it can take effect. Obviously, this childhood incident had a strong emotional impact on you at the time. Of course, you could do nothing to stop those boys. You were completely innocent of wrongdoing. Nonetheless, you experienced the incident through helplessness and passivity. Now, with just the memory of it, you can resurrect those old feelings. Your unconscious loves it. It devours those old feelings, though consciously, of course, they are painful. As you understand the secret purpose for serving up this memory—your wish to experience yourself through that old, familiar feeling of passivity—you will stop replaying it. The memory will fade away. When you are free of the passive attachment, the memory, should it reoccur, will be neutralized. It will not carry an unpleasant emotional charge."

Paula had struggled for years with compulsive overeating. Now in her forties, she was increasingly concerned for her health. She often felt swept up by the impulse to raid the refrigerator or the cookie jar. She observed: "I say to myself, 'Paula, don't do it!' It's a joke! My resistance collapses. You'd think I was a zombie heading into the kitchen. I'm such a willing participant in my own sabotage."

Her parents, both heavy smokers and drinkers, were not nurturing or supportive to her and experienced her needs as an intrusion and a nuisance. Paula often said, "If only I'd had normal parents." (This expression of wishful thinking in itself denotes a victim mentality and underlying passivity.) She remembered as a child of six stepping on a nail one day and limping around for hours in pain. "I stayed at school and I didn't talk or say anything to anyone about it. I just took it all—the abuse, the pain. I think it was just more of what I was used to. I guess it didn't occur to me that even this need would be met with sympathy. How passive can one be!"

The following example indicates how quickly an individual can put together an inner "blueprint" that represents the major issues in his life. Once that inner configuration is created and made conscious, the individual can quickly emerge with new energy, purpose, and creativity.

I was finishing a session with Chuck, a plumber in his thirties, when I asked him to consider before I saw him again all the different ways his passivity was acted out. At that point, I had seen him for only about five sessions, so I was impressed when he came in the following week with a list of major areas of passivity. His list, revised here for purposes of elucidation, included:

1 - He usually waited a week or more to discuss a point of contention with his current girlfriend. Before talking to her, Chuck would "check in with friends, getting their opinions about what was happening and what I needed to say." During this time he was "belabored with thoughts" that became increasingly painful. Often he was thoroughly confused and, by the time he did speak to her, quite angry.

2 - Chuck frequently overbooked himself, and ended up "having to apologize to a lot of people." If the appointments he cancelled weren't emergencies, his customers were usually patient. He procrastinated in returning calls and in returning to customers' houses to complete his projects or make final adjustments. "Then I do get people annoyed, and I live in fear of their annoyance."

3 - He was a handsome man and had a pattern of becoming quickly intimate and sexual with women that appealed to him. Once a sexual encounter occurred, the women became attached emotionally to him. "This is how I get into relationships," he said. "Now I feel I'm in control. I can decide—am I going to stay with her or not? Am I going to live with her or not? Am I going to see her twice a week or what? That's how I like it." Without this control, Chuck felt passive.

4 - He had lost $12,000 on a recent investment. A friend of his had encouraged him to invest with a particular group. "I just slid into it," he said. "It wasn't a legitimate, healthy organization. I didn't check their references. I was

unreasonably trusting. I'm not good at following up on details."

5 - Chuck was an amateur musician (his mother had been a musician) and he owned a valuable piano. He met a musician that he admired greatly and wanted to ingratiate himself to this person. Chuck volunteered to lease him the piano and have it transported to the musician's recording studio. The musician said he would start making the lease payments when his expected funding became available. Meanwhile, he showed little interest in Chuck and resisted Chuck's attempts to spend time at the studio playing with him and his friends. Chuck let this situation drag on for more than a year. "Of course, I was not getting what I wanted. But I was never clear from the beginning. I expected something from him that was never clearly expressed." He finally called for his piano and got it back after some unpleasantness about the terms of the agreement.

From the beginning, Chuck showed considerable determination to work out his emotional issues. "I've been putting things off all my life," he said. "To have it called something [passivity], and to see how readily I go there to experience it, makes me feel a lot better." His progress in therapy has been impressive and is reflected in new-found inner harmony and integration.

Through our passivity we often feel uncomfortable with the experience of having and expressing our power. One client, Jeannie, insisted to her artist friend that she not use Jeannie's forks but a screwdriver instead to open cans of solvent. The friend begrudgingly obliged. The following day, as they were preparing again for a painting session together, the friend asked Jeannie to walk across the room and get the screwdriver for her. Jeannie detected annoyance in her friend's request, apparently leftover from the previous day, and Jeannie felt herself tempted to say, "I know I'm being fussy about using the screwdriver—I'm sorry to be such a bother." However, because of her growing understanding of her passivity, she refrained from making such a statement. Had she done so, she would have been giving her power away. Passivity creates the impression that the exercise of one's power and rights is not appropriate.

Paradoxically, passivity can also be found on the other extreme, where we insist (likely with some belligerence or rigidity) that our rights are sacrosanct and must be defended at all costs. Handgun advocates, when they imagine themselves without their weapons, can react with protest and fervor to an underlying feeling of powerlessness.

Finally, here are four more examples of passivity, briefly outlined:

1 - A middle-aged woman's fear of flying was associated with her terror of being out of control in a perilous situation. As an adolescent, she had screamed in fear when her insensitive older brother drove her around on twisting mountain roads. Her parents had been insecure people who never discussed with her the possibility of having inner resources to fall back on. She had been conditioned to doubt herself and to believe in external safety as an ultimate value.

2 - A male in his fifties, who complained of feelings of being "ravaged by self-doubt," remarked on how he would "zone out" and become quiet and passive whenever he visited his parents. He had grown up with very little parental recognition and validation, and had felt

emotionally abandoned by them. Now, in their company, he did to himself what he felt had been done to him; in failing to be present to himself and the situation, he was abandoning himself.

3 - A woman, also in her fifties, was feeling confused and anxious following a trip home to care for her dying mother. She was plagued by doubts over whether her handling of her mother's care and finances was adequate and by fears of running out of money. She spent hours every day planning for contingencies and speculating about possible problems, while playing down the significant contribution she was making to her mother's well-being. She was also identifying with her mother's fear and helplessness. She experienced herself through a sense of helplessness, through feelings that she had little of value to offer, and through a conviction that she didn't have the inner resources to support herself emotionally and financially.

4 - During our discussions a young client would frequently take verbal detours in which he would pose some imponderable question that he would appear intensely puzzled by. Examples included, "Why did my parents do that?" and "How can people be so insensitive?" These questions were not merely rhetorical. I realized after several attempts to answer them that he wasn't interested in answers. He would soon be back, as stumped as ever, with other such questions. His search for clarity was a pretext. His real intent was in being up against feelings of uncertainty, confusion, and helplessness. When I pointed this out to him, he gained new insight into his passivity.

Chapter 3
Self-Aggression and Passivity

Many social reformers contend that the oppressive actions of the powerful cause much of the world's suffering and injustice. I believe oppression and injustice in the world are a reflection of a power struggle within our own psyche between positive and negative forces. I also believe that the oppressive actions of the powerful are a symptom of a deeper cause of human misery: unconscious passivity.

Noted trial lawyer and author Gerry Spence writes in his book, *Give Me Liberty! Freeing Ourselves in the Twenty-First Century*, that we are all enslaved to corporate and political interests—the "new slave masters"—who control our airways and media, decide how our children will be educated, and who will be elected to office. "The slavery of which I speak," he writes, "reveals itself in our social values, in our apathetic, often unconscious acceptance of the way of things."[vi]

Spence writes, "Man is the only mammal that enslaves his own." Why does man do that? I believe it's because man is a creature who enslaves himself.

We have grown used to contradictions and accept them, Spence writes, adding that, "Democracy and the corporate ownership of our politicians is a contradiction. Free speech and the control of the airwaves by the corporate few is a contradiction."[vii]

There is, I contend, a greater contradiction to consider: those of us in the United States and other democracies proclaim how free we are, even as we fail to see clearly how we're inwardly enslaved. To see this is a painful contradiction of our self-image. We aren't willing to acknowledge that we're under the influence of an inner tyranny of which unconscious passivity is a large part.

Spence writes that our social and economic system is based on the master-slave model: "The New Master represents the most dreadful accumulation of power the species has yet encountered. It eats up the landscape, the deep jungles, the prairies, the pristine forests. It consumes anything growing, anything alive, to satiate its insatiable appetite for profit. It devours the people who labor for it. The thing is so enormous that it casts an endless shadow upon the earth that the people have grown to accept . . ."[viii]

But the problem is not so much the power of the oppressors as it is the passivity of the oppressed. It is an axiom of depth psychology that power and abuse fill the vacuum created by passivity. This master-slave model has its roots in the relationship we each have with ourself. We are all passive to our own self-aggression. Sigmund Freud wrote about this in 1930, in *Civilization and Its Discontents*. But like children who repress their fear, we have basically ignored (in this case, chosen unconsciously to be ignorant of) this knowledge. Freud wrote the following:

> And here at last an idea comes which belongs entirely to psychoanalysis and which is foreign to people's ordinary way of thinking . . .Every renunciation of instinct now becomes a dynamic source of conscience and every fresh renunciation

increases the latter's severity and intolerance. . .
The effect of instinctual renunciation on the
conscience then is that every piece of aggression
whose satisfaction the subject gives up is taken over
by the super-ego and increases the latter's
aggressiveness (against the ego). . . By means of
identification he takes the unattackable authority
into himself. The authority now turns into his superego and enters into possession of all the
aggressiveness which a child would have liked to
exercise against it.[ix]

Freud is saying that our innate or biological aggression,
which is an instinct for survival, usurps the role of our
moral conscience. This negative energy is directed at our
unconscious ego, itself an inner center of intelligence that
accommodates and integrates competing or conflicting
psychic energies. The aggression often swamps or
overruns our unconscious ego, creating not just an inner
disharmony but also an inner tyranny. Inwardly, we can
be very much at the mercy of this alien, negative energy,
and much of our inner resources and energy are mobilized
in trying to fend off this psychic oppression. This negative
force opposes our conscious aspirations, even our very
being. Psychology calls it the shadow, the dark side, the
harsh inner conscience, the inner critic, or the superego.
The American elder Robert Bly calls it both the superego
and the Interior Judge. In this book I generally refer to it
as self-aggression.

Self-aggression is a source of much of our irrational fears
and is what people have projected outward when they talk
about the devil. It is the part of us that we are reacting to
when we become cruel, vicious, or evil. It is also in the
ascendancy when we feel depressed, dispirited, and
defeated. We are like children wanting to believe in a

fairy-tale existence—not wanting to acknowledge this inner terrorist and regarding all allusions to it as make-believe. In refusing to consider it, however, we place ourselves at its mercy. It is an element in criminality, psychopathic behavior, violence, paranoia, and hatred. It is also a factor in anxiety, depression, apathy, self-doubt, and failure. Under its influence, our life can feel like a series of skirmishes and battles in our own civil war. Often the inappropriate aggression we send outward to others is a projection of our rebounding self-aggression. This mechanism, when not tempered by our awareness, has serious social consequences, as I explain in later chapters.

Self-aggression comes at us in varying intensity, in the form of self-doubt, self-disapproval, self-criticism, self-rejection, self-condemnation, and self-hatred. It tells us what is "wrong" with us, and what we should and shouldn't do. Often as it bullies us it is a vicious caricature of how our mother and father related to us. At its most intense, when self-aggression collides with the fog bank of our passivity, it feels as if it is about to negate or annihilate us. However, self-aggression is only as imposing or vicious as our consciousness and our passivity allow.

Until we become more conscious, we are intimidated by our self-aggression. The more passive we are to it, the more we absorb its negativity and become negative in ourselves. Thus, the more hostile we can be toward others when we project this negativity outward. Often with shy or otherwise repressed people, the aggression is projected silently as they keep their angry, hostile feelings to themselves.

Conversely, when we respond to our true inner authority, we have subdued our self-aggression and will exhibit emotional independence and true power in the world. We are no longer held ransom by a part of ourself. One client, a lawyer who was coming to terms with his passivity, found he could check his self-aggression with the statement: "No, you're not coming into the house. You have no search warrant. Off you go!"

We must remember, however, that the goal is not to fight against self-aggression. Fighting against it, like defending against it, only energizes it. We can engage the self-aggression in a dialogue (see example in Chapter 9) but not in a duel. Instead, we simply observe it, a silent witness who sees its exaggerations and lies. We shine the light of our awareness upon it. The witness that we become is empowered by clarity and truth. We understand our self-aggression for what it is—an expression of unadulterated negativity. Exposed to our consciousness, it loses power and retreats. We have to be vigilant, however, because it is known for its stealth and can quickly return as an assailant in other guises.

A client described one way she reacted to her self-aggression. Every time she left her apartment or her car, she repeatedly checked her pocket to make sure she had her keys. In the instant that her hand moved toward her pocket, she felt a jolt of anxiety, a lurch in her heart. Calm was restored the moment she felt her keys. She was reacting to her hair-trigger readiness to feel self-aggression viciously impugn, "You fool! Have you lost your keys again!" She had locked herself out of her car several times and each time had assailed herself for such a "foolish, stupid thing." She experienced similar feelings of anxiety and panic concerning the location of her purse and the balancing of her checkbook. While she was afraid of her self-aggression and was protecting herself against it (i.e., by constantly checking for her keys), she also was willing unconsciously to experience herself through that "sick, sinking feeling of terror" because of her attachment to passivity.

Like passivity, self-aggression is an inner aspect that is very real and yet very much denied, even by the psychological establishment. Freud identified self-aggression more than seventy years ago, although he never clearly incorporated it into his concept of Thanatos, the death instinct, and Eros, the life instinct. Psychologists and most people in general will not understand self-aggression until they plunge into their own psyche to expose the irrationality of it along with their emotional attachment to it. Doing so is a heroic undertaking known in mythology as "the hero's or heroine's journey," involving the courageous passage into the psychic underworld to expose, confront, and neutralize one's self-aggression and impulse to self-annihilation. This undertaking is often presented metaphorically in drama and literature as the hero's encounter with vicious villains or psychopaths, in mythology as the struggle against life-threatening demons, ogres, gremlins, and dragons, and in dreams as the effort to thwart various evil forces that threaten us physically.

In overthrowing inner tyranny, we become the hero in the drama of our own life. Our heroism is especially apparent when we own (become responsible for) our deep willingness to live through the intimidation and subjugation of our self-aggression and begin the process of liberating ourself. Otherwise, we are like children when dealing with self-aggression—vulnerable, naïve, and ignorant. We can't bring ourselves to take seriously the existence of this psychic malevolence and its crippling effect. One client said, "I realize that self-aggression is real, but I am still surprised every time I get hammered by it. I'm caught off-balance. It has me all tangled up in anxiety and defensiveness before I know what's happened." Her naivety, I told her, was unconsciously maintained for the purpose of keeping her in her familiar place of passivity, accepting of her condition of inner authoritarianism.

I believe the primary reason that we humans have been so reluctant to come to terms with our self-aggression, despite all that has been written about it in psychological literature (and all the allusions to it in world literature), is our unwillingness to fathom and take responsibility for our passivity. It's easier to try to debunk Freud, as do many pundits, clinicians, and academics. Even more than the existence of self-aggression, the fact of our passivity is the truth we most abhor. Much self-deception or unconscious deal making goes on to hide this condition from ourself.

We are all born with an aggressive drive. This energy or drive was required by our ancestors to survive in the world. It had to be immediately available in any emergency, as instinctive as a bird's quick flight from danger. We need it to seek out our mates and even to say, "I love you." Like all energy, however, it can be misapplied or misappropriated, and it needs the application of greater consciousness to establish its balance or find its best use.

Most of us come into the world with more aggression than we can comfortably deal with. Babies try to throw off the excess of aggression with temper tantrums—screaming, physical thrashing, and vomiting. However, it can't all be ejected in that manner, and since it has to flow somewhere, it is introjected, meaning it is turned inward and directed back at us, like a backwash.

Accusations of inadequacy, foolishness, and passivity are the ammunition that self-aggression fires at us. Without deeper awareness, we resonate emotionally with the accusations and implications. Despite mental attempts to the contrary, we believe deep within us that these accusations have validity, that they are somehow merited or deserved by our failings, mistakes, and weaknesses, even when we know intellectually that we are good people trying our best to do what is right. We "buy into" the allegations and resonate with the negative feelings and toxic shame.

At this point, our self-aggression comes up against our inner passivity (centered in our unconscious ego), which tries to deflect or neutralize it, but does so ineffectively and not with our best interests in mind. The unconscious ego protects itself at our expense. It is not able to defend our essence but only itself. Our ego mobilizes defenses to protect itself, and behaviorally these defenses run the gamut from withdrawal and apathy to hyperactivity and aggressiveness. Our self-aggression is mollified when enough emotional suffering in the form of our fear, depression, guilt, shame, tension, and anxiety is offered up as a defense, in sacrifice to our well-being. The deal our unconscious ego strikes with our self-aggression creates our emotional suffering, self-defeating behaviors, and personality disorders, along with the suppression and denial of our own truth and power. This inner deal-making is transacted in thousands of ways, and one can learn more about the process in psychoanalytic literature. One brief example, mentioned earlier, shows the unconscious ego offering up the defense of laziness, with its accompanying guilt and shame, to deflect the self-aggression's objection to our underlying passivity.

The inner tyranny that is subsequently established in the devil's pact between self-aggression and inner passivity can be compared to a political tyranny. A political tyranny maintains power, in part, through corruption of the media and the judiciary (represented inwardly by the unconscious ego), while we, the population (our self) remain ignorant and passive. Because we are so unconscious, this devil's pact can become our fate. It means we "buy into" an obfuscation of the truth about ourselves and live in a dream world in which we are lost to ourself. The hero's plunge into the unconscious is the process of our discovery, recovery, and restoration. When we see self-aggression for what it is, we understand that it does not represent our truth. In fact, it is an attack on the essence of who we are. We have to become smarter than the self-aggression in order to transmute it, to turn it into creativity and consciousness. But it won't happen if we are fooled by our defenses. (Chapter 4 provides insight into how our defenses work.)

We become defensive as we resonate with accusations and insinuations, whether they come inwardly in the form of self-aggression or externally from others. The worst way to interact with self-aggression is to be defensive. It's like being defensive all the time with a partner or spouse, or passive-aggressive with others and ourself. It just feeds the negative energies and causes us to feel and do things that are self-defeating. However, it's very hard not to be defensive when we don't understand these inner dynamics.

In his book, *The Superego*, Edmund Bergler wrote, "Without exaggeration, one can speak of the superego's 'twenty-four-hour schedule of torture.'" Bergler adds, "we think, feel, act, work, love, are moody, become irritated with trifles, bore or amuse ourselves, and to some extent even dream in an unconscious attempt to construct a convincing unconscious alibi and defense."[x] These reactions are part of the array of inner compromises that our inner passivity makes to cope with our self-aggression. Though it's our inner passivity that makes these compromises, we have to become responsible for its doing so. Thus, it is more helpful to accept the notion that *we* make these compromises, rather than an unconscious part of us.

We can see how different people deal with their self-aggression. All of the following personality types are passive to it—they just have different ways of reacting. Shy people have a very passive relationship with it. They absorb it and feel beaten down by it. Outwardly angry people, often "injustice collectors" and so-called "victims," exhibit the intensity of their own self-aggression—they take it in, absorb it, and viciously throw it back out at whoever or whatever becomes a convenient target. "Jokesters" are people who try to undermine their self-aggression through humor, making puns, wisecracks, and jokes that reduce to absurdity the allegations contained in their self-aggression. Optimists are stoics who numb themselves to the inner assault, pretending through this persona that they are somehow above it all, while pessimists and cynics concede to its validity as it sours and embitters them. "Blamers" desperately try to deflect it and pass it on to others before it sinks too far into them. All of the above personality types are passive or passive-aggressive because their behavior constitutes unconscious reactions to a perceived higher, albeit negative, authority—our self-aggression.

We can see the effects of self-aggression on Tom, a fifty-year-old state employee. Tom's girlfriend, Deborah, complained that he often wasn't attentive or present to her. "He has these different personalities, and when he goes into one of them I just don't know who he is. It feels so bizarre, like I'm in some never-never land. One time he's a baby, then a giddy joker or court jester, then a pompous ass, then a beaten wimp, then a raging maniac, and finally a gooey lover who wants to make everything okay. It's very painful for me when this happens."

In our next session, Tom and I explored the significance of these subpersonalities. He admitted he acted out these different roles, although he didn't see that all of them were necessarily inappropriate. "I'm caught between feeling that I've got to stop and feeling that she is blowing it all out of proportion. When I see how hurt she is, though, I know I've got to try to change this."

We looked for how he would begin to slip out of "that centered place," as he called it, "when I feel on top of things, good about myself, and at peace with Deborah." One morning several days earlier, after a week or more of being composed and in harmony with Deborah, he noticed that he had begun to criticize himself for not having taken care of some overdue paperwork. That afternoon he also encountered a few work problems that he felt could have been prevented with more diligence on his part. By that evening, out shopping in a department store with Deborah, he slipped into the baby subpersonality. From here he raised his voice a few octaves, adopted a sing-song harmony, and said about a tricycle they passed, "Oh, isn't this a sweet little thing. We can ride it down the aisles." At times in the past, Deborah had reacted in a neutral manner to this behavior, but more and more she found it repulsive.

"What do you think is behind this baby subpersonality?" I asked.

"Well, it feels cute, even charming. I do often get people to smile and laugh when I slip into that persona."

"When did you first start to use it?"

"I remember doing it in high school. I'd come home and approach my mother, usually in the kitchen, and say as I drooped my head on her shoulder, 'Oh, mommy, mommy.' Mother would kiss me and hug me, so my behavior was certainly validated. My sisters and I used to compete a lot for what little of my parents' affection was available. Being a good, sweet boy was one of my devices."

"This subpersonality and all the others," I said, "reflect the master-slave relationship you have with your self-aggression. First of all, from what you described this past Tuesday [and from what I knew about Tom from previous sessions], you find yourself being weak and defensive against inner attacks. Next thing you know, you're in the baby subpersonality. You've gone there for protection from your self-aggression, hoping your self-aggression won't beat up a defenseless baby. Let's look at the other subpersonalities. The giddy joker is like a court jester who can tease or tweak the self-aggression in the attempt to reduce it to absurdity. While an actual court jester could tease his sovereign the King, it was clear who had the power. Next you're the pompous ass. From this place, you try to ignore Deborah (or your self-aggression) and proclaim your own reality, emphasizing from your soapbox the validity of your impressions. The beaten wimp, meanwhile, has capitulated, accepting the slave position, while the raging maniac is all pseudo-aggression, trying to look tough to cover up the passivity. Finally, the imploring lover comes to Deborah looking for her to make it all better, like a parent kissing a nick on your finger, so that through her forgiveness the self-aggression can be mollified. All these subpersonalities are passive parts of you that you use, largely unsuccessfully, to hold off or deflect your self-aggression. You have this wardrobe of subpersonalities, and you try on whatever works."

Tom was pensive for a moment. "In the light of this I have to admit that there is a motto that has governed my life. And that is, 'Direct me. I'll do whatever you want.' That just came to me." Tom remembered at that moment an incident from earlier in the day. A businessman had tried to charge him $100 for a service that was never provided. Tom called the man, and it was agreed that the charge was improper. "Suddenly, as I heard him admit his mistake, I felt his cheeks go red," Tom said. "And then, you know what, I became passive with him. I said to him, 'Hey, these things happen. It's no big deal—don't worry about it.' I went on and on like that, like I was apologizing for even bringing it up." After our discussion, Tom called the man again and "made sure" the money was credited to him.

Once Tom saw how his many subpersonalities originated out of his passivity and understood how self-aggression lurked within his psyche and struck from out of the darkness there, he began to drop these personas. Now he could be himself, and he became someone who, as Deborah said, she could more fully trust to be real.

Self-aggression is a biological drive, while passivity, as I've said, is an emotional attachment. As mentioned, understanding emotional attachments presents a cognitive challenge. An attachment consists of our unconscious willingness, or temptation, to experience a given situation through an old, unresolved, negative feeling (such as being deprived, refused, controlled, helpless, criticized, rejected, and so on). These attachments are extraordinarily powerful—yet people don't know they have them. We erect various defenses (blaming, excuses, denial, and so on) to try to prove that we are not secretly willing to come under the influence of our unresolved negative emotions.

Our inner predicament mirrors our collective experience. Our political, social, and economic forms and interactions, as well as our experiences of family life, are based on how we perceive the world through the filters of our own psychology. There is no other way it can be. As long as we are passive to our inner authoritarian aggression, we create an external situation that mirrors this inner dynamic. For instance, even in a democracy we can be apprehensive or fearful of government officials and agencies, the police, the legal system, doctors, parents, teachers, and various authority figures.

We also project the inner aggression outward to others, either physically, verbally, in our imagination, or in our dreams. A young client named Bill had a dream in which he hit Sonny, a friend of his, over the head with his guitar. Bill had dreamed that he and Sonny were at a party where Bill's ex-girlfriend, Eve, and her new boyfriend showed up. At that point, Sonny made a wisecrack to Bill about how Eve's new boyfriend had got the best of him, and Bill, who had been playing his guitar, angrily hit Sonny with it.

I told Bill, "Sonny's sarcastic comment and your retaliation represent your own inner conflict. You have been depressed about losing your girlfriend, and that depression has come about because you have been berating yourself or, more harshly, mocking yourself, for letting that happen. This inner attack on you for allegedly losing your girlfriend is represented in Sonny's comment, and your retaliation against Sonny reflects how painfully you yourself take in the self-aggression, allowing it to have its way with you. Freed from it, you would be kind and supportive of yourself as you go through this difficult experience of losing your girlfriend."

As we become more conscious of self-aggression, we see it for what it is, a rogue energy that has not been brought under our conscious mastery. Soon we are able to deflect the accusations harmlessly aside. In time, such is our growing power that the accusations cease altogether.

Banishment from Our Self

The circumstances that induce much of our self-denunciation are innate or biological. We come into the world with aggression because we need it to survive and thrive. Once turned inward against us, it instigates unhappiness, at the same time that it can prod us toward greater self-understanding and wisdom. Children feel their self-aggression acutely when adults mishandle situations involving them.

When George was four, he initiated some genital exploration with his three-year-old sister. George's behavior may have been induced by the particularly fastidious manner in which his mother bathed him and kept his penis washed and clean. One day their mother found them in the act of innocently childish sexual exploration and condemned George in a most unforgiving manner. He was shut in his room for a day and a night, and on his release his mother continued to regard him with disgust and hostility for several more days.

Forty years later, following reminiscences with family members, he began to remember being locked in that room. He had burned in utter shame and self-loathing, he recalled, as he heaped on himself the utter condemnation he felt from his mother. With her condemnation internalized as such, he had likely experienced a more severe punishment than his mother intended to confer.

George had sat there alone in his banishment, rocking back and forth on his bed with his arms folded around his legs. Out of his inner turmoil and confusion one thing at least came clear—at last he knew who he was. His self-aggression, fortified by his mother's disgust and scorn, let him know he was truly worthless, like one of those ants or other bugs his mom smashed with the fly swatter. How could he expect to live with himself? It was simply too painful. He felt the need to disown that part of him that was so bad. He wanted nothing more to do with himself. When he was finally allowed out of his room, his head hung dismally on his chest and he could look at no one. He didn't need to see the condemnation in their eyes—he was infused with self- condemnation. The self-aggression in that moment was annihilating. Kilowatts of negative energy scorched his soul. He would be a good boy now and hope they would accept this new redeemed version of him.

George's curse of self-banishment had lasted forty years. Over that time he managed well enough—he got married, raised a family, and had some success in his career. But satisfactions and happiness were always fleeting, replaced by a great void in his life that left him feeling somehow inadequate and unworthy. And he was especially sensitive to feelings of being overlooked, discounted, or rejected by others, the very experiences to which through self-aggression he subjected himself.

Whenever he did something that he felt looked bad in the eyes of others, his self-aggression returned in full force, burning his face in intense shame, draining him of spirit, and leaving him feeling sick to his stomach. During this time, he also lacked sensitivity for others, and people often experienced him as being cold, remote, and indifferent. Since he wasn't sensitive to himself, and was unaware of his self-banishment, he could not really be sensitive to others. He could only honor their being at the rather superficial level at which he acknowledged himself.

George's story is our story, for self-banishment is common to us all. When self-aggression is fueled by harsh parental condemnation, it causes a break or "disconnect" from ourself. Usually this break happens in a process that is more covert and subtle than George's. Often it involves being subdued through fear, shame, scorn, guilt, and humiliation. We become disconnected from ourself, and we go through our lives, day after day, year after year, without checking in with ourself, without remembering ourself or being present to ourself. It's like having a friend who seldom calls or says hello. This friend takes us for granted, like we take ourself for granted. This condition of knowing ourself superficially, as if we are simply an old acquaintance with whom we are familiar, is an element of inner passivity. Our life is half-lived. Our relationship with ourself is inconsistent—antagonistic in one context, cheerful in another, and nonexistent in still another.

As George put it as he was breaking free of his identification with his false self: "In trying to gain acceptance, you extinguish the person who is you. You grow up to be comfortable with the false you. When the real, vibrant you tries to emerge, you feel wrong or bad. When I started to feel powerful, a part of me would say, 'No, no, that's wrong. This is not who you are.'"

Problems of passivity can be acute for individuals who experienced sexual molestation and abuse in their childhood. A child forced to submit to sexual abuse is thrown so deeply into passivity that often dissociation occurs, experienced as a temporary break in consciousness as in slumber or a coma. This form of dissociation is an internal protection from horror, pain, and helplessness, similar to the lapses into unconsciousness that can occur during torture. An adult's self-hatred can be a consequence of early childhood abuse. Here, as a lingering effect of the acute passivity, the capacity for self-protection is so weak that self-aggression encounters little opposition and overwhelms the person's sense of self. The person can't distinguish himself from the rejection and hatred of his self-aggression.

We all grow up identifying with a limited, often painful, sense of ourself. Our egotism and our attachments to unresolved negative emotions leave us feeling separate and fragmented. Unless validated by outside sources or authorities, we are unable to recognize and support ourself, and so we feel and act like orphans, slaves, or beggars. We can feel that we have no voice and no say and that our very being is of no consequence. Or, conversely, as a compensation for this deep attachment to feeling inconsequential, we identify with our ego and an overvalued sense of self, and become narcissistic. We go back and forth between these two extremes. Meanwhile, our self-aggression finds a new way to torture us. Not only are we passive to our self-aggression, but also our self-aggression begins to berate us and condemn us for our affinity for passivity. This mechanism is based on the anti-hedonistic principle: our self-aggression objects to anything that we indulge in, and our passivity in its many variations is high on the list of our secret indulgences. Thus, much of our "acting out" and various behavioral difficulties, as well as emotional reactions such as annoyance, anger, and hatred, are cover-ups or defenses against this accusation from our inner critic that we emotionally attached to our underlying passivity.

We might say in our inner defense: "No, I'm not attached to my passivity. I want to have power, I want to be powerful." To make this defense work, we are desperate to feel power. We often create a sense of power by acting out inappropriately or else by imagining situations in which we are manifesting it. The phenomenal international success of the Harry Potter novels by the author J.K. Rowling offers evidence for this inner condition. Harry Potter is an English orphan who, rescued from wicked relatives and sent off to study at the Hogwarts School of Witchcraft and Wizardry, rises from the helplessness of his abandonment and subjugation to acquire supernatural powers. Millions of readers, all of whom are steeped in childhood experiences of passivity, thrill to the feeling of acquiring such power as they identify with Harry and his wizard friends.

Early Childhood Helplessness

Psychoanalysis, of all the psychological approaches, has made the best attempt to understand passivity and its significance. Freud discussed passivity in many contexts, including that of childhood helplessness. In a 1994 book, *Freud's Concept of Passivity*, Russell H. Davis wrote that Freud used the words passivity, passively, and passive a total of 239 times in forty-four of his works.[xi] Freud wrote that fear of death, fear of life, and fear of nature are an emotional continuation of the state of helplessness of the small child and constitute the need for religious belief.

"As we already know," Freud wrote in "The Future of an Illusion," an essay published in 1927, "the terrifying impression of helplessness in childhood aroused the need for protection—for protection through love—which was provided by the father; and the recognition that this helplessness lasts throughout life made it necessary to cling to the existence of a father, but this time a more powerful one. Thus the benevolent rule of a divine Providence allays our fear of the dangers of life . . ."[xii]

Unconscious passivity is at play in the psyche whether or not we believe in God, whether or not we are spiritual practitioners, and whether or not we are participants in organized religion.

Freud devoted much of his thought and writing to the subject of aggression, particularly in relation to the superego, the death instinct, and suppression. At the heart of psychoanalysis is the idea that we are shaped emotionally when our biological impulses and psychological drives, including the unrestrained impulses and fantasies of the id, interact with the authority of the family and by extension the authority of society and the state.

The noted literary critic Lionel Trilling, in a commentary on the poem written in 1940 by W.H. Auden in tribute to

Freud, had this to say in explaining the position of psychoanalysis:

> The individual in the course of his development incorporates this authority into his emotional system, in both its conscious and its unconscious parts. If the authority thus internalized is excessively strict—as it may be either because it mirrors the actual repressiveness of the parental control or because the individual for some reason imagines the external authority to be more exigent than it actually is—there will result a malfunction of the instinctual life, inhibiting the healthy development of the personality and causing great emotional pain. The malfunction begins in earliest childhood, though it may not manifest itself until a later time, and Freud's method of therapy is to bring the patient into the light of consciousness of the particular circumstances, actual or fancied, that may serve to explain where his emotional life went wrong, why the "internalized authority" is devoted to causing pain.[xiii]

Later in his essay, Trilling writes, ". . . it will be plain that it [psychoanalysis] is antagonistic to authoritarianism, though not to rational authority."[xiv]

If this "internalized authority" is so irrational and antagonistic, as I agree it is, then what constitutes the part of us that appears to fail to stand against it? If internalized aggression is a major negative influence upon us, then isn't it obvious that some part of ourself is being passive to it? Indeed, this inner aggression is self-negating, and it is our passivity that allows it to limit us, confine us, and inflict suffering upon us. Before we examine this further, let us return to more consideration of the child's passive experience. Many of our experiences in our first few years are passive in nature. The following experiences of infancy and childhood have been observed and recorded by Edmund Bergler.[xv]

The child:

- is completely dependent on the mother;

- feels passively "victimized" even when being fed (in contrast with the womb where everything was provided "by himself");

- is passively subjected to a time schedule for his meals;

- must undergo the passively experienced "tragedy" of weaning;

- feels in toilet functions that something irresistible drains parts of his body;

- feels helpless to the forced movement of his body during handling and diaper changing; feels that "something" forces him to sleep;

- feels in toilet training and early socialization that he is being forced to submit to mother's rules and requirements, hence the rebellion of "the terrible twos";

- begins (in the case of boys) to fear his father as a competitor for mother's affection, and (for boys and girls) to fear father as a source of imagined or real punishment.

Birds and mammals are independent in the first year or two of life, while humans spend many years in a state of relative helplessness and dependency, during which our passive condition is imprinted on our psyche. Geza

Roheim, author of *Psychoanalysis and Anthropology*, wrote about the significance of this biological reality:

> I think nobody will dissent if I say that the period of immaturity or helplessness is more protracted in man than in any other animal. . . Now it is a curious fact that while man's delayed infancy is universally admitted hardly anybody uses this fact in the sense that I do. . . How is it that nobody recognizes that in this one fact we have one of the most important keys to the understanding of human nature?[xvi]

The child's relationship with the mother is complicated, and it incorporates some fear and aversion surrounding the impression that he or she is at the mercy of "a powerful giant." By the time of the Oedipal stage beyond the age of two, father's presence begins to have more impact on the child. A new order is now set up, consisting of mother, father, and child, replacing the mother-child duality of the earlier stages. A boy is now able to demote the "threatening and fear-inspiring mother figure," the giant of the nursery, by identifying with the father's strength. In fact, the boy is able to shift his impression of his mother dramatically. She becomes an image of his own frightened and passive self.

The boy now sees his mother as being completely dominated by his father. Bergler wrote that the boy, now identifying with his father, "finds the once frightening Giantess of his babyhood to be completely 'weak, passive, helpless,' just as he had been in the past. . . In general, the Oedipus complex is frequently misunderstood to mean only that 'the boy desires his mother sexually.' Its prehistory, which is suffused with fright, terror, massive passivity, is entirely disregarded."[xvii] The boy's identification with his father's strength serves to counteract passivity by demoting the role and influence of mother.

Within a few years, however, passivity is again reinforced when the boy begins to experience his father as a source of potential or real punishment. The boy also has been experiencing his father as a competitor for mother's affections but realizes he must renounce any designs upon his mother, who, in any case, does not take his interest seriously. The boy, in unconscious feminine identification, feels that he wants to be loved by his father, as his mother is.

A girl's experience of childhood is similar. It appears, however, that a girl is able to digest the passive experience more easily, more successfully, without the boy's desperate need for a countervailing effort against it. In the Oedipal stage, as a girl identifies with her mother, her urgent need is for her father's validation and love, and she suffers greatly if she and her mother are not getting it. Because passive traits in women have more social sanction, women are usually less assailed by self-aggression for having these traits. It may appear that the social sanction of passivity in women makes it more difficult for them to overcome it. However, men have a corresponding hardship in their rigorous opposition to considering it in themselves. In any case, when passivity is acted out in self-defeating ways, it is certainly equally painful for both sexes.

Even sophisticated, liberated women may not feel, on a deep emotional level, their equality with men because many of them still experience themselves through fear, doubt, and distrust. Men do too, of course. Both men and women are perfectly willing to use each other to feel oppressed, and this sense of oppression is usually subjective and emotional, self-created and co-created with one's partner.

"I Don't Want to be Passive."

At least one school of psychoanalysis says we have an inner wish to experience our passivity.[xviii] This wish or attachment derives from the fact that any unresolved psychic conflict is going to be sought out, acted out, and repeated compulsively by us. A conflict involves the compulsion to experience ourselves repeatedly through a negative impression, i.e., feeling deprived, refused, helpless, ineffective, and overwhelmed. Consciously we dislike and try to avoid the pain associated with passivity, while unconsciously we seek it out because we still identify with ourself through the feeling. As we begin to dislodge and eliminate our passivity, we discover that letting go of the attachment (or working it out) involves a monumental shift in our identity or sense of self. In this process, our passivity becomes less abstract, less like a phantom and more like a state of internal affairs that we can access with our senses and our intelligence.

If we don't know ourself through what is familiar, even if painful, it feels as if we don't know who we are at all. Our sense of identity is based on what is familiar. We orient ourself in the world through our appearance, beliefs, habits, emotions, memories, skills, fears, pleasures, and self-image. Even though our passivity is unconscious, it is an accepted or at least a habitual part of our experience of ourself, like the smog youngsters in East Los Angeles grow up thinking is normal. Inner passivity is dissipated gradually as it is exposed as an alien element and as we begin to see the manifestations of it in our life.

The "unconscious repetition compulsion" illustrates the appeal of the passive experience. This compulsion refers to our active repetition of passively endured experiences. In other words, in this conflict we repeat actively an experience that in childhood was felt by us as a hurt in the passive position. A child who was beaten repeatedly and viciously by his father is far more likely to become a child abuser when he grows up than is a child who was raised appropriately. An adult who is now beating his own children identifies with the passive experience of the child being beaten, thus transplanting himself back emotionally to that old, familiar experience of himself being abused and violated. He is compelled to find some way to experience himself through passivity, and violence against children is, through identification, one of his unconsciously chosen forms of passivity.

The classic example of the unconscious repetition compulsion, presented by Freud, involves the little girl who sits fearfully in the dentist's chair, where, despite her protests, she is forced to open her mouth and have the dentist's fingers and tools inserted. She comes home and plays dentist with her younger sister. The older sister is now the dentist and the younger is the patient who submits, at her older sister's insistence, to the passive experience that the older sister endured earlier. The older sister repeats the passive event, this time taking on for herself the sense of power, in order to cover up or defend against her attachment to the passive experience: "I don't want to be passive—I want to be the aggressive dentist." This illustrates not only the impact that the passive experience has on us but also our underlying emotional attachment to it and the measures we will take, in this particular case, to hide it from ourselves (by reversing roles), while, at the same time, to experience it (through identification with the younger sister).

Another perspective on passivity involves the anal-retentive characteristic. Toilet training is a time when the passive experience is quite acute for a child. The child initially may feel fear in being unavoidably "drained" in the elimination process, although at the onset of the anal stage, beginning at eighteen months, he normally finds gratification in the unregulated elimination of feces. However, he is now being forced by his mother to renounce that pleasure and control that function. The anal period of childhood development is the time of the "terrible twos," when children object strenuously to being told what they can and can't do.

The child reacts passive-aggressively to this feeling of being controlled. By stubbornly refusing to release feces, he is rebelling against the feeling of being forced to submit. The rebellion is based on the child's subjective impression that toilet training is an imposition, something forced upon him that he has no choice but to endure passively. Later in life, the adult often misconstrues various experiences as an imposition upon him, an attempt to make him submit, when that is not the intention of the other person or the situation. Through our passivity we are under the impression that we are being acted upon by external events or forces. It seems some outer circumstances cause us to feel a certain way or that someone's behavior makes us react in some manner or other.

I don't know how many times clients of mine have said something to the effect of, "His behavior made me angry." To this I reply, "His behavior didn't make you angry. He was a catalyst for your reaction, and you have to take responsibility for becoming angry. When you trace the anger within, you see that it covers up deeper negativity that you are willing to take on. That is why you want to blame the other person, so you don't have to face this aspect of yourself."

The Argument Culture

A social symptom of this inner sense of oppression is the "argument culture," spotlighted by the verbal jousting of TV and radio talk shows. When passivity lurks in the background, we are more desperate than ever to win the argument. Why? If we lose the argument, we feel beaten, defeated, and forced to submit to the other person's point of view. Who we are, it feels, is negated; what we stand for is demoted or dismissed. We also feel that if defeated by the other (representing a different personal, political, religious, or social persuasion), we will be forced to submit to the programs, beliefs, and processes that the other, in victory, will want to impose upon us.

Just as we resist with our argumentation in one context, we submit in another. Either way it is passivity. Demagogues and zealots are often easily able to implant their ideas and beliefs into individuals, particularly under conditions of group excitation. Instances of mass capitulation to the ideas and beliefs of others involve brainwashing, indoctrination, fanaticism, mass hysteria, and cultism. The extraordinary passivity of cult members is evident in documentaries and books on the subject.

Madison Avenue and big business know of the degree to which we can, in a sense, be bought. The cunningly crafted images and language of advertising influence our desires and manipulate our behavior. The advertising message may be most effective when we, as consumers languidly ensconced in front of our television sets, are at our most passive. However, we can't blame advertisers. The problem is our passivity. Call it the Law of Inertia: wherever passivity exists, outside energy, even in the form of goofy commercials that exaggerate and lie, will invade and overtake its space.

We won't be sensitive to the feelings of those who oppose us when inner passivity is present in our debates about civil rights, abortion, euthanasia, missile defense, affirmative action, genetic manipulation, homosexuality, and so on. The more passive we are, the more we fear and condemn the other side. Hostile arguments are manifestations of the split within ourself that is acted out with others. Ideally, we want to understand those who oppose us and how their opinions are formed. From an enlightened perspective, we can see stubbornness and willful ignorance in others as a part of ourself, representing our own inner resistance to deeper understanding of human nature and ultimately of nondual reality.

Truth and understanding are found in the individual himself, far below the surface, something known through his own being. Passivity is a blockage to the accessing of that source. We are mechanistic and our humanity is compromised due to how we react to self-aggression. This represents our lack of evolvement, of course, not the human norm or ideal. We stand in the shadow of our false self, shoring up an illusion, acting out our fate, and protecting our defenses.

Chapter 4
Demolishing Our Defenses

Passivity must be made visible if we're going to overcome it. We need to track this phantom to its lair and scorch its ugly countenance in the illumination of our awareness. Learning how to penetrate our defenses is one of the best ways to do this. Our defenses are unconsciously erected and maintained in order to protect the inner status quo, meaning our illusions, our egotism, our passivity, and our capitulation to a tyrannical underworld.

Variations on defenses number in the thousands, and issues involving work and money are a factor in many of them. Jack, a client in his thirties, described various symptoms of passivity with respect to his job at an electronics and computer company. "It all seems so burdensome. I never feel comfortable at work. The assignments aren't that hard, but I don't feel excited or motivated, and it's hard to get started. It always feels as if I'm doing something I don't want to be doing. I often daydream about being in some kind of business of my own, or else living in a cabin in the woods somewhere with no responsibilities at all.

"When I was growing up, I did chores only when they were forced on me. My mother was always there, criticizing it, finding fault. Now I hate the feeling of somebody telling me what to do. But then I end up slacking off, and, sure enough, somebody comes along and tells me what to do.

"I would like to feel passionate about my work. But rather than looking for a vocation I choose jobs that pay the most money. Money is a major concern. I feel the need to save at least twenty or thirty percent of my paycheck. I feel very anxious when I'm not saving at this rate. It feels as if I need to get more, get another raise, and save even more money."

Jack had erected a money defense against his passivity. He associated money with freedom and had hopes of being in a position financially to retire in fifteen years. Unconsciously, he was willing to go on feeling passive, in this case feeling forced at work to do things he felt he didn't want to do. His unconscious defense claimed: "I don't want to be passive. I want to be free and that's why I'm saving so much money, so I can retire early." To keep this defense in place, Jack was required to continue to worry about his retirement account: "Look how worried I am that I might not be able to retire early." In trying to defend against passivity, we often throw ourselves into a deeper, more painful experience of passivity. In a sense, we can become passive to our defense. In Jack's case, not only did he feel controlled at work, but now he was also controlled by his defense: he was required to go on saving a high percentage of his income in his attempt to prove it was freedom he wanted, to cover up the fact that he experienced a boss's or supervisor's authority through his passivity.

As a psychotherapist, I need to be skillful in penetrating the defenses of my clients. As I do this, they often find it quite disconcerting to be left with little wiggle room. In the process of adhering to and acting out our defenses, we unconsciously prefer to be deceived and to do ourself harm rather than to see the truth about ourself. We fight constantly against the full affective understanding of our passivity.

We shy away from our own truth because, emotionally, we associate it with exposing something unsavory that long has been repressed. We learned as children that our parents disapprove of some of our behaviors and beliefs, including matters concerning sex. To gain their approval, we repressed our own sense of truth and reality, and now looking inward is associated emotionally with what is forbidden. We also harbor ambivalent feelings toward our parents—loving them in one context or at one moment and hating them and having aggressive impulses toward them in another. "Step on a crack and break your mother's back," one woman said, remembering as a child "seeing" her mother's spine in the sidewalk cracks she gleefully tromped on. As children we don't understand that this ambivalence is normal. So negative thoughts or hateful wishes that occur to us about our parents are felt by us to be bad or evil. Little boys and girls imagine how scandalized their parents would be were they to learn of their children's secret thoughts, impulses, and wishes. There is no need to act on these wishes to feel guilty— the wish alone is sufficient to create guilt, and sometimes the wish is even unconscious. To curb our guilt and shame, we institute repression to store the "forbidden" material in the unconscious, thereby eliminating it from our awareness.

Later in life, when it would be appropriate to "look inside" oneself for insight and understanding to remedy painful emotions and behaviors, what we encounter in the way of self-knowledge is felt to be forbidden, the stuff of self-accusation and non-acceptance, and thus we feel resistance to accessing it. Enormous resistance underlies the joke in a cartoon in *The New Yorker*: a man lying on a couch says to the psychoanalyst seated behind him, "Look, call it denial if you like, but I think what goes on in my personal life is none of my own damn business." It is no joke how many people have that attitude, in the form of their unconscious resistance to exploring valuable knowledge about themselves.

Because of self-aggression, self-knowledge can be quickly turned into self-accusation, to which the unconscious ego becomes passive and quickly defends. We associate truth about ourself with the prospect of exposure and punishment, with being bad, inadequate, and not deserving. We also fear this truth because we are afraid it will hurt others, afraid we will be disliked or hated for expressing it, and afraid it will cause us to lose everything, especially the false or limited self with which we are identified. As we take the plunge, however, the inner space of our unconscious opens up before us, becoming intriguing, then fascinating, and then the magical pathway home to our source.

Knowledge That Penetrates Defenses

Defenses are enmeshed in our self-deception. We succumb to inner processes and dynamics that distort perception and impede our ability to be objective. For the most part, we are unaware of how we are deceived and how we deceive ourselves. For example, when we blame others or life in general for our self-generated problems and failures, we are, of course, refusing to acknowledge our own contribution and complicity. More than that, however, we aren't even seeing how blatantly we are lying to ourself.

According to the traditional interpretation, defenses are inner mechanisms established to protect us from being overwhelmed by threatening and even destructive thoughts, impressions, and impulses—like something a person might experience on a bad LSD trip. If our defenses suddenly disappeared, we would certainly be swamped emotionally and mentally by all of our repressed material. But defenses can also be understood in another way, as an inner system of chicanery through which we block out deeper truths about ourself. Why would we want to do that?

Our so-called defenses are not protecting us but instead are guarding an inner status quo that includes a secret power structure and our attachments to negative emotions and impressions. We are, as I have indicated, like naive inhabitants of a fantasy land, wandering around in what we believe to be a democracy—but which instead is a secret despotism. We settle for the illusion of democracy, an illusion that protects our ego but keeps us weak and subservient. Our ego is like a puppet prince sitting on his throne, reveling in his ascendancy, while the real power resides with the Machiavellian minister of state—our self-aggression—lurking in the wings. Through the ego each of us is convinced that "even if things are going badly for me, I am still running the show." We settle for this arrangement, in large part out of ignorance, rather than challenge and overthrow the secret power structure. As long as we remain ignorant of our defenses and what they block from our awareness, we are simply acting out the prompting of unconscious forces. We are not voluntary creators of our thoughts, emotions, or actions. This inner predicament of ours is the foundation of our passivity.

Projection is one of the defenses through which we deceive ourselves. In this defense, we see (and dislike or hate) in others those negative attributes that we refuse, for the reasons stated, to see in ourself. Projection is often behind personality clashes, where two individuals dislike each other because each holds up to the other a mirror of the other. Projection is often imposed upon children by their parents. The children then feel judged or criticized and believe they are at fault because of something bad or wrong in them. Typically, such parents feel annoyed or upset at their children for the traits the parents see or imagine in their children that they don't like in themselves (i.e., a father projects his own passivity onto his son and then experiences disapproval, dislike, and even rejection of his son). In understanding this dynamic, we can see how unfair and even how abusive it is to children, who take their parents' projections against them at face value and begin to identify with themselves in a negative way. One day, when we all become more conscious, parents might be held accountable for this emotional mistreatment. Commonly, parents also project their ego ideal onto their children, resulting in the imposition on the children of high expectations and standards of performance.

Transference, another defense, also clouds our attempts to see what is real and true. In transference, we experience others according to our own unconscious expectations and attachments, based on infantile misperceptions and childhood experiences with our parents. Transference is the unconscious compulsion to experience current events and relationships in a manner that revives emotional attachments and hurts from our past.

For example, we might consistently feel that we don't get anything of value from others, or from life in general, when the main problem is our transference of this expectation onto others based on feelings from our childhood that mother or father, or both, never gave us anything of value. Now the feeling is, "My partner never gives to me, my kids don't give to me, health providers don't take care of me—yes, and even the universe doesn't care about me or give to me." Meanwhile, we are unconsciously attached to that unresolved emotion, meaning we are tempted and even determined to continue to experience ourselves through that familiar old feeling of being deprived and refused.

The defense is, "I'm not looking for that feeling of being deprived and refused. Look at how upset I am that I'm not getting what I want from others. That proves how much I want to get!" All the while, stoking a bonfire of self-deceit, we are throwing our energy into creating and maintaining such detrimental defenses and allowing our intelligence to be sapped, conned, and manipulated, depleting our capacity for worthwhile endeavors.

Avoidance of certain people (or situations) with whom one feels passive is a defense based on this premise: "How can I be passive! Look, I don't even want to be around that person." Acting out this defense limits an individual's options and generates missed opportunities for friendship and other benefits. It can also have other self-defeating spinoffs, such as fear of flying. The defense contends: "I'm not looking for the feeling of being helpless, at the mercy of the airplane, the pilot, the weather, or whatever. Look, I don't even want to get on an airplane." Through his imagination, this individual feels the terror of dropping out of the sky in an out-of-control airplane. What we are attached to arises as fear or loathing of external circumstances in which the negative emotion is experienced. In this case, the person is emotionally attached to the feeling of helplessness and being out of control, even though consciously he hates the feeling. He then "uses" his avoidance or fear of airplane travel as a means to "prove" he is not attached to helplessness.

We also avoid dealing with certain subjects, particularly our own behaviors and feelings, when we're afraid of being exposed to a critical onslaught or overwhelmed by repressed feelings. A typical avoider is someone who changes the subject or evades a direct question in order to stay clear of threatening material. "Diverters," ramblers, and weasels have mastered the art of being evasive and protective, often in order to feel in control of situations.

Attempting to feel power, or taking a bold action, is often a defense against passivity. A man in his fifties, a gentleman and professional, experienced himself passively in an encounter with friends, although he wasn't aware at the time of being passive. Fifteen minutes later he was in a department store and shoplifted an item of clothing. The action was completely out of character. As he related the experience, he described the moment he decided to take the item and leave the store: "It felt as if taking this item—I hate to use the word stealing—restored my balance. I felt strong again, and thrilled to have been so gutsy and daring. In fact, I felt invincible, that there was no danger of being caught. I was smiling to myself as I walked to my car. But within five minutes, feelings of guilt and remorse and foolishness descended on me. I was miserable all day."

The more daring the action, the more we can feel that our power has been restored. The defense is, "I'm not interested in experiencing myself passively—I want the feeling of power!" This is a reason that some teenagers, who are floundering in their struggle for inner autonomy, join gangs and engage in ritualized acts of vandalism and violence. Typically, such self-defeating reactions can produce an even more intense experience of what we are defending against. In other words, if the shoplifter had been caught and arrested, the sense of helplessness and passivity in the experience of being detained by authorities and charged with theft would have been enormous.

We can also react to our passivity by adopting a behavior or action for which we make the claim, "I did it my way." An example would be a passive husband who is hounded by his wife to achieve a higher income from his work. To oblige her in the manner she expects creates in him the impression that he is being passive to her. So he looks for a way to appear to comply with her request—allegedly based on his choice or his decision. Typically, when we react to passivity or defend against it, the result is self-defeating. In this case, under the pretext of trying to make more money, the man goes out and invests in a dubious scheme that promises huge returns but ends up going bust. He feels guilt and shame over the outcome, and by focusing on his blunder he manages to overlook completely his underlying passivity. He finds only slight solace in telling himself, "I was only trying to make more money, like she wanted." This individual sabotages himself in that, unconsciously, he fails in his endeavors in order to remain passively subjugated to his wife's expectations and demands.

A variation on this defense is, I believe, a factor in childhood learning problems. Faced with an intellectual challenge, the child doubts himself, questions his abilities, and slips into a feeling of helplessness. Now he's in a downward spiral: the more he feels helpless, the worse he does with his learning challenges and the more he feels helpless. The inner imperative is to cover up his passivity, and he does so with the defense of pleading guilty to what in his unconscious is a lesser crime: "I am not looking to feel helpless. The problem is that I am stupid." (Or, "My parents say I have a learning problem.") Now he feels bad about himself, to the point of intense shame for allegedly being stupid or defective, while the true instigator of his difficulties—inner passivity—is covered up.

With passivity, we latch on to an impression of deficiency or weakness and unconsciously create a situation in our life through which we remain entangled in these feelings. One of the ways we do this is through addictions, compulsions, eating disorders, and other failures of self-regulation (see Chapter 7). I also believe that functional illiteracy, which affects one American in five older than sixteen, is a consequence, at least in part, of passivity. The problem is particularly acute in families that are poorly educated, where the parents do not feel confident and powerful. When illiterates and semi-illiterates try to learn to read, they encounter shame and fear, a sense of failure, and an impression of being overwhelmed. A child feels a surge of power at that moment when he or she penetrates into the meaning of words on a page. I remember the day in Grade One when I learned to read my first words: it was an enormous delight and a sense of triumph to have broken through this layer of mystery and penetrated into the realm of adult comprehension. Some children and adults can't cross that bridge because of the limitations they feel about who and what they are. Then they erect the defense of pleading guilty to the lesser crime: "I am not passive. The problem is that I am incompetent or stupid." Again, as they plead guilty to this lesser crime to cover up passivity, they feel shame and a sense of failure for allegedly being stupid. I believe much helpful research can be done investigating a correlation between inner passivity and intellectual capabilities in general.

Our defenses are always shifting. Over its lifetime, our core passivity can have a variety of defenses. It is easy to be fooled into believing the inner core has changed when only the defense strategy or the symptoms have changed. Defenses are dynamic, not static, because the same defense won't always be accepted by our torturing self-aggression; the decline in a defense's effectiveness leads initially to anxiety and then escalates to fear and panic. Pleading guilty to the lesser crime (the defense in the above example) may be exchanged for a defense of pseudo-aggression.

The Defense of Pseudo-Aggression

Becoming inappropriately aggressive or angry is another common defense. This is pseudo-aggression, a defense that often consists of provoking someone or being rude, or carrying out some behavior for the sake of looking active or forceful rather than passive. This defense is invariably self-defeating. It contends: "No, it's not true that I'm wanting to feel controlled, to feel helpless, or to feel refused, criticized, or rejected. Look at how aggressive (or angry) I have become (at whoever or whatever is causing me to feel this way)."

Pseudo-aggression is very different from self-aggression (as discussed in the previous chapter). The former is a defense, the latter a drive. Pseudo-aggression can take many different forms and is related to much more than just anger. Stealing the article of clothing in the earlier example was a pseudo-aggressive reaction. Even passive-aggressive behaviors, through which we procrastinate, withdraw, become sulky, work deliberately slowly, and protest, are forms of pseudo-aggression. The man, for instance, who purposely works slowly, may feel that he is exercising power—"I have decided to do it this way, and I don't care what anybody says." The main objective of pseudo-aggression is to try to prove through some action, emotion, or conviction that we are not attached to the feeling of being deprived, refused, disappointed, overwhelmed, submissive, dismissed, or passive in some other way.

Someone who becomes overly angry because he can't fix the lawnmower or get it to start, for example, or gets furious at someone who won't do his share of housework or office work, is exhibiting pseudo-aggression. This person might believe that his anger is the problem in itself, and he might feel guilty for his anger. Many mental-health practitioners try to treat anger directly, through anger-management techniques ("Hold your breath and count to ten"), without understanding the underlying, deeper emotions that prompt the anger in the first place.

So what are some of the differences between pseudo-aggression and appropriate or normal aggression? Normal aggression or assertion is used only in self-defense, or as an appropriate gesture of self-interest, or for the sake of true justice or compassion. In contrast, pseudo-aggression is used on innocent bystanders to cover up an infantile pattern. In normal aggression, the object of aggression is a legitimate enemy or antagonist, while in pseudo- aggression the object of aggression is an enemy created by our transference, projection, or emotional imagination. We feel no guilt when we respond to a situation with normal aggression, while pseudo-aggression is always a reaction and is usually followed by guilt. Finally, the expression of normal aggression is appropriate to the degree of provocation, while pseudo-aggression overreacts to the slightest inducement.

The brutality of a wife-abuser is an example. A wife might get a beating from such a husband for serving dinner five minutes late. The perpetrator himself feels victimized in some fashion (misunderstood, not appreciated, not respected—either at work, at home, or wherever) and lashes out at his wife as a reaction to some alleged injustice against him. His behavior is neurotic aggression, which is the same as pseudo-aggression. The more passive the wife, the more "liberties" this type of man takes. Meanwhile, the more vicious he becomes, the more he is identifying with the helplessness of the abused.

A pedophile's sick behavior is a form of pseudo-aggression. The pedophile is propelled by his passivity, by his desire to identify with the helplessness and vulnerability of the child. These are feelings that, like the sexual masochist, he has "libidinized" (made sexually pleasurable). Often he feels remorse and shame for his conduct. He will plead guilty, at least in his own mind, to being a sexual aggressor, to seeking forbidden sexual encounters with children. Underneath that, however, he feels his passivity acutely through identification, by being emotionally "in the skin" of the children he renders helpless.

Passivity can be highly alluring when it is experienced as sexual pleasure, as is the case with sexual masochists. However, anyone who can assume a submissive role in sex play, whether in fact or fantasy, can experience the libidinization or "sexualization" of passivity. The dominant partner in sex play can experience pleasure either through the feeling of healthy aggression or by identifying with the submissiveness of his or her partner. This experience is harmless enough in adult lovemaking, particularly when individuals can switch back and forth from passive to dominant, enjoying either role. It is not likely to be healthy, however, if a person is completely dependent on the passive experience for sexual pleasure. The quest for sexual pleasure through passivity can be a powerful compulsion in borderline or psychotic cases, and it is a factor behind crimes such as pedophilia, rape, and the consumption of child pornography.

Passivity and pseudo-aggression, incidentally, know no political boundaries. From the left wing, for instance, violent anti-globalization demonstrators are reacting to the feeling that they will be swallowed up and rendered impotent by a monolithic corporate constitution. From the right wing, prolife advocates, who identify with the powerless of the aborted (or soon-to-be aborted) fetus or with the feeling of the fetus being rejected or devalued, can have a similar belligerent reaction as a way to cover up their own entanglement in helplessness and rejection.

More Cunning Cover-Ups

Our defenses are cunning. If we don't learn precisely how they operate, we'll be fooled every time. The following section provides more examples of our defensive efforts to fend off awareness of our passivity.

Joan was hesitant to approach a woman for money that she was owed. "I'm afraid I'll get angry," she said, explaining her avoidance of approaching the woman.

"Yes, getting angry would be a defense against feeling passive," I said. "And the woman could become determined not to pay you once she was exposed to your anger."

"But I wouldn't go that far. I'm afraid of getting angry, but I wouldn't actually get angry when confronting her. I'm afraid of having any power one-on-one with another person. I'm more powerful when I do something that doesn't involve someone else." Joan told of the time she actually had gotten angry with an elderly woman who had delayed returning Joan's security deposit on an apartment lease. Joan wrote several angry notes and finally went with her father to confront the woman at her house. Joan learned that the woman was deathly ill and had not been able to perform any duties. Joan's father then told her, "See, you shouldn't have gotten angry." Joan felt terrible guilt, and since that time, "I've always been biting back my words."

This experience put her up against another defense that protected her attachment to passivity. Emotionally, it felt to her that to be powerful was to hurt others. She also had another emotional conviction that blocked the expression of her power: when she asked for something from someone who seemed reluctant, she felt wrong for asking. If we give credence to this impression of being wrong for expressing our rights, we remain passive. An emotional impression such as this has to be seen for what it is, a protector of our passivity and a keeper of the keys to inner freedom.

Joan's defense of feeling wrong for asking for her due involved two inner layers of operation. Through her self-aggression, she was berated for her anger. Consequently, she erected a second line of defense against her passivity, in which she claimed, "Yes, it's true, anger is bad. Not only do I feel bad for my anger, I feel bad for even asking for what is due to me in the first place. I'm not going to ask for it in the future."

Gloria, an artist in her fifties, helps us understand the relationship between passivity, rejection, and shame. She described how timid she felt when she attended grade school: "The other kids were noisy, more aggressive, and I couldn't even talk to them. My mother dressed me funny, so that I looked like a displaced child right off the boat. I didn't feel as cute or lovely—almost as if in my appearance I was disabled. I wanted to disappear, be invisible, so that nobody would notice me. I was so ashamed to feel that way, as if I had a defect."

Much of Gloria's shame concerned her subjective, negative impression of her own appearance and, ultimately, her own essence. She was convinced that others saw her as being completely unacceptable. Her impression stemmed from her attachment to self-rejection, experienced in herself through the rejection she felt from others. From this attachment emerged self-loathing and then shame. In her shame, Gloria believed that she was indeed deserving of the scorn and rejection she was experiencing. Her punishment was her shame. Consumed as she was in her shame, she did not see the real problem: her underlying emotional attachment to rejection, often experienced most intensely as self-rejection.

Gloria's shame had persisted for many years, during which she felt completely unable to improve her emotional circumstances. The deeper her passivity (in this case the conviction of her ineptitude and hopelessness), the more intensely she experienced self-loathing for it, and then the more deeply ashamed she felt of herself. The unconscious defense she had erected was acutely painful: "Can't you see how much I'm suffering for my passivity. Isn't that proof enough that I'm not attached to passivity?" Generally, we will accept intense suffering to avoid seeing deeper into ourselves.

As she understood her attachments to passivity and rejection, she freed herself of the suffering she had endured to cover up any awareness of these attachments. She gradually began to embrace the self she had struggled so hard to discover.

John, a clothing designer in his forties, saw an opportunity to create a new line of clothes, based on a theme he felt sure could become popular. His idea seemed sound, although it did involve some risk in time and money. He was at a standstill in his career, and a change of direction did seem appropriate.

His defense against an awareness of his attachment to underlying passivity was his fear of failure. "The minute I think about starting to do this," he said, "I get this awful feeling in my stomach. I feel small and my voice gets weak and squeaky, almost 'mousy.' And I begin to think of all the ways this might not happen for me. At the same time, I'm pining away for it. I want it to happen, but if I fail I know I'll be devastated."

"Fear of failure indicates the expectation of failure," I told John. "Your fear covers up how much you are aligned emotionally with the prospect of failure. Also, in a sense, it signifies how much you are secretly looking forward to the experience of failure. I know that sounds harsh, but that's how our unconscious works. Just thinking about the possibility of failure throws you into two of your emotional issues. The first is self-condemnation, and we can trace that back to your experience with your critical mother. The second is passivity, and that is what you picked up from your father and his relationship to himself and the world.

"So, were you to fail, you would likely turn on yourself quite viciously with this condemnation. That would be completely unfair to yourself, of course, but that is what you do—you look for opportunities to be harshly critical of yourself. Thus, you feel blocked with this idea of yours because, although you are unconsciously attached to the condemnation, your defense is to fear it and to try to avoid it. So you hesitate to go forward with your idea.

"You also made a comment to the effect of, 'I keep thinking of all the ways I am likely to fail.' That statement reveals your passivity. Whenever you think about moving forward, you stop yourself with thoughts such as this. You need to see that such feelings or statements represent an expression of your passivity. Such statements are not rational—they are emotional. But you buy into them, believe in them, because you are identified with that sense of yourself. In that very moment of doubting yourself, your passivity has you in its clutches."

"Maybe my passivity is that evil voice I hear," John replied. "It says, 'Now John, are you sure you wouldn't sooner lie down. It's too much work today. Besides, you need to think more about this. Maybe you should wait until tomorrow.'"

"Yes, when passivity rears its ugly face like that, you can see it for what it is. Then you can eliminate it."

Larry, another client, felt angry that the contractor who was building his new house had fallen behind schedule on the project. It appeared that he and his wife would be moving in almost two months later than expected. Larry had been visiting the site a few times a week, talking to the builder and expressing his discontent.

"I'm certainly not being passive in this area," he said. "I've been pushing them hard to get this project done."

"Tell me again how you've been feeling during this construction process."

"Annoyed. Frustrated. And angry."

"So this experience of having a house built has been an ordeal for you, is that right?"

"Yes, I suppose it has. I certainly wouldn't do business with that builder again."

"Do you think your attempts to prod him along have been effective?"

"It's hard to say. I really don't know. I'd like to think so."

"Let me suggest, Larry, that you have felt compelled to intervene and get your builder moving on the project because you were too distressed to sit by and do nothing."

"Are you telling me that it's better to do nothing? That sounds like being passive."

"Of course prodding people is sometimes appropriate and effective. In this situation, however, the main clue to what is happening internally, within yourself, revolves around the considerable distress you have felt during the construction process. You felt this distress because you experienced yourself in a helpless situation, unable to do anything about the building schedule for your house and forced to endure your builder's slowpoke timetable. As a defense against that painful feeling, a feeling that you are emotionally attached to, you take on an air of being assertive and even aggressive in going after the builder to speed things up. I gather from what you've told me that he probably has experienced you as a nuisance, if not a downright pain-in-the-butt. It's quite possible that in experiencing you in an unpleasant manner, he might passive-aggressively retaliate and slow down the project even more. Your efforts could be counter-productive, and typically when we react pseudo-aggressively from our emotional issues the results are indeed counter-productive."

"So what I am supposed to do? You're right, it is painful to sit around and wait for him to get it done."

"Use the experience to identify your passivity. It's a chance to see your passivity in action. If the situation with the builder becomes too difficult, sure, go over and have a talk with him. Or, if he really falls seriously behind his schedule, you might indeed be well advised to take further action. If you do so while keeping an eye on your passivity, you will be more likely to make choices and behave in a way that serves your best interests and makes the experience merely an annoyance instead of an ordeal."

Another client felt he had to submit to his wife in many of their everyday interactions. He made the statement, "Why can't she compromise more—I'm always looking for compromise and she isn't." Underneath this statement, however, was the defense of, "I'm not tempted to feel passive. Look, I'm interested in compromise with her. I'm trying to resolve this." Compromise can be an acceptable choice, of course. But his frequent and fervent claims of innocence because his wife wouldn't compromise betray his use of this approach as a defense.

Yet another defense involves the trait called compulsive goodness. Here the individual is locked into a restricted persona or character manifestation that was chosen unconsciously at some point in his life. In using compulsive goodness as a defense against self-aggression, the individual claims, "Look how good I am," thereby covering up how wrong or bad this person feels when stepping out of his emotional straightjacket of compulsive goodness.

When he does step out, he swings between extremes, being the "good boy" in one context and in another context swerving over to the complete opposite and acting out, often with drugs, sex, and lies. The swing to the "bad" subpersonality is tempting because this kind of person feels, in doing so, that he is taking power and exercising freedom. In other words, it feels better to be "bad" than to be passive. Soon, however, this person begins to feel guilt and shame for the "bad" behaviors. When the guilt for being "bad" becomes too intense, the individual swings back to compulsive goodness. This inner mechanism can be a factor in the "born-again" religious experience.

A variation on this defense is pseudo-spirituality, in which an individual claims, as a rationalization for passivity, that he was just doing the "right" thing, turning the other cheek, and avoiding confrontation. True spirituality, however, involves the desire to honor one's integrity and to express one's compassion and courage. The counsel to turn one's cheek represents the wisdom of not being reactive. It is also the admonition to avoid seeking revenge, for the vengeful person is being pseudo-aggressive, reacting out of his helplessness, sense of loss, and egotism.

One of the most effective defenses protecting our inner status quo, often adopted by pseudo-spiritual types, is the claim that we know all that is significant about ourself. Paradoxically, though we go to a therapist to learn about ourself, we unconsciously hate to be told facts we have been repressing. For doors to open on the secrets of our soul, we need to approach our psyche with humility, receptive to whatever the truth may be. Our aversion to inner truth is irrational. No "horrible" truth can taint the essence of our true Self.

Ironically, even doing nothing can be a defense against passivity. Such is the condition in which an individual, mired in painful ambivalence, moves hesitatingly in one direction, stops, backs up, tries another direction, and again hesitates. He is more likely to wander off along some dead end than the path that leads to fulfillment. Here the defense reads, "I am neither passive nor aggressive. I simply can't decide." Although that inner statement in his defense looks straightforward, he limits himself and risks feeling tormented as he keeps afloat his juggling act of options, possibilities, doubts, fears, and regrets.

Another defense is to become enthusiastic, hopeful, or optimistic about some project or endeavor that the individual's passivity, in the form of disappointment in oneself and a sense of failure, will later scuttle. The defense goes like this: "I'm not anticipating the feeling of disappointment or failure. Can't you see how enthused I am about this new project of mine?"

The Power of Resistance

Behind human nature is our colossal resistance to understanding it. The closer we get to self-understanding, the more resistance we feel. Resistance is our unconscious opposition to inner freedom and enlightenment. It often surfaces in the form of angry, mocking, or scornful rejection of any relevant knowledge about the contents of our unconscious and how it works.

One aspect of our resistance is our unconscious refusal to absorb the meaning of such basic tenets of psychology as projection, transference, identification, and narcissism—especially in terms of how these devices or mechanisms apply to ourself. Some of our resistance is learned behavior. We imitated our parent's lack of self-knowledge, as well as their restraint in being open and in sharing of thoughts and feelings. Thus, as our parents did before us, we close ourselves down and disconnect from our innermost being, effectively hiding from ourself.

Resistance in itself is a kind of overall defense. It is represented by our unconscious refusal to look inward and to understand the details of unconscious functioning. It is incorporated in our hesitation to let go of our old way of knowing ourself— "hanging on for dear life"—even though our identification with our false self is painful. One client said, "It's as if I'm determined to stay in the Old World instead of moving to the New World." It is also implicit in our reluctance, once we do see the inner dynamics, to let go of our attachments to negative emotions and move beyond our conflicts. We experience it as the feeling that no matter how hard we try to understand ourself, we still can't "get it." We can say, in a sense, that resistance stops us from surrendering to the realization of our deep attachment to inner passivity. I recognize it in my clients when they "forget" to write down dreams or the details of pertinent events, as well as in their "forgetting" therapy appointments or showing up late for them. The following example of resistance illustrates this tendency.

One client in his forties had been severely beaten by a neighbor in the city where he had lived four years earlier. One leg was broken, and he was hospitalized for several weeks. He had experienced a deteriorating relationship with this neighbor over several months and had failed to prevent the growing animosity. Even though the identity of his assailant was established, the client had to persist over a period of almost one year to bring the case to court, at which time the assailant received only probation.

Now, years later, my client remembered the event within minutes of awakening each morning, and on and off throughout the day he visualized with some intensity the face of his assailant. These memories returned to haunt him for several minutes at a time. "I feel like I'm still being beaten up," he said.

The reliving of intense painful memories is a universal problem that has a secret purpose. "You're using this event for a hidden reason," I told him. "Of course this was a dreadful experience, and getting past it, moving beyond the pain of it, would take time even under the best circumstances. But you are impeding the passage of the pain. Unconsciously, you're willing to maintain and replay memories of this event for the purpose of experiencing yourself through the helplessness of what happened. With your attachment to passivity, you are tempted to use this highly charged scenario to create that inner effect. You have to see that this is the ulterior motive behind these memories and flashbacks. Whenever you're having a memory of this event, 'flash' on the awareness of this secret intent, which is to experience yourself through the painful helplessness. As this attachment is exposed, you will find greater strength to avoid the temptation to indulge in it."

For several months this client was unable to grasp this concept. He continued to replay memories of the assault in a way that was utterly painful. "Your resistance is the problem," I told him. "Your resistance is your unwillingness to apply this awareness. You are reluctant to give up your passivity. Watch for your temptation to walk out of here when this session is over and forget, or fail to reflect upon, the knowledge about this passivity and your emotional attachment to it. This understanding is like medicine, and if you are not 'taking it' you're being blocked by your resistance to getting better."

Susie was in her forties and thirty pounds overweight. She had been working on her psychological issues for many years, and in the past year she had focused on her inner passivity, seeing how she used food to numb herself and how her struggle with weight served as a way to experience herself passively.

At times, she began to feel more powerful and effective than ever, and she was able, as she put it, "to really get a taste of who I am." However, she found that she couldn't sustain these feelings; they were "too much to handle." She could feel herself slide back into the old sense of herself, the feeling that who she was really didn't matter that much and that she didn't deserve better than the familiar frustration and pain of hopelessness.

Susie had a dream in which a movie actor she liked approached her passionately. "He was all over me, hugging me, very loving, holding me from behind, not just sexually but with great affection and love. I could feel my resistance. I wasn't letting that love come in. I could feel how much I didn't want his love. I said to myself, 'He has a girlfriend, so he's not really being sincere.' It felt somehow foreign to allow his love in."

"What would happen if you did allow that love in?" I asked her.

"Well, I just wasn't going to let it come in. That resistance to feeling love seems very cellular, like I've been feeling it my whole life."

"But suppose you had no choice, that you couldn't resist the love. How would that feel?"

"It's so different from how I know myself. It would feel very empowering. It just feels as if I wouldn't even be the same person. Feeling all that love, I guess I would be someone I don't know."

"That's right. You have resistance to letting go of that old passive way of knowing yourself. Feeling love is to feel connected to life, to existence, to yourself. That is very empowering. It can be hard to seize that feeling because the old way of experiencing yourself is so familiar, so deep-rooted."

Susie's resistance was also experienced in another way. In the past few weeks, she had been telling herself, "I'm not getting any better. I'm failing completely. I'm not in the game. I haven't even come out of the dugout."

"Susie," I told her, continuing the metaphor, "a lot of people never even get to first base in the struggle for inner liberation. You have to appreciate what you've done for yourself over the years. It has been very heroic; you have fought and clawed your way, in my opinion, to third base. All you need is a little bunt to get home. But look at what you've been doing. By convincing yourself that you have not made any progress, you are throwing yourself back into the old experience of passivity. I can sense as you talk how much you are feeling stuck. Look how weak that makes you feel and how convinced you are that this feeling represents the truth about your situation. This impression of weakness is another expression of your passivity and also indicates your resistance to moving beyond it."

"Yes, because I have been feeling how I don't want my strength to show. I don't want people to see what I've done, that I do have it together."

"That's more resistance. Just try to step back from it and look at it. Otherwise, when you're caught in the feeling, it's as if you're just a big ball of resistance. Look at your resistance—and respect it. You don't even have to fight it.

Cultivate the feeling that you are going to be moving right through it. This resistance can't stop you. Your destiny is on the other side of it. How could anything stop you now?"

Donna was also going through a difficult experience of resistance, both in herself as well as in Jeff, her husband, who seemed unable to become more open and intimate. "I've been weepy, sorrowful, and feeling defeated. It's like I'm wilting, not withering on the vine, exactly, but wilting. I guess that's not quite as bad."

At the first sign of Jeff's resistance to her amorous advances, Donna would hesitate and back away, and then feel sad or angry with herself and with him. "I can feel my resistance kick in. And then I also get so scared that I'm not going to make it."

"Passivity and love are related," I told her. "Dropping the passivity is taking in the love. Your husband mirrors your own resistance to coming out of passivity. Unconsciously, you hold him at bay. In passivity, we block both the giving and the receiving of love."

"I know I block it," Donna said. "In fact, I feel as if I'll be destroyed by it. And I guess I will. Certainly, that old me that has kept love at bay all these years will have to go."

Another client expressed his resistance this way: "I find the process of trying to get better to be so stressful in itself. I have to think about this stuff all the time. It's like another chore I have to worry about. On top of that, it's not happening fast enough."

After pointing out his resistance, I gave him a pep talk. "Look at it this way: your mind is being challenged. You

117

can take satisfaction in the feeling that you are operating at a high level of effort and determination. Try to feel the gratification of knowing that you won't give up."

We can also be resistant to feeling our grief and sorrow. Of course, we don't want to indulge in grief and sorrow. But often we have to feel deeply into ourself in order to release our pain. In a typical example, a man who is abusive toward his son is not likely conscious enough of his repressed hurt from having been abused by his own parent. If this man gets past his resistance and accesses these feelings deep within himself, he becomes more sensitive to what he endured in his childhood. Now he is able to be sensitive to his son's experience. When deep grief and hurt are cleared, compassion arises.

Resistance is such that, unconsciously, the seeker after psychotherapy doesn't want to be cured but only to strengthen his defenses so that inner guilt is abated. Often, rather than having his core issues addressed, the client flees from therapy, agreeing to himself and to others to eliminate a few of his more self-defeating symptoms or those symptoms that his spouse or partner objects to the most. He manages to "behave" for a time, but soon the underlying conflict reasserts itself and he is back to acting out in some self-defeating manner.

Feeling like a Victim

One of the most common defenses and purest expressions of passivity is the feeling of being a victim. Sometimes, of course, we are innocent victims of a situation. But very often, in the process of acting out our issues, we plan, write, produce, direct, and star in scenarios depicting our own victimization. As a defense, the victim mentality goes like this: "I am not interested in feeling passive to this person (or situation). Can't you see how awful I feel, how much I hate it? I am clearly being victimized. And can't you see how much I want revenge (pseudo-aggression)?"

Paula, a massage therapist in her forties, walked into a spa that just the previous day had opened in her town. Paula introduced herself to the owner, a woman who also was a massage therapist, and said she might be interested in doing some massages in the new facility. A few minutes after her arrival, a man came in looking for a massage, and the owner, seemingly unprepared and acting flustered, asked Paula if she would do it. "You do it, you do it," the woman said. Paula agreed, although she had second thoughts a few minutes later when she found out that no massage oil was available. However, she felt pressured by the woman's "overpowering insistence" and the fact that the man was lying on a massage table under a sheet in the next room. So she proceeded to do the massage with baby oil that the owner managed to find, although it was a poor substitute for massage oil.

During the next week, Paula did eight more massages and was paid her commission on six of them. But the woman told her at that point that she didn't want Paula to continue working for her. When Paula insisted on knowing why, the women told her that, because Paula worked independently with her own clientele, she feared that Paula was going to steal the spa's clients. Paula insisted that she had never considered doing this and had told those spa clients who wanted to see her again that they would have to make appointments through the spa.

The experience of being "let go" was very painful for Paula, and she felt a lot of anger toward the woman. Paula wanted to retaliate somehow and, though she felt nervous about confronting the woman, insisted she be paid for the last two massages. Around the same time, she received a phone call from her father-in-law on some unrelated subject, and he was harsh and critical of her during this call, insisting on information that she wasn't prepared to divulge. Paula was passive to her father-in-law in not addressing his harsh tone, although it felt to her that withholding the information he wanted constituted power.

"I felt like a little kid being yelled at, and I felt like a horrible person," she said of the phone call. "After we hung up, I went and ate two muffins, and I slept very badly that night. That was four days ago. I've been having a very difficult time since. Both these incidents have been very painful for me. I feel so badly treated. It brings back the feeling I've had all my life of being victimized by others."

Both experiences were influenced by Paula's passivity. The passivity may be more obvious in the example with her father-in-law, but it is also the basis for the negative feelings she endured with the spa experience. Paula was passive in the manner in which she agreed to do the first massage. She reacted to the woman's anxiety, what Paula called her "overpowering insistence," and the presence of the customer wanting immediate attention.

Asked to re-experience that moment when she agreed to do the first massage, she said, "There was the sense that this woman was needing me and that I was going to be in charge. I was coming to the rescue. It felt very powerful."

This feeling was a defense, a claim to power to cover up her passivity. Later in our session, Paula said in reference to this incident, "It's true. In that moment when she asked me to do the massage, I really had no choice. It never occurred to me to say no. I think that even if I'd had an appointment somewhere else, I still wouldn't have said no." Later she said about the incident with her father-in-law, "I feel like I'm always responsible for everything. And then I feel so impotent, that I have no right, that everyone is an authority over me."

She divulged another aspect of her passivity. "In my mind I'm always saying to people something to the effect of, 'Don't worry— I'm not so great. Don't worry—I'm not that good-looking.' I'm always making myself less important than they are. It shows how much I'm not comfortable with feeling my power." In another incident, Paula was diverted off the subject in a conversation with an acquaintance. She was telling this woman of her concern about the amount of traveling she did to get from client to client, lugging her massage table around. "I'm getting too old for this work," she told the woman. "I would like to be in one place and maybe work out of a spa."

"I'm older than you," the woman said.

"No you're not."

"Well, how old are you?"

And so the conversation went, lurching off in a direction that was not Paula's original intent. "I never got back to the point I wanted to make," Paula said. "In fact I didn't even realize I had deviated from it until much later in the day. And then I said to myself, 'Paula, you didn't even give yourself the satisfaction of expressing those feelings.

You let yourself be cut off.' That's one way I don't take very good care of myself."

Being a victim corresponds with the widespread, universal beggar-slave-orphan mentalities. We go through life like beggars (feeling deprived and refused), slaves (feeling controlled and helpless), and orphans (feeling rejected and unloved). Feeling like a victim has a certain appeal. We can use it to attract attention to ourselves and to garner sympathy. When victims connect with other victims, they can commiserate with each other and feel close and even intimate through their bonds of misery. Many of us would sooner have sympathy and even pity than what is felt to be the alternative—to be anonymous and invisible. Children and adults often profess to be sick, or make themselves sick, in order to get attention and love.

Some of us seem forever bound in the victim's quandary: "If I say what I feel and go for expressing my rights, I will offend the other person and pay for it in the form of disapproval, rejection, and banishment. I'll be seen as bad. Yet, if I submit, I'll get nothing and go nowhere. I'll be lost to myself and miserable." A man, an artist in his thirties, was concerned because his homeowners' association planned to install a gate and make his subdivision a gated community. He wanted to be able to sell his art from his studio in his home, and he was afraid an attempt was being made by others to block access and prevent any commercial activity in the subdivision.

His wife wanted him to "play hardball," to hire a lawyer and fight the attempt to curtail his business activities. However, he felt intimidated. "I feel I'm in the wrong," he said. "Who am I to go against the wishes of the majority?" He also felt neutralized by his fear. "It feels as if I lose my ability to reason. I imagine trying to present my side to the others, and it feels as if I can't present it logically or rationally, that what I say won't have any impact."

He added, "I don't know in which direction to go, so I don't do anything. Do I try to force them to keep the gate open during the day? I don't know. It just brings up a lot of fears." This man frequently used the expression, "I don't know," accompanied by a helpless shrug.

Later he told me of clauses in the homeowner's agreement that appeared to support his right to have customers or clients visit his home. Such visitors are permitted, the agreement stated, "providing there is not an appreciable increase in traffic volume." Despite this legal support, he still hesitated to challenge the other homeowners. Although he was "philosophically opposed" to gated communities, his main protest was a passive form of pseudo-aggression, consisting of holding off payment for his share of the new gate.

Victims either have a fear of confrontation or else charge pseudo-aggressively into confrontations, worsening a situation or wrecking it beyond repair. In healthy confrontation, we stand up for ourselves, asserting our perceptions, feelings, and needs. We are honest with others, have no intent to hurt them, and refrain from overreacting. We also wait for the best time to make our stand, and we expect success in the form of resolution. Unhealthy confrontation, in contrast, is a form of protest designed to make someone else responsible for our feelings or reactions. This kind of confrontation is used for the purpose of intimidating, judging, and controlling, as well as imposing revenge, guilt, and shame. The healthy individual is able to express his feelings or perceptions and state his boundaries, while the passive individual wants to defend himself, to secure his own self-approval, whether by blaming others, making them wrong, or by justifying his retreat or anger.

The Passivity of Terrorists

Terrorists do have a common psychology, despite what many experts say. Whether Islamic extremists, members of the IRA or the KKK, Earth First arsonists, abortion-clinic bombers, or mass killers, they are all steeped in a victim mentality.

Unconsciously, they are prone to experience certain challenging situations through feelings of deprivation, helplessness, domination, and defeat. In other words, despite their vicious behaviors, they are inwardly very passive.

Their interest is not in achieving reform or creating a better world, or even accomplishing political goals, but in continuing to experience themselves and the world through a sense of victimization and oppression. Their violent reactions are intended to blame others for their negative feelings, thereby covering up or defending against their emotional investment in various forms of unresolved passivity.

Some terrorists have indeed experienced forms of injustice. But their extreme reaction is a problem of their psychology and is fated to be self-defeating. The terrorist experiences the power and in some cases the abuse of others, whether nations or individuals, through feelings of being humiliated, overlooked, deprived, pushed aside, and otherwise victimized. Unconsciously, he is attached to such feelings. That means that, inwardly, he knows himself through these feelings. The feelings originated in his childhood and now represent a large part of what is limited and painful in his experience of himself. They are part of his identity. The terrorist hasn't liberated himself inwardly from this impression of himself—this feeling of being overpowered and forced to submit—vis-à-vis others and the world. Rather than see his subjective participation in his experience, he wants to believe, as a defense, that his painful impressions are an objective guide to truth and action.

His unconscious defenses repress any awareness that he is prepared to experience himself in this negative manner. From deep in his psyche, he covers up or defends against his emotional attachment to this old, familiar way of knowing himself. (All of us cover up our inner passivity and try to repress awareness of our attachment to it.) By striking out in anger and with violence, the terrorist can claim in his unconscious defense, "I am not experiencing my situation through passivity. See how powerful I am as I strike back at my [alleged] oppressors."

Other characteristics common to terrorists are also symptoms of inner passivity: profound denial, oversimplification of issues, lack of patience, desperation, self-righteousness, and an authoritarian mentality.

Though the terrorists' behavior is irrational, it can nonetheless be understood according to psychological principles. Terrorists are individuals who resort to the ultimate psychological defense—the murder of innocents—to cover up their secret attachment to their own identification with helplessness and victimization. This has a parallel to the person who commits suicide: in murdering himself, he "successfully" covers up his own unconscious collusion in feelings of hopelessness.

Terrorists have their own inner terror, created through their feeling of powerlessness or their impression of being at the mercy of some alien force intent on doing them harm. Thus they do to others what they themselves fear—being terrorized, rendered helpless, and defeated. What they fear is what they anticipate. On a deep, unconscious level, they are masochistically attached to the feeling of being terrorized and defeated. Invariably then, they act out this emotional attachment by bringing terror and defeat to themselves when justice comes calling.

Evidence of terrorists' passivity can be seen in their suicide missions. Suicide is the ultimate act of passivity. It is an act steeped in helplessness, alienation, hopelessness, and despair, as well as the conviction that no other alternative is available. Fanaticism, too, is an externalized expression of inner passivity. The fanatic's mind and emotions have been taken over by dogma or by the agenda of others. He is enslaved by a belief system. He is so powerless that he isn't capable of thinking for himself. His way of knowing and experiencing himself is through separation from his own truth, his own self, even his own species. Such an individual will align himself with whatever action makes him feel powerful and real. The goal is to feel powerful to cover up the affinity for feeling powerless. The more dramatic and significant the action, the more substantial and real the person feels. Dramatic effect, not value or benefit to himself or society, drives this individual's actions. Obviously, tragic consequences result when individuals operate from this base of internal disorder. The same psychological mechanism operates among members of violent gangs who, when not attacking and murdering each other and innocent victims, deface and destroy property.

Like the gang member, the terrorist also experiences himself through feelings of being pushed aside and rendered invisible, and his antisocial behavior, his cover-up of his attachment to such feelings, says, in effect, "I exist! Now you will pay attention to me!" He is very sensitive to feeling disrespected. This means he has little respect for the sanctity of others. On the bottom line, he sacrifices others in an attempt to cover up his attachment to feeling insignificant.

The terrorist is best known for his hatred and rage. These emotions, however, are simply other symptoms, other defenses, of this individual's identification with knowing himself through hopelessness and inner passivity. The greater his passivity to his self-aggression, the more extreme is the hatred, first of self, then projected onto others and external circumstances. The greater the hatred, the more likely this individual will act on it. Here the defense professes: "I am not passive! Can't you see how much I hate what is being done to me and how much I hate those who are doing it! And look how I am planning to go after them!" This is a defense against his seeing, feeling, and owning his own sense of worthlessness and self-loathing. This hatred can be cloaked behind self-righteousness or religious extremism.

To maintain this defense, the individual has to carry the hatred within him and look for targets on which to project it. Though carrying this anger inside is very painful, the individual willingly pays this price to embrace the illusion of power the anger gives him and to cover up his inner passivity.

A terrorist's rage also emerges from his feeling of having no power. He attributes his sense of powerlessness to external circumstances, but the true source is his subjective, emotional interpretation of his situation. Ordinary people who feel such powerlessness in themselves and in their circumstances can also feel rage. This powerlessness is a subjective inner experience based on the existence of inner passivity and the corresponding lack of connection with oneself. The resulting rage, which is a defense or a cover-up for the emotional attachment to passivity, creates the illusion of having power. Rage is not an effective or true power because it leads straight to suffering and self-defeat. True power, which can be felt and accessed even when one is being oppressed or unjustly treated, does not require dramatic display. It is a felt quality, a sense of peace and liberation that emerges through the overthrow of one's ego and inner terrorist (self-aggression).

It is also a defense for the terrorist to claim that he is fighting for reform or for legitimate political or religious goals. This claim is a rationalization, a cover for the aggressive and hateful impulses that spring from his deep passivity. If reform were truly his aim, he would come out into the open and use discourse and the power of persuasion to advance his cause. He would work toward inner healing to build up his sense of self-worth and true power.

True power is not destructive; rather, it is creative. It reforms and heals. It inspires, compels, and directs us to be courageous and to struggle to bring out the best in ourselves. In comparison, being destructive and blaming others is the worst kind of weakness, involving a failure to take responsibility for one's own negativity and unresolved emotional issues.

In the aftermath of the September 11, 2001, terrorist attack on the United States, many Americans felt acute helplessness. Television images and our own imagination drew us deeply into the horror of the victims, and we identified with feeling trapped in such a hopeless predicament. "I couldn't stop thinking about what it was like for them, and it was unbearable," said one client who had relapsed into his passivity in the week following the attack.

We felt we had to do something, and in many of these instances our responses were conscious and active, benign and beneficial, including displays of solidarity such as donating blood, writing letters to the editor, volunteering for relief efforts, contributing to charities for the victims, and flying the flag. Less benign reactions arising out of inner passivity included the wish for immediate retaliatory action, feelings of fear and depression, rising hatred for unidentified enemies, revenge fantasies, and irritability and anger at friends and family members.

We carry a terrorist inside us in the form of our self-aggression. This inner terrorist doesn't hesitate to attack us for minor infractions or even for imagined crimes. Our deep passivity allows this arrangement to continue unabated. It is this negativity in our own psyche that is the ultimate source of terrorism. The collective consciousness of our planet has to be raised—or refined—so that the terrorist, like his brethren the racist and the fascist, is restricted to his lair. Our ultimate victory over terrorism will come when we understand and expose the psychology that underlies it.

The real enemy is irrationality in all its forms. Like hurricanes and tornadoes, the wrath of irrationality is a force of (human) nature we need to respect. It is expressed in terrorism, other forms of violence, injustice, lack of civility, and failure of self-regulation. The United States was founded on a faith in reason. Reason produced the Constitution and our foundation in law, giving us domestic safeguards against our own emotionalism and irrationality. We have now been invaded by irrationality in the form of international terrorism. Our attempts to respond can be off balance—underplays or overreactions that themselves are forms of irrationality. Unless our understanding of the psyche penetrates deeply, we could be swamped by irrationality and dragged down into its depths. One way to prevent this from happening is to expose the defenses beneath which it lies.

Chapter 5
Passivity in Relationships

Deep, committed love is not to be found like a talisman beside the road. It has to be created. And passivity is a major obstacle to creating love. Through passivity, we are afraid to take the risks that creating love entails. We hesitate to push through our resistances to love. We fail to uncover our hidden niches where we play it safe, where we withhold ourself, where we are willing to live out our expectations of being deprived, disappointed, controlled, and abandoned. All the while, we can get very angry at our partner when his or her expectations or requests of us require that we extend ourselves to grow in wisdom and love.

A client marched into my office bristling with annoyance. He had just been arguing with his wife on his cell phone while driving to my office. He plunged into his feelings: "I needed some parts to fix our dishwasher. I told her to write down the numbers I was going to give her and call an 800 number to order the parts for me. She just kept interrupting and wanting to know about this-and-that, which wasn't relevant. I feel I'm losing whatever scrap of control I have. This is my domain—fixing things. Here at least I should be able to call the shots. I told her, 'This is what I know—will you just do what I say for once?'"

It is very helpful for us in such a situation to understand that, because of our emotional readiness to experience passivity, we read into our partner's actions and words the intent to control or manipulate us, to resist us, or to impose certain expectations upon us, and thus we misinterpret situations in ways that cause us to become resentful, withholding, or angry at our partner. Even if our partner is actually trying to control us, we won't get triggered or upset if we manage to avoid experiencing the situation through our inner passivity.

However, before we worry about handling our relationships, we first have to establish one. Passivity can impede even this first step. A single woman in her forties, who had never married, told me she was "terrified of being dependent on a man." Her relationships had seldom lasted more than a few years. She worked as an accountant but wanted to have more time for her paintings and had always dreamed of a career as an artist. Yet a few years earlier, when the man she was dating offered to marry her and support her financially while she painted, she declined the offer. Fear of being dependent covered up her attachment to passivity. Through her passivity, she had suffered in her previous relationships with feelings of submission, being controlled, and forced to submit. Now, as a defense, she avoided relationships. Of course, relationships need not be experienced this way. A person's integrity and power are not threatened by this situation unless passivity is present.

In another instance, Julie, a client in her thirties, was anxious to be in a relationship. Yet she was hesitant to leave her catering job, with its long hours and weekend work, for a nine-to-five job that would give her more freedom to socialize.

"I've been in that situation before," Julie said, "where I wasted away my weekends, not making plans and feeling alone and abandoned. I didn't know what to do with myself—I'd hang out at home, take a nap, watch TV, have dinner, go to sleep early. It's okay to spend a weekend like that once in a while—but I was doing it every weekend. I'm afraid that I'll get back into that routine. Maybe too much unstructured time just doesn't work for me."

"Unstructured time indeed won't work for you if your passivity takes over," I said. "As you imagine having weekends off, you slip into the feeling that you won't be able to make anything happen for yourself. You don't feel you can take charge of your life or take the initiative to make plans to get out of the house and be involved with other people. Try to see that your secret interest is to experience yourself through this feeling of passivity. When the passivity is in place and you don't see it, it gets the best of you."

Julie also felt she was not able to meet the "right kind of people." She felt she had little in common with the men she did meet. "I'm beginning to think twice about extending myself."

"Extending yourself is exactly what you need to do," I replied. "Growing out of your hesitancy and uncertainty, and feeling more confident in who you are, is a process of extending yourself. Life requires that we do this, or we won't find the fulfillment and happiness we want."

As Julie saw her passivity and understood it more clearly, her situation improved dramatically. Within months she had left her catering job, found more suitable employment, and discovered how fulfilling her weekends and her love life could be.

We can also fail to get to first base when we don't know or can't determine how we feel about our significant other. Love or the potential for it may exist one for another, but that love may not be felt or expressed because of passivity or other issues. One client said of his girlfriend, "I'm depending on her to make up her mind (about the relationship). It's really up to her. I can't make up her mind for her." His girlfriend, however, appeared to need a strong indication of the man's true feelings before deciding whether to commit to him. This man said, "I'm always asking her what she wants to do [about the relationship]." True, he did so, but that was an expression of passivity. He wasn't expressing with any conviction or passion his feelings for her. I did many sessions with him before these feelings finally emerged, and fortunately she was still around to enjoy his passion and commitment.

A man whom I was seeing for the first time came to my office with his girlfriend. He wanted her to be present for the session. I didn't object, although I knew her presence would likely make him more defensive when I presented my interpretation. She expressed her chagrin in the session, telling me that he planned to walk away from their five-year relationship without making any serious attempt to save it. He shrugged his shoulders and said, "Let's face it—she's better off without me." When I suggested that inner passivity was at play in his lack of commitment, he indignantly denied he was in any way passive and informed me that he wouldn't be coming back for more therapy.

One of the most common feelings associated with lack of commitment is the fear that others will see us as a disappointment, as inadequate and defective, which is how we are ready to feel about ourself. Or else we believe that the other will let us down and that we will be burdened with providing his care and emotional support. Passive issues also include fear of being trapped and controlled, being held accountable, having to submit, and losing the essence of who we are. Keep in mind that almost always our emotional attachment to these feelings is unconscious.

Sometimes we just drift into a relationship, as if the experience, to express it in the passive mode, is happening to us. One woman told me: "I didn't want to think about my relationship and my impending marriage. I just wanted to be taken care of. And I guess I was ready to take anybody who wanted me." When it came time to unwrap her wedding gifts, she passed all the presents and envelopes over to her parents to open. In another case, a man told his girlfriend, "God has put us together, so who am I to end it?" Often we look for excuses for why a relationship won't work. A new client, speaking about his difficult relationship with his girlfriend, told me, "I want this relationship to go forward—but it doesn't seem that it can."

"Why not?" I asked.

"We live eighty miles apart. We see each other only on the weekends."

"That's no excuse. Of course it can go forward. You're using the physical distance between you as an excuse for maintaining the emotional distance." Overcoming the emotional distance was the real challenge, I told him, and that was where he hesitated because it required that he plunge into himself to discover the reasons why he wasn't successfully securing the relationship.

This man also had a series of complaints about his girlfriend— such as, "She doesn't have a sense of direction in her life"—all of which were projections of his own passivity upon her.

Passive factors can block growth in a long-established relationship. Annie and Gus were in their sixties and had been married more than thirty years. Annie complained of how Gus ignored and disappointed her, how he constantly failed to listen to her, to respond to what she was saying, and to show her through his actions that her feelings and points of view mattered to him. "It seems so hopeless with him," she said, in quite a state of anguish. "I don't know that he'll ever get it."

Occasionally I saw this couple together. At those times Annie expected me to zero in on Gus to get him to see his "misbehaviors" and help him to curtail his negative outbursts. Of course, I did try to get him to look at his issues, particularly his transference (he transferred onto his wife the old, negative expectations that were still unresolved with his mother). Gus always made what appeared to be a sincere attempt to see and understand his contributions to their disharmony. He professed to be "very sad" that his behavior was so painful for his wife, but he didn't know how he could make it different. (It can be harder for older people to make fundamental changes, though they sometimes use this as an excuse not to try. I have had clients in their sixties who made significant progress working out deep issues.)

Gus's emotional "misbehavior" was more apparent, while Annie's was subtler. She was also inclined to experience Gus as she had her mother, a woman with a narcissistic personality disorder who never did learn to relate to Annie in a caring, affectionate manner. All the years with her mother, Annie had despaired of ever getting her to change and become more appropriate. In her marriage Annie began to experience Gus through the same sense of frustration and helplessness. She would often say, "I might as well give up because it's not worth the fight." As long as Annie continued to experience Gus through passivity, the chances of Gus achieving any substantial growth were limited. Unconsciously, we give to each other what the other unconsciously expects: as long as Annie was willing (unconsciously) to continue experiencing Gus through her passivity, he would (unconsciously) deliver what she was willing to endure, however painful that was for them both.

I saw this couple for only a few months, and the therapy may not have been particularly effective. Annie could not get a grasp on her passivity, or a feel for it, and she may have felt that I was being ineffective by shifting some of the responsibility to her and not focusing enough on "fixing" her husband. Unless people are willing or able to explore the deeper regions of their psyche, a negative pattern like this couple's will remain largely intact. It was a tribute to their love that they had stayed together all those years, and I'm inclined to believe they have since remained together. How much sweeter their lives could have been if they'd had an opportunity at a younger age to work out these emotional issues.

Clark, an office worker, described how his long-ago relationship with his mother had contributed to a profound passivity that was now entrenched and painful in his adult life: "The only thing worse than disagreeing with my mother was to be angry at her," he said. "My father also was passive to her. He would tell me, 'Son, just let her have her way—it's not worth fighting about.' I didn't have a chance to be a man and feel my power. Whatever she said ended up being right. Meanwhile, she painted herself as this loving mother who did everything for her children. Anything I accomplished she jumped in and took credit for.

"After a while," he continued, "all the fight was gone from me. I would just say, 'Well, all right, whatever.' I got good at it—when anger arose, I could stop it dead. I managed to preserve myself, although I was like a tree dying of thirst. I retreated into a core place inside me, a secret place she couldn't find. My only recourse was to disconnect on the surface. If I was myself, somehow she would swallow that up and take all the credit for anything I did. My power had been usurped and my enjoyment taken away. So I withdrew and went numb."

Now, whenever Clark emerged from his passivity to engage his girlfriend in a powerful way, "she gets so excited and becomes so passionate that I get the same old feeling. I read it as if, like my mother, she is going to take me over. I won't be myself. She will usurp me. So I disconnect again and withdraw, leaving her very upset. Then she accuses me of not loving her or wanting her. But that's not true. It's just that it's so easy for me to disconnect. I had to do it to save myself, and now I don't know how to stop."

Clark did learn to hold on to his power as he realized that the power was not taken away from him—but that he relinquished it, he deflated himself. "I've been in a constant search to give my power away," he said. Seeing the problem as an unconscious attachment to passivity, and understanding the passivity as a deep identification and not the essence of himself, Clark eventually secured his own autonomy.

Another man, who was trying valiantly to save his relationship, told me: "In the past, I've always walked away, just left the woman. What I'm fighting is the 'give up' in me. This time I'm not going to walk away."

A prominent passive theme in romantic relationships involves the unconscious willingness of one partner to give inordinate or inappropriate significance to the words and actions of the other partner. One woman said, "My first husband was so easy-going that I couldn't turn him into an oppressor. He let me do just about anything I wanted. Of course, as I now realize, I chose him for that reason. The problem was that we didn't connect. There was no passion. Now I can feel my current husband trying to control me. However, I'm giving less power to his words and actions. I'm starting to see more clearly that controlling me is not his intention. He just gets scared of losing me when I act independently, and that's why he can start to act bossy and controlling."

We live in reaction to the statements and demands of others. We spend our time defending ourselves against the perceptions others have of us (or that we think they have of us, or that we have of ourself). We aren't free enough to experience ourself more securely. We don't know ourself well enough yet. We don't feel solid enough and so spend a lot of time reacting to what others say about us. Through passivity, we review conversational content over and over, second-guessing ourself, looking for validation, insinuation, even accusation, seeking to quell our gnawing insecurities and to subdue our doubts about ourself. When we are entangled in self-doubt, we often don't like people simply because we feel this self-doubt when we're around them.

The compulsion to control others, whether in romantic relationships or everyday interactions with friends and coworkers, stems from underlying passivity. One client was struggling to stop calling chat rooms where he tried to induce women to talk about sex. "I don't like it if they're too eager to talk about sex," he said. "I like it better when I have to get them in a mood to talk about it." This man became sexually aroused as he identified with the passivity of the women who he felt were submitting to his agenda.

The controlling person, paradoxically, feels passive if he suspects that in any way he is being controlled. As in the above case, he is also secretly willing to identify with the passivity of the person he is controlling. Invariably, it feels to him like a case of control or be controlled. Typically, such a person will be controlling in one context, in which he is triggering or annoying others, and will feel passive in another context, in which he is being triggered and annoyed by those he feels are doing the controlling.

To complicate the picture, we may secretly be inviting control when, for instance, we ask someone, "So, what do you think?" or "What would you do in this situation?" Here we may be flirting with the feeling of coming under the influence of the other person. There's also a good chance that if this person does tell us what he thinks, we will passive-aggressively resist accepting what he says, even if it's the best advice around, and perhaps resent him for saying it.

Another tendency in relationships is for one partner to become a "problem-solver" or "problem-fixer," ready to jump into any discussion to try to fix something, rather than to listen to the other person and be truly present. Often there is nothing to be fixed: all the other person wants is for someone to listen. But listening can be difficult when we feel helpless or overwhelmed by the intensity or urgency of what is being communicated. To cover up this passivity, we want to take action, to fix the problem. This reaction only contributes to shallow communication.

Any challenge that takes us out of our comfort zone, demanding that we "show up" and make our presence felt, can feel too imposing. An article in the *Psychology of Women Quarterly* reports that, although safer-sex campaigns have targeted women to encourage them to take responsibility for condom use, many women are unable or unwilling to accept this role.[xix] While I couldn't find a comparable study on men, I received the next best thing, this comment from a woman who read an early draft of my manuscript: "How many men are also unwilling or unable to accept this responsibility?"

The following list reveals prominent relationship patterns and experiences that result from passivity. Many of these provoke our partner into controlling us more. This list is taken from the chapter on passivity in *LoveSmart: Transforming the Emotional Patterns That Sabotage Relationships*. (The book, seven years in the writing, was completed in 1999 by my wife, Sandra, and published that year):[xx] Here are these examples of passivity:

1 - Feeling it is our duty or obligation to give to our partner what he or she wants; going along with his requests, agreeing with his opinions, and accepting his negative behaviors, even though we do not agree with him; avoiding any kind of argument or confrontation while prostituting ourself for love;

2 - Believing our independent thoughts, feelings, or behaviors make our partner upset or angry, or will cause him to leave us; consequently, not speaking up and squelching our feelings and reactions; finding it difficult to say no or to refuse our partner anything; responding in a vague non-committal fashion that causes our partner to disregard us, since he's not clear what we want or feel;

3 - Setting it up for our partner to support us and take care of us; allowing ourself to be emotionally and financially dependent on our partner; feeling that we couldn't live on our own without him or her;

4 - Feeling powerless and helpless in the relationship, that we have no say or influence; needing permission to be ourself or to express what we want or need; being unable to ask for help or support; allowing our partner to silence our opinions, feelings, and aspirations through intimidation, guilt, or physical retribution;

5 - Putting our partner on a pedestal and believing he represents an ideal, thereby setting ourself up to feel controlled or deceived when he reveals his true feelings and perspectives;

6 - Feeling we have to be accountable for everything we do; feeling forced to explain or defend our behavior;

7 - Rearranging our life to accommodate our partner's needs and aspirations; doing his dirty work; that is,

carrying the burden of his problems in the relationship, serving his interests, not our own, and taking responsibility for his emotions; denying our needs, desires, and viewpoints so as not to upset him. Meanwhile, serving our own best interests feels wrong to us and punishable by guilt, rage, and abandonment;

8 - Being suggestible and believing everything our partner says about us; distrusting our own ideas and perceptions;

9 - Enduring unhealthy or painful situations and not taking action to change our circumstances; producing creative excuses or rationalizations for our lack of initiative; complaining behind our partner's back to friends or relatives and telling them how badly he treats us; eliciting sympathy and emotional support from others to make the hurt go away; setting ourself up to be rescued by others rather than relying on our own internal resources;

10 - Allowing our partner to make all the decisions, then resenting him for it; waiting for things to happen or for our partner to fix a situation; refraining from making decisions on our own without first getting advice from several different sources; letting someone else be responsible for the outcome of our life; blaming our lack of progress on our partner;

11 - Remaining in a state of confusion over what to do about our relationship;

12 - Giving in to our partner because we feel sorry for him; feeling guilty when our partner pouts and looks dejected; assuming he's fragile and will break apart if he doesn't get his way.

The solution to these difficulties rests, of course, in changing oneself, not one's partner. It's hard enough to change oneself; it's impossible to change one's partner. If growth is going to happen for us, we each have to want change for our own sake and to be willing to be responsible for the progress of our inner work.

A great relationship with another person is icing on the cake. The need for quality starts with the cake, which is the quality of our relationship with ourself.

There are many sources for more examples of passivity in relationships, including Sandra's relationship books. At this point, I want to move on to the relationship we have with ourself. We prepare the soil for a successful relationship out of our willingness to examine our relationship with ourself.

My Passivity and Me

Most of us know ourself through the false self, the limited and painful identity in which we are trapped emotionally and mentally. Our passivity is a major component of this false self. Before we can be free of passivity and begin to realize our potential, we have to get into the heart of this false self. We do that by seeing its many facets and aspects.

In the following pages, I lay before the reader intimate intricacies of my own psyche. My intention in doing so is to illustrate the kind of inner reckoning or psyche-searching that penetrates to the core of dysfunction or neurosis. It is a process of uncovering, discovering, and recovering our authentic self by patiently and lovingly learning about and overcoming the emotional beliefs and attachments that block our psychological growth.

144

This material reveals the kind of relationship I once had with myself. The following notes pertain to my struggle to become successful in my career as a writer and psychotherapist. I was quite neurotic just 15 years ago. I now feel the satisfaction of being successful, though not so much in terms of worldly accomplishment or external validation (as I once thought success would be experienced), but in the moment-to-moment harmony and self-acceptance in which I live.

From a young age I was emotionally attached to feelings of being a disappointment to others and myself. I have many childhood memories of feeling myself to be a failure in the eyes of my mother and father. Many times I have felt the old shame as I continued to replay those negative expectations with Sandra, my three children, and others. I harbored nagging feelings of being less than others, of being unworthy, insignificant, and—most painful of all—a loser.

On the surface, however, I clung to my illusions of pseudo-enlightenment, believing that my brilliance and wisdom penetrated into the mysteries of life. Magical thinking and ego-in-the-clouds dreams of fame and financial riches buoyed me along. A New Age believer, I chanted my mantras, communed with Father Sky, and contemplated walking on hot coals.

But I couldn't avoid those inner storms of discontent. I never knew when the next existential crisis would blow in, assailing me with blustery insinuations to the effect of, "Why aren't you succeeding like you're supposed to? How come you're such a bum, anyway? Look at you—you screwed up again. What makes you think you're so smart and evolved?"

Finally, beginning in 1985, I began to get some really good psychotherapy. I started to expose and study the conflicts, attachments, and inner tapes that were sabotaging my success.

Here is a summary of what I discovered about myself with respect to my difficulties in advancing my career and finding peace and fulfillment. Written in note form as I composed it more than ten years ago, this section is somewhat of an interruption in the narrative flow of this book. It is presented in this manner to give readers an abbreviated impression of the psychic bugs and quirks we encounter and acknowledge in this process of inner liberation. Many of the statements appear to be infantile and contradictory. Nevertheless, they represent the language of the unconscious and the irrational processing of the neurotic mind.

Peter's Passive Portrait

Part A. I have an emotional attachment to deprivation, refusal, and loss, which affects me in the following ways:

1) I try hard but never get anywhere;

2) I am easily discouraged, not persistent, little follow through;

3) Things don't work out for me; I will not get what I want, so why try;

4) I always manage to miss out;

5) I see others get rewards and benefits and I feel they are less deserving; I feel cheated out of what I deserve;

6) I don't really want it badly enough; becoming successful will take too much from me; I will be drained; success represents a loss rather than a gain.

Part B. I have an unconscious attachment to feeling controlled, squelched, and rendered helpless, powerless, and ineffective:

1) By failing, I thwart mother, wife, and boss, so as not to have them triumph over me; failing, I make them look bad; thus they are not as good as they claim to be:

>   a) I unconsciously equate success with mother (father, wife) feeling vindicated or validated, that what they did was right (and I was wrong);

>   b) Being successful is also equated with being what mother wants me to be—good, obedient, and subservient to her needs and desires;

>   c) Success means pleasing others (parents) and submitting to their agenda or expectations of me; success means giving in and capitulating to others;

>   d) Parents did not give me what I wanted; therefore, I reject them and their advice, and make them pay by not giving them what they would like for me—my happiness and success.

2) Success takes too much effort.

>   a) Parents did most everything for me; therefore, others should continue to do for me; I expect to get what I want without expending any effort; it is my due;

b) Parents did not do much for me; now in retribution, I make others do it for me to compensate for what wasn't done for me;

c) Effort drains me, takes from me; I feel dominated and controlled by what I need to do to become successful; I will lose my freedom; to become successful, I will have to give up time for play, fun, and doing things I really want to do; failure is associated with freedom, while success means enslavement;

d) I need to be pushed and forced into changes, even into areas that will be positive and good for me;

e) Parents did everything for me; therefore, I did not develop my own personal initiative;

f) Parents resented me doing things based on my own efforts; they resented my independent expression which i) made them feel not needed; ii) made them feel inadequate; iii) was never good enough and I (or my choice) was constantly put down.

3) I fear my own power; underneath, I am attached to someone holding me back and preventing me from being myself;

a) Parents squashed my autonomy and made me feel it was bad or sinful;

b) The expression of my power would invalidate or even destroy one or both of my parents;

c) The expression of my power would make my parents angry because they would take it as negation of who they are and what they believe in;

d) The expression of my power will cause others to abandon me, not like me, resent me because I am no longer there with them and for them;

e) Spontaneous independent expression of any kind was immediately squelched and not allowed because it put a burden on my parents; it was too inconvenient for them;

f) I should be squashed because they also were squashed and controlled as children; this is the way it should be.

4) I am unconsciously attached to being up against an immovable, intractable object (usually in the form of a person) that refuses to respond, listen, understand, or give to me; this object, which originally represented my parents, I now transfer onto others or life itself;

a) This attachment renders me powerless, hopeless, stuck in a despair that has no cure; I must swallow whatever crumbs are available to me and suppress my creative urges and drives.

Part C. I have an emotional attachment to feeling criticized and rejected. My self-concept does not include success.

1) I don't deserve success:

a) Because I am inherently bad, worthless, and undeserving;

b) If I express myself in any way, I will be seen as stupid, idiotic, inadequate, and a failure. So why take that chance; by keeping myself hidden, no one gets an opportunity to put me down;

c) Receiving help in any fashion makes me feel weak, inadequate, and uncomfortable; I must do everything myself; to become successful, I may need help from others; asking for help makes me feel that what I have already attained or who I am is invalidated; that is, anything good that comes from others invalidates my limited accomplishments and me.

2) No matter how good I am, I still do not receive any recognition or acknowledgment. (My parents rarely acknowledged or rewarded my good efforts.)

3) My parents did not expect anything good or superior from me; thus I produce only up to the level of their meager expectations.

4) My parents often times expected too much from me; I was to be great to validate their worth; they did not see me for who I was; by not being successful I thwart them and disappoint them to the degree to which they thwarted and disappointed me.

5) My sisters see me as inadequate and let me know I will never amount to anything.

6) I unconsciously identify with both of my parents and act out their success-failure issues; for example, my father's pattern was to work hard but never attain the status or recognition he felt he deserved; my mother felt that she could never hope to be understood or loved.

a) One is supposed to work hard just to get by; that's all that can be expected in life;

b) I unconsciously become my parent, subjecting my partner to an impression of emotional neglect that I felt subjected to as a child; I thwart my spouse and skimp in my affection and emotional support of my children;

c) I unconsciously become my parent to myself and subject myself to the same feelings to which they subjected me; thus, I feel they negated me and discouraged my talents; now I do the same to myself;

d) I unconsciously transfer my parents on to my partner and imagine she is squelching me or putting me down in the same way my parents did; for example, I force my partner into a parental role and feel she requires me to do things I don't want to do; then I refuse and thwart her, causing us both to feel as if we're drowning in failure; I would rather fail than submit to my parents or spouse and have them win over me.

7) If I am successful, more will be expected of me; I'll have to keep on performing and looking good; there will be more pressure to continue my success and thus less freedom.

8) If I am successful, others will benefit; they will use my success and me; I equate success with giving to others, not giving to myself; thus what I give to others takes away from me; it robs and drains me; they will like me or want to be with me only because of my success.

9) If I am successful, others will be jealous and hate me; they will no longer be my friends.

10) If I am successful, who will take care of me? But failing, I ensure that others will take care of me and attend to my needs.

I had absorbed the meaning and significance of each of these notations over many years. The knowledge had to sink in, wiggling past my resistance in a "psychic osmosis," and be absorbed—sometimes consciously, sometimes unconsciously—down into what feels like a cellular level. However much my parents or society might have contributed to these facets of my psyche, I have had to accept responsibility for them. These were my psychic bugs and quirks. If I ever hoped to dissolve them and realize my potential, I had to study them, "own" them, and strive to move beyond them.

People are amazed when they realize that we are bound in place by such emotional, irrational, and infantile impressions. This is one of the more difficult facts to accept and understand about our human condition. We want so much to believe that our common sense can rule our lives and lead us to success and happiness. But common sense is not the language of the unconscious.

Discovering Your True Friend

What does it mean to have a good relationship with oneself? Many of us have difficulty imagining or feeling that such a relationship is real or viable, partly because we don't even think in terms of having a relationship with ourself. Yet why shouldn't we? We have relationships with others and with animals. When we pause to consider it, we know we can be our own best friend or our own worst enemy.

Most of us, as I said, either take ourself for granted or have an antagonistic relationship with ourself. Often we only feel ourself when the sensation is pronounced—when we're feeling happy, sad, or bad. That's a sensation or experience of ourself—whether pleasant or unpleasant— but not a true connection. For the most part, we are like second cousins to ourself: we are not conscious of how much we are not conscious of who we are.

Much of the time we look for ways to distract ourselves with a thousand trivial pursuits because, first, we dislike who we are and want to avoid ourself; second, it feels that, below the level of our thoughts and feelings, we are immaterial and therefore unworthy of our attention; and, third, to look into ourself is to expose fearful and forbidden elements. The speed of modern life, with millions of us hurrying mindlessly from point to point, is a measure of our need for distraction to escape the challenge and responsibility of being human: digging in the roots of our existence, cultivating our self, our garden of divinity.

"We wish to be swallowed up," writes Gerry Spence. "'Swallow me up,' we say to the system. 'Swallow me up,' we say to belief. 'Swallow me up, take me. It is better to be taken than to be alone. It is better to be a slave in the presence of slaves than to be free in the presence of only the self, the frightened, and lonely self.'"[xxi]

Our common everyday experience is passive when we are idle receivers of the ruminations of our mind. In this condition, we have no attunement to the moment, to the here and now, and to the pleasure possible in our experience of ourself. If we believe what the wisest people tell us, the present moment is the richest point of contact with reality, and reality starts with our relationship with ourself. When we strive to improve our relationship with ourself, we can live in satisfaction and fulfillment even if, for various reasons, we are not as prosperous or successful as we would hope or not in an intimate or romantic relationship with someone.

When we emerge from passivity and become connected to ourself, we enter into a unified knowing, a state of grace where negative thoughts and feelings are kept at bay or simply dissolved in the truth of ourself. We feel that our moment in existence is too precious to let slip by without our being present to it, like a father who wants to be sure his daughter's wedding is filmed and photographed. There is great joy in the feeling of being master of our experience.

From this perspective, we are honoring ourself, but not in an egotistic sense. In egotism, we feel separation from other humans and from existence. We compare ourselves to others. It feels like "them and me," as if who I am is different from who you are. We may feel better than others or inferior to others—either way is an egotistic perspective. When we truly honor ourself, we feel our oneness with other humans and with existence—there are no more comparisons with who we think is better or who is less. We experience fulfillment beyond our current limitations, knowing ourself as an extended being, receptive to whatever life and spirit might bestow while not expecting or needing anything more than the beatitudes that our awakening reveals in the present moment.

In contrast is the kind of experience familiar to codependents. Codependents, enablers, or emotional caterers are reeking with unconscious passivity, revealed in their denial or negation of self and in their inability to create healthy relationships and positive circumstances in their lives. They represent psychic impotence, the condition of spinning one's wheels to get nowhere. They are also emotional bingers, deeply steeped in the sense that much is missing from their lives. They do not expect recognition, validation, and love (although they are desperate for it), which reflects the poverty of their relationship with themselves. Codependents often play the role of emotional rescuers, perpetually at the service of troubled individuals. Often, their true motivation is not altruism as much as their unconscious identification with the helplessness or ineptness of the ones they are attempting to rescue. Their sense of responsibility for rescuing others also covers up the helplessness they feel in not being able to "fix things" for others. Through their engagement and involvement in the lives of others, codependents create an illusion of power. They feel as if the other person really needs them. In their passivity, however, they not only cater to others but also accommodate other people's opinions of who they are.

Of course, codependents are not by any means the only classification of people who negate themselves and feel unworthy of a loving inner relationship. The Nobel Laureate Czeslaw Milosz observed this as a general condition of humanity when he wrote, "Today man believes there is nothing in him, so he accepts anything even if he knows it to be bad, in order to find himself at one with others, not to be alone."

Functioning in such a manner, we may be barely tethered to our humanity. *In Unspeakable Acts, Ordinary People: The Dynamics of Torture*, journalist John Conroy investigates three incidents of torture instigated by those in authority—in Northern Ireland, Israel, and the United States—that reveal the potential in each of us for absolute brutality. Following orders or obeying authority is a primary inducement for ordinary people to commit unspeakable acts.[xxii] A lack of connection to ourself means a lack of connection to understanding, compassion, joy, and love. Psychologists have also established that we look to others to define events. We judge by the behaviors or actions of others whether a certain event constitutes an emergency or depicts unacceptable behavior.

Even our relationship with God reflects our relationship with ourself. If we are not connected to ourself, we may feel that God is absent, distant, or nonexistent, and we may be more desperate than ever to feel recognized and validated by God. If we are convinced of our own inadequacy and unworthiness, we are likely to see God as disapproving and punishing. God, as we know Him, tends to be a projection of our relationship with ourself.

I remind myself, at this point, that our world seems to have become quite inarticulate about the inner life of spirit. So here—whether articulate or otherwise—are some passing reflections on the subject. I am after all writing about the psyche, and I do sometimes wonder, as have many thinkers, whether psyche is the seat of the spirit or the soul—or vice-versa. Certainly, psychology's advocacy of inner harmony draws comparisons with spiritual advice on upkeep of the soul.

Some people say, "We only have to believe in God." But continuing psychological and spiritual evolvement requires more than this. Just as we want our children to grow powerful and autonomous (if we are healthy enough to want that), so God or some divine consciousness wants this for us. God becomes known through the divine in ourself, and the divine becomes known through inner purification, the psychological working out of negativity. Our inner work produces higher consciousness which is a process of inner transcendence. Experiencing God now happens directly, on an emotional level, through our loving connection to ourself and others.

So believed the Gnostic Christians, who formed an important part of the early church in the years following the death of Christ. The Gnostics said that whoever remains ignorant of the Self cannot obtain fulfillment. As the Gnostics saw it, the royal road to God is through a connection with our true Self. God will be an abstraction, an idea, or a hope, something external to us, or separate from us, as we feel separate from ourself and each other, if we can't feel or see something of the divine within ourself and each other.

In the Gnostic Gospels, discovered in 1945 by an Egyptian peasant along the Nile River, Christ is quoted as saying to Judas Thomas the Twin, "Rather, the kingdom is inside you and outside you. When you know yourselves, then you will be known, and will understand that you are children of the living Father. But if you do not know yourselves, then you live in poverty, and embody poverty."[xxiii]

Later in these Gospels, Christ says again to Thomas, "For whoever does not know self does not know anything, but whoever knows self already has acquired knowledge about the depth of the universe."[xxiv] Humans have known of the Self for a long time. The Upanishads, sacred Hindu texts the oldest of which were written in Sanskrit between 800 and 400 BC, make numerous references to the Self. It is written in the Isa Upanishad, "Who sees all beings in his own Self, and his own Self in all beings, loses all fear. When a sage sees this great unity and his Self has become all beings, what delusion and what sorrow can ever be near him?"[xxv]

Through the psychological method described in this book and with spiritual help, I have been moving toward a deeper connection with myself. The more I am able to clear away my emotional debris, especially passivity and ego, the deeper I go into life and the more I know, through a subtle, intuitive assurance, of my own immortality. I was raised a Catholic, shifted to atheism in university, and later, during the winter of 1975-76, became a Catholic Worker on the Bowery in New York. In my present understanding, I consider that I am God, that we are all God, that all is God. Passivity has stood in my way of this realization, as has ego. Unconsciously, we prefer to cling to our limited self. We cling to our sense of separateness, despite the suffering it entails, blocking us from realizing the comfort and joy in understanding that, in all likelihood, all is one. Through our ego and in our resistance, we fear the demise of the old self, as if death and destruction will accompany our attempt to discover our true nature.

As we struggle to become extended beings and search assiduously for the sacred essence within us, it is, as one of my clients said, "like trying to touch a butterfly on the wing." Even as we are succeeding, we find it difficult to say what we are succeeding at. In these realms, words are like falling leaves, with little impact or substance.

Occasionally, I apply these cross-over thoughts (between psychology and the spirit) in my therapy sessions. Doing so depends on a particular client's set of beliefs or open-mindedness. James was agonizing over a woman who hesitated to be romantically involved with him. He told me in a session, "My desire for her, my longing to be with her, has become very painful. Maybe it's trite to say that I can't live without her, but that's just how it feels."

We exposed his attachment to the feeling of missing out and being deprived, and still he continued to pine for her. "Take that energy of longing for her," I told him, "and turn it inward, as if it were a spear of laser light that you hurl into your depths. It carries the same longing, only now for yourself. This is a conscious attempt to transmute negative energy, to give it a higher purpose. Instead of suffering, you take that intense longing and use its potency to connect with what is available—love of your own self. Do this each time your longing for her arises, and you will lessen the frustration. Moreover, you will be expressing your determination to feel more support for yourself from within. In your persistence, you will be asserting a deep belief in yourself, that fulfillment and happiness are available within you. It is important while doing this technique to see your resistance to connecting with yourself in this powerful way. Try to see this connection: the pain and frustration of not connecting with her is also the pain of not being there for yourself."

Though he never did establish a romantic relationship with her, James said several months later, "I like this new sense of myself. I'm not on the back burner anymore. At the same time, I don't put myself ahead of anyone else. It's the feeling that I can easily rest, or find repose, in myself. There is a sense of incredible value in that relationship."

By the fourth century, orthodox Christianity had won out over Gnosticism. This happened, in my opinion, because individual Christians could not resist orthodoxy's authoritarian model—that Scriptures, the apostles, and the Church represented absolute truth—because their passivity prevented them from believing deeply in themselves. The people of the time were not ready for inner freedom, not yet ready to embrace their divine essence. To some degree, we remain in this state to this day.

Without this new relationship with ourself, all our relationships suffer. If we don't know who we are and what we are feeling, our ability to be present to others is limited. We will always be reacting to them or to some unconscious issue within us—even when we are trying to be kind—rather than being truly present to them. Connected to ourself, in comparison, we become our own source of understanding and compassion. We fully accept responsibility for our choices and do so without self-recrimination when those choices are brought into question or appear to have been wrong or ill-advised. In our alignment with the Self, we become both our own authority and an instrument of divine will.

In summary, our present experiences of ourself, others, and the world are based in large measure on (1) a personal and cultural belief in ourself as separate from others and above nature; (2) an emotional desire for self-aggrandizement stemming from childhood impressions of inadequacy, unworthiness, vulnerability, and insecurity; (3) the success of our inner defenses in blocking awareness of our passivity and our collusion in unhappiness and self-defeat; (4) an unconscious association of the false self with the imperative of self-preservation and physical survival; and (5) our resistance to understanding our spiritual nature.

Chapter 6
Passivity and Health

Health problems often are an indication of a needed change in our attitude toward our life and ourself. Illness can be a physical representation of the forces in all of us that victimize us, stop our progress, and render us powerless. We know that stress can cause disease and that suppressed anger or fear can make us sick. Negative thoughts and emotions can depress us and affect our immune system.

Most of us agree that psychosomatic conditions do exist, and a great deal of new studies and literature, including a growing number of studies appearing in mainstream medical journals, supports the body-mind connection. In my practice, I have seen such body-mind (or body-emotion) connections between passivity and hypochondria, hypertension, addictions, compulsions, eating disorders, migraines, constipation, skin problems, obesity, impaired intelligence, attention-deficit disorder, stuttering, herpes, lupus, chronic fatigue, insomnia, hyperactivity, frigidity, impotence, and premature ejaculation.

It has been reported that stress hastens the onset of AIDS in men infected with the virus.[xxvi] Another study, published in 1998, found that people who suffered abuse in childhood, who had a parent who was an alcoholic, an addict, or a battered woman, or who endured other stressful situations were two to four times more likely than other adults to suffer serious illnesses such as heart disease, emphysema, and stroke.[xxvii] Another study, of 942 middle-aged men, found that feelings of hopelessness, failure, or uncertainty about the future could cause a faster progression of atherosclerosis.[xxviii]

Emotional Resistance to Physical Health

Pain or illness can be seen as the manifestation of an embedded emotional conflict. We can respond to illness to mobilize ourselves for further psychological growth and enhanced physical health, or we can react to it in a way that mires us more deeply into disease and a victim position.[xxix]

For example, the manner in which a person is affected by the herpes virus may correspond with a part of himself that is entrenched in feeling defective, contaminated, unwanted, unlovable, and rejected. This virus can be associated with unconscious sexual conflicts and feelings of shame and lack of forgiveness pertaining to sexual conduct and sexual identity.

We may harbor a buried conviction that we really do not deserve health, success, or happiness. Health and happiness feel foreign to us because they do not correspond with our expectations or who we think we are. Sickness may be indicating the depth and magnitude of our self-rejection, self-loathing, and despair. Loss, deprivation, and feelings of neglect are more familiar to us than prosperity or feeling loved. Even the good in our life causes anxiety in some of us because we anticipate, whether consciously or not, that it will be lost or taken away.

An important way to activate self-healing is to understand the emotional causes of sickness as well as the emotional uses of sickness after its arrival. Sickness can be a way to connect with other people. Children may observe that, when sick, they get more attention and affection from their parents. Many individuals, and especially children, cannot seek such recognition from a position of strength. Children don't usually walk up to their parents and say, "Mom and Dad, I feel that you have been ignoring me and taking me for granted. I would really like it if you would speak to me with more sensitivity and show me that you truly do love me, as you claim." Many if not most adults are unable to say this to one another.

Love and attention are so important to children that, if they see a passive way to attain it, they are willing to resort to that method, becoming sick or staying sick for a longer period if that serves the purpose. At the other end of the spectrum, being healthy can bring up for a child or an adult the emotional sense of being alone, having to be independent, particularly if it is observed that siblings or others get more attention for being sick.

Sickness can be cultivated as a passive way to get back at a parent or spouse. An individual, for instance, may exhaust himself through overwork and approach the point of illness, all the while covering up inner resentment against a spouse or parent who he feels has not recognized or supported him. The following irrational, yet emotionally convincing inner clause can support this form of self-defeat: "Okay mother, you insisted that I work hard and succeed in life. You didn't care about me, only about my success, so you could feel good about yourself. Well, I'll show you the price of that kind of mothering. I'll do what you want, and if I kill myself in the process you'll finally regret what you've done to me." When sickness develops in this emotional climate, the individual has the satisfaction, however limited it is in reality, of inducing guilt in those who he feels have failed to appreciate him. In effect, however, this illness is the acting out of his passivity, the feeling of having been neglected, controlled, or rejected by mother or father.

Codependents often feel themselves to be the victim of neglectful people. Though codependents go out of their way to support and care for others, they can be very sensitive to the feeling that their care is not appreciated or reciprocated. Should they get sick, they can intensify the feeling of being neglected, thereby acting out with more emotional intensity this very feeling to which they are attached. Their unconscious defense is, "You see how much I help you. I'm willing to sacrifice myself, even my health, to show you how much you matter to me. If only you would give me just a fraction of the support I have given you."

Through illness, the individual puts the other person in the role of the neglectful parent, recreating the childhood experience of feeling overlooked and unappreciated. A variation on this theme could be expressed as follows: "My husband doesn't want to help me. He has no respect for who I am. I have to do it all. Now I'm getting sick. I don't know how long I can go on like this."

Sickness can also be a form of retaliation against someone close. If the individual feels that the other is not available, then through sickness he himself becomes unavailable. This passive maneuver is common among the partners of alcoholics and drug addicts. In another variation, the person who is sick is able to reverse the situation in which he feels controlled or helpless and thereby place others at the mercy of the conditions or requirements of his sickness, such as developing food disorders.

Sickness can be a way to express dependency. Rather than being responsible for himself, the person's sickness makes others responsible for his well-being. There are many chronic "dependees" who sacrifice their careers and health and act out their substantial inner passivity "guilt-free" because, allegedly, "it's not my fault I'm in this passive position—it's the fault of my sickness." This situation is an infantile recreation through which others are set up to be pseudo-parents.

Still others become emotionally invested in their disease, which becomes the primary way they know and experience themselves. In its most passive expression, the feeling can be, "I don't know who I am without my disease." One perpetually sick woman stated, "Nobody knows what it feels like to be sick like I am." She seemed to adopt a sense of validation for being the greatest sufferer, the biggest martyr. Because of her passivity, she has little inclination or energy to improve her circumstances.

We create an emotional climate for a disease when looking for a way to experience our passivity through loss of energy, loss of strength and physical functions, and the sense of being overwhelmed and defeated by physical or medical conditions that seem impervious to treatment. An individual who becomes angry at his body could be manifesting this emotional condition. The anger is a defense, making this statement: "I am not 'into' (or resonating emotionally with) the feeling of being overwhelmed, rendered powerless, and defeated by my disease or illness. Can't you see how angry I am at my body for letting me down?" Another clue was provided when a client with lupus expressed the emotional distress of these frequent recurring thoughts: "If I could do something differently, I'm sure I would get well," and "I just don't have the wherewithal to deal with this." Both statements expressed her deep entanglement in passivity.

Sickness can also be a passive way to avoid obligations or commitment. Rather than being direct, many of us have used the excuse of sickness to get out of something that we didn't want to do. Others take it a step further and develop the symptoms of genuine illness. If we are incapacitated in some way, the feeling is that others will not expect much from us. On the other side of the ledger, we may feel that in being healthy or successful, others will place too many demands on us. So illness is a passive way of saying *no*, or a way of isolating ourselves, or an excuse for an emotional predisposition to failure.

If we feel that improvement in our health depends on the actions of others, we are taking a passive approach. Others can't necessarily be relied on. And we don't always have to change the outer circumstances. What we need is to moderate or change our emotional alignment, to put an end to our own willingness to feel passive or somehow victimized. We resonate with this painful feeling, as if our psyche is an old Marconi radio with just one frequency.

Even free of physical disease, we may still exist in a negative condition, consumed by worry, stress, and feelings of being deprived, controlled, and unloved. Older people can worry about becoming disabled and immobilized, and when in fact this happens they often experience this physical hardship through passivity, in this case the feeling of being helpless, restricted, and at the mercy of others, thus making their situation much more painful and fearful. True health is a state of freedom, a physical, emotional, and spiritual condition in which harmony, compassion, presence, and joyfulness radiate from within us. Doctors, medicine, or loved ones can't create this condition in us. We have to do it for ourself.

Breathing, Sexuality, and Elimination

Ill health and passivity are also associated with shallow breathing and the repression of sexual energy. Deeper breathing is tremendously important for vitality, creativity, and joyfulness. Often people breathe only into the upper part of the respiratory system, with little or no flow of air into and out of the abdomen. We wear belts and waistbands that are too tight. The respiratory musculature can become fixed on this shallow level, and a concerted, conscious effort, combined with massage or bodywork, can be required to deepen one's breathing.

In Bioenergetics theory, both the ease and quality of breathing and movement are hampered in the emotionally ill person by chronic muscular tensions. Shallow breathing can start in childhood when the expression of feelings is discouraged by parents. As children, we get angry or excited or frustrated, and we breathe deeply in our expression of these emotions. We are told to stop the emotional display, to shut it down, and the only way to do so is to restrict our breath. Even before that, pacifiers are jammed in our mouth when we are fussy, noisy, or crying. What message does this deliver to the infantile psyche?

Dr. Alexander Lowen writes of people who have difficulty breathing fully and easily: "As children, they held their breath to stop crying, they drew back their shoulders and tightened their chests to contain their anger, and they constricted their throats to prevent screaming . . . Now, as adults, they inhibit their breathing to keep these feelings in repression."[xxx]

Most people find it difficult to breathe out fully. The chest is generally held in an expanded position, while the lungs contain reserve air. Breathing out can be felt to be passive because it is the equivalent of 'letting go.' Lowen writes, "Full expiration is a giving in, a surrender to the body. Letting go of the air is experienced as a letting go of control which the neurotic individual fears."[xxxi]

When we become more conscious of breathing and able to breathe more freely, we become more conscious of our voice. Our voice is an instrument of self-expression and self-assertion. Both power and passivity are recognized in our voice. An indicator of emotional health is the ability, when responding rather than reacting, to use the voice in all ranges and registers.

Our sexual nature is also repressed when we are scolded or shamed for exploring the pleasure that comes from playing with our genitals. We now begin to inhibit ourselves, for if we breathe deeply we will feel alive, wild, and sexual. So we shut down our breathing and with it our vital energy. Sexual energy is associated with the flow of energy through the pelvic region. That same energy, when it flows through other centers in the body, generates other feelings and effects such as confidence, compassion, creativity, self-expression, and insight. If the energy is blocked at the sexual center or elsewhere, it will not be available for the expression of our full humanity. (A powerful breathing exercise is described in the Appendix.)

Passivity can impede our ability to experience pleasure. A significant percentage of us can certainly feel our pain, and we complain loud and long about it. When acting more on our own behalf, we make an effort to be attentive to the subtle pleasures inherent in our body. The satisfactions that come from alertness to our senses and a spiritual sensitivity for the wonders of life begin to awaken. Passivity blocks the ability and desire to maintain a more acute attention to our experience of the world and thus to the possibilities of pleasure in any given moment. The ego-based pleasure so many of us experience, based on self-admiration or the validation of others, provides a shallow and fleeting gratification. We often pursue distant goals that we feel will bring pleasure, yet we fail to experience real pleasure in the moment.

In relation to the terms anal stubbornness and anal retentiveness, many health experts concur that a sluggish, constipated bowel affects our health in many ways, including undermining our immune system. The *Merck Manual*, the medical industry's standard diagnosis and treatment text, reports colon degeneration on the rise. Cancer of the colon and rectum is the second leading cause of cancer deaths in the United States, after lung cancer. This cancer develops in a sluggish colon over many years and has a long precancerous stage.[xxxii] A sluggish bowel can retain on the walls and in the pockets of the colon pounds of toxic, poisonous fecal matter. The retention and absorption of this waste can often be the primary cause of sickness.

Evidence suggests there is a common lack of concern for, and attention to, regular elimination of fecal matter. I believe this situation is influenced, at least partially, by passivity. As mentioned earlier, in Chapter 3, a major aspect of our experience of childhood passivity is centered on toilet training and our resistance to it. Power struggles are common in the difficult months of toilet training. The child stubbornly refuses to release feces in his rebellion against the feeling of being forced to submit, a feeling that is deeply offensive to his infantile sense of autonomy and independence.

Refusing to release feces is a passive-aggressive reaction. Withholding in this way feels like an expression of power, but, as is typical of passive-aggressive behaviors, it is actually self-defeating. Passive-aggressive behaviors, widespread among adults, are forms of indirect resistance, including procrastinating, being stubborn, working deliberately slowly, being intentionally or unconsciously inefficient or inattentive, avoiding obligations and forgetting, failing to do one's share of work, frequently complaining, scorning those in authority, withholding affection, and using verbal boomerangs to thwart the wishes of others.

The psyche makes no allowance for the space of time in the years between childhood and adulthood. What upset us in our childhood fifty years ago we can feel again in this moment, just as fresh, just as disturbing. Everything is present tense. When we are indifferent to taking care of proper elimination, we are back in the passive-aggressive saddle, acting out our resistance to an old feeling of being compelled to please some authority. If getting or staying sick is passive, wanting to be healthy and doing something effective about it is an expression of our power. Eat your apple a day, skip around the block, and drink lots of pure water.

Time Is On Our Side

Millions of us have become "human electrons," zipping hither-and-yon to keep this electronic age humming. Pushed by high workloads, social pressures, and our psychological predisposition, we hurry from one deadline to the next commitment to the next crisis, as if trying to outdo the speed of our computers. This speed mania is apparent in many areas of our lives. We want faster computers, food, travel, and returns on our investments, as well as faster-acting medicines, cars, and athletes.

Behind our obsession with speed is the feeling that we need to save time. Dr. Larry Dossey, a prominent physician and best-selling author, believes we have created a clock-conscious culture that makes us the servants of time and seriously impairs our health. Dr. Dossey has for the past twenty years been a leading exponent of a more holistic and less mechanistic approach to medicine. In his book *Space, Time & Medicine*, he says we are generating more illness and may even be destroying ourselves by perceiving time in a linear, one-way flow.[xxxiii] Mechanistic time has now enslaved many of us, and the schedules and timetables of civilization are run like the 100-yard dash. Animals may have a more realistic sense of time than we do.

We can sense in meditation, in the silence of our inner space, that time stands still. If we succeed at calming our mind, we can feel as if we begin to dissolve into existence. Deep in meditation, there is little or no sense of time. Back on the surface of ourselves, however, where we identify with our mind, personality, ego, and body, we again start ticking to a sense of past, present, and future. We see change happening in the material world, including our own aging process, and we believe that these material changes can be explained only by the flow of time. What we are seeing, however, is limited to what our senses observe about the nature of time and matter. Moving in space, particles of matter flow, disperse, interact, and come together in new forms. It appears that time is acting upon matter, but time is irrelevant to the essence of matter. Matter is dynamic, and even apparently solid objects are shifting and spiraling within the confines of their space, while time is the vortex of the eternal present. The notion that time flows is comparable to the illusion that the sun rises in the east, crosses the sky, and sets in the west, when in fact the sun is not moving relative to the Earth. The impression of the sun's movement is created by the Earth's rotation on its axis in the direction we call eastward.

Most cultures and most humans had, until the invention of the first reliable clock, a cyclical (based on the rhythms of nature) rather than a linear sense of time. The days and seasons come and go with regularity, as the moon orbits the Earth and the Earth the sun. Everything returns again to the beginning, we sensed, and the process renews itself. We were participants in the spiral of energy and life, not followers of a straight line running off to the horizon. However, our mind, enthused by the Age of Reason and dazzled by the Industrial Revolution, shifted to a mechanistic, linear mode of function, and our sense of time, in breaking away from the natural world, began to reflect the intoxication of these new powers and the lust for a life-span, however limited, that glorifies our ego, the alleged creator of these powers. Our ego can't exist in timelessness; though it wants very much to exist, like linear time it is an illusion.

We created time in this new self-image, based on our narcissistic sense that, in being special creatures apart from nature who are able to dominate life and perform feats and create machines that make us gods, time is thus what we now perceive it to be. Like travelers lost in the woods, we've circled back on ourselves, restoring the child's sense of omnipotence in the ego's credo: "I, through my own impression, make it so." Our infantile sense of omnipotence, dashed by the countless humiliations of passivity, is repatriated through the power of science and technology. Now, by means of the genetic revolution, we will be perfect gods, recreating ourselves.

Our passivity and our ego have formed a partnership with reconstructed time. T.S. Eliot's "The Love Song of J. Alfred Prufrock," a duet of time and passivity, portrays our sorry state: Time for you and time for me / And time yet for a hundred indecisions / And for a hundred visions and revisions / Before the taking of a toast and tea . . . / And indeed there will be time / To wonder, 'Do I dare?' and 'Do I dare?' Do I dare / Disturb the universe?

Newton held to a cyclical view of time, and his impression of it was tied to nature. However, as Dr. Dossey writes:

> . . . the linear view of time was increasingly popularized by such figures as Leibnitz, Barrow, and Locke. This view of time gathered momentum in the three hundred years following [Dutch scientist Christiaan] Huygen's invention of the pendulum clock, such that we now generally believe it to be intuitively obvious that time flows; that it is divisible into past, present, and future, and that once an event has happened, it will never occur again. Our lives are so chronometrically dominated that we not only have become unconscious of the cycles in nature, we have become inured to the cycles within ourselves. We no longer eat when hungry or sleep when sleepy, but follow the dictates of the clock.[xxxiv]

An underlying sense of urgency is illustrated by Dossey's observation about the emotional reactions of terminally ill patients: "Of all the predictable responses of patients who discover they have a terminal illness, panic is one of the most characteristic . . . 'How much time do I have?' 'How much time is left?' In the panic state the consideration of time is paramount. Time is running down, it is being played out. The time sense becomes heightened. Moments, heretofore unnoticed, are savored—but usually with a dread: soon they will be gone, and I with it."[xxxv]

Health experts now say that three emotional or social components—time pressure, hostility, and lack of human connection—contribute more to the incidence of disease than even such physical influences as high cholesterol and cigarette smoking. These three components are all related to aspects of passivity.

Our sense of time is skewed by another factor: we experience the present moment as unsatisfactory because we don't have enough (of whatever). This creates an emotional preoccupation with future goals—only in the future will we finally have enough to be happy. Of course, the future never comes because only the present is real. Meanwhile, we don't see how deeply, through our passivity, we are prepared to live through the feeling that something—some vague essential—is missing.

We have built our culture on a foundation of orality. Orality describes a vital aspect of our experience of life in our first eighteen months, when our pleasure is experienced through the mucous membranes of our mouth. In this period, we begin to experience displeasure too. When the breast or the bottle is not immediately available, a baby can quickly become frustrated. The baby does not understand the relativity of time, so a ten-minute wait for food while mother runs around the house taking care of other things can feel like an eternity. Waits such as this are extremely offensive to the baby's self-centeredness and sense of omnipotence. The baby's illusion of power demands instant gratification. To maintain this illusion, the baby believes that the delay in waiting for food is what he or she wants—"If it is happening to me, this must be what I have wished for." In this manner, we acquire lifetime emotional attachments to feelings of being refused, deprived, and missing out.

Consequently, our aim is not *to get* but to *not get*. We cover up this secret attachment to not getting by running around trying to get everything we can. In other words, we are under the influence of a powerful temptation to "prove" that we want to get. The very nature of such desires is that they remain unfulfilled. If something external is provided or fulfilled, we want something else. The harder it is to get, the more we want it; the easier it is, the less we value it. We seek to maintain the experience of wanting something, while remaining unfulfilled. This is one way we know ourself, through this fixation. We take this deficit feeling for granted, as if there is no other way to experience ourself. Marketers and advertisers may not understand the underlying factors this clearly, but they surely can see the desire, entitlement, greed, and envy in our eyes. "Say yes to everything," says a department-store solicitation for its credit card.

Psychoanalyst Erich Fromm said of this condition:

> A passive person is . . . an eternal suckling babe. What he consumes is ultimately of little consequence

to him. He simply waits, with open mouth, as it were, for whatever the bottle offers. Then he is gradually sated without having to do anything himself. None of his psychic powers is called into play, and finally he grows tired and sleepy. The sleep he experiences is often a narcosis, an exhaustion induced by boredom, more than a sleep of healthy regeneration. . . . And the media involved in producing our false needs keep reassuring us that it is our level of consumption that demonstrates the high level of our culture."[xxxvi]

Our orality is dissatisfied with the *here and now*. The future holds the promise of succulent sensation. Our defense says, "I'm not attached to the feeling of not getting or being deprived. Look at how anxious I am for the future to get here so that I will be fulfilled. If only time would pass more quickly." From beyond the horizon we hear future's siren call, promising us riches, recognition, fulfillment, and love. Of course, the future has no substance in itself. In our passivity, however, we cannot make the present real. We lack the power to secure the deeper satisfactions that lie in our own consciousness and existence.

Not only do we become passive slaves to the clock, but also through our religious beliefs we accentuate the sense of time quickly running out. Christians, Jews, and Moslems believe we have only this one life to live, in contrast with Hindu and Buddhist doctrines that profess a belief in reincarnation. Whatever the truth may be, we in the West are imbued with the conviction that whatever our purpose or business on Earth, we had better move fast to take care of it. This impression is so pervasive that even agnostics and atheists probably come under its influence.

The belief in one life is conscious, but its negative effect on us is unconscious. We are not aware of how much we are willing to use this belief to heighten our sense of time being lost and our helplessness to do anything about it. This impression accentuates, for the sake of our attachment to passivity, the feeling of being at the mercy of forces beyond our control. We are greatly under the influence of impressions that leave us feeling overwhelmed and powerless.

This above-mentioned panic denotes not just our fear of our psychological death-passage into the unknown but also the experience itself of dying. In other words, in many instances the panic is a defense against realization of our passivity. No power on Earth can save us from death. When through terminal illness we see it coming in the distance, approaching quickly, our sense of helplessness can be acute. The defense is, "I'm not wanting to go into this profound state of helplessness. Look at how panicky I am that such a prospect is approaching in the form of death."

The implication is that passivity can cause a much more anxious or fearful death than would otherwise be experienced. Dossey writes, "The constricted time sense in the terminally ill is apparently part of a psychological dynamic resulting in early death. It is associated with desperation, panic, and giving up. This coping path is a malignant path for the terminally ill. It should be dealt with as surely as we would employ drugs and surgery and irradiation in treating an underlying cancer."[xxxvii] Opportunities to suffer and become ill abound in the many, many things we can feel helpless about.

Meditation is very helpful for dealing with the stress of modern living. Through meditation, we experience time in new, friendlier ways, and we access a more expanded sense of ourself. One problem is that many of us simply won't meditate. For starters, our mind is too active and refuses to be dislodged from its starring role on the stage of our experience. If we get past that problem, we encounter others: our fear of the feeling of emptiness, and beyond that the possibility of merging with the whole, and thus death to the ego and all the limited and painful attachments with which we are identified and reluctant to give up. To merge with existence in the present moment requires that our ego disappear, at least temporarily. Our ego, as I said earlier, wants no part of such an arrangement. If anything it wants to be solidly and permanently at the center of our experience of ourself. Under the influence of the ego's fear of being exposed and diminished, we back off, not trusting this process to lead us to safety and freedom. How can we trust in existence to support us? Won't we be annihilated? Are we strong enough, we wonder, to come back intact?

Meditation, when it brings us to an undisturbed center, is indeed an antidote for anxiety and stress. For the frenetic Western mind, however, it may not be as beneficial or work as quickly as absorption of the psychological knowledge and truth about our own individual psyche. The best psychology offers this level of insight, the full power of liberation, if we can allow it to penetrate past our defenses, our resistance, and our fear of the death and rebirth process.

Doctors and professors are among the most orthodox of professional people. A large cadre of doctors is still faithful to Descartes' conception of mind-body dualism and scoff at the notion that treating psychological issues can improve physical health. Although traditional medicine has sought to fight disease from the outside—by attacking the invading viruses, bacteria, and germs—we are nevertheless well on our way to establishing a medical model that recognizes ethereal elements at man's center—consciousness, harmony, destiny, and the will to live.

Our extensive reliance on pharmaceutical drugs reflects our passivity. We allow ourselves to be conned and lied to. We are conned because we pay too much for medications to cure ailments that many natural herbs and other products can treat more successfully. Dr. David G. Williams, in his monthly newsletter Alternatives, writes:

> I am honestly shocked at how gullible the American public has become in regard to issues concerning their health. The hundreds of millions of dollars being spent on advertising by the giant drug companies seems to have convinced the public that safe pharmaceutical answers exist for practically every possible health complaint or concern. Unfortunately, the truth is that most drugs and hormones fail to live up to this image of "safe efficacy" . . . they are not without dangerous side-effects and they are not always the most effective methods of dealing with the problem over the long term.[xxxviii]

The pharmaceutical industry has also been telling outright lies about the needs and benefits of mood-altering drugs, claiming as well that the psychological components of depression have not been determined. Depression, as well as guilt, fear, anxiety, and shame, are byproducts of our unresolved emotional conflicts. These conflicts are deep negative beliefs with which we resonate. They are contaminants in our psyche, and can be compared to bugs or quirks in a computer system. They are the guardians of our limited sense of self.

Evidence that inner passivity is included in this toxic mix is seen in the erratic peaks of manic-depression. These peaks involve feelings of power and creativity followed by plunges into apathy and powerlessness. Unfortunately, most psychological methods do not work deeply enough in the unconscious to access much of this negativity and give us the chance to work it out. Properly accessed, our unconscious is a gold mine of insight that empowers our intelligence and reveals our truth. It's not drugs we need as much as this truth and intelligence, without which we risk losing what makes us human—dignity, integrity, wisdom, freedom, and a friendly sense of self.

To get to the roots of depression, a therapist has to show his clients how they secretly collude in their misfortune. The compulsion to repeat patterns of self-defeat has to be exposed and understood. Our defenses have to be penetrated and dislodged. Unwittingly, many therapists shore up their clients' defenses. They feel their role is to listen to their clients and to comfort them, to commiserate with their plight, even to validate their perceptions concerning the apparent injustices of others and the world. This handholding is not going to produce emotional health and inner strength. The best therapists are freedom fighters who strive to help their clients establish inner freedom.

I observe with concern the ineptitude of many therapists and the skullduggery of drug manufacturers. But I'm not anxious or unhappy about it. It is important in overcoming passivity to allow others their life choices and delusions without unduly troubling oneself or taking on their burdens. Each of us is responsible for the lies we believe and the choices we make. The world is perfect as it is, perfect for the purposes of providing each of us the support we need to be where we choose to be and to learn and grow. The line we draw against ignorance and evil is in the sand of our psyche.

Another aspect of our health concerns the health-insurance industry. We would have a better health-insurance system as well as better medicines if we were not so passive and so afraid of death. If we were not so beholden emotionally to the pharmaceutical and insurance industries, its leaders would be obliged to adopt more enlightened practices.

Psychiatry Abandons Causes

Experts estimate that medical care for unhealthy habits and other modifiable health risks such as smoking and obesity cost the nation about $250 billion a year. Much of the expense is for stress-related diseases or ailments such as gastrointestinal disorders, diabetes, heart ailments, back pain, and migraines.[xxxix] Anxiety is considered the western world's number one mental-health problem, costing the United States $42 billion a year in doctors' bills and workplace losses, and experts say the situation is getting worse.[xl]

The odds of developing an anxiety disorder have doubled in the past four decades, says a World Health Organization study. Harvard Medical School epidemiologist, Ronald Kessler, who co-authored the study, gives a reason for this rise: "It's a scary place and time. People are moving to strange cities, taking jobs in new industries; there's a lot of uncertainty about the future. Bad things that happen to people are on the rise. Look at the evening news: murders, car accidents, and terrorist bombs. This stuff is out there in the popular imagination and making us worried."[xli]

Dr. Kessler's explanation is undoubtedly correct. However, it doesn't penetrate very deeply into the mystery. Why do some of us go through disruptive life experiences and not feel nearly as anxious as others? A common thread in Dr. Kessler's explanation is the feeling of being overwhelmed, a primary symptom of passivity. It is the terrifying feeling of losing control of one's environment and of oneself. If we are living on the surface of ourself, we may be able to anchor ourself somewhat through a stable environment— living and working where we have developed friends and roots. If we start moving to strange cities, we lose that external anchor. Without a solid connection to our inner core, we can indeed feel displaced and overwhelmed.

As mentioned, depth psychology has claimed for decades that anxiety, stress, tension, fear, guilt, anger, and depression are surface symptoms of psychic conflicts. These deep conflicts can be accessed and successfully treated through knowledge and insight, by making conscious the unconscious. (Academic psychologists claim that research shows insight by itself is not effective in eliminating symptoms. What they offer in the way of insight, however, is knowledge that is quite shallow. They do not present their research subjects with deep knowledge concerning inner conflict, psychological defenses, and emotional attachments.)

Modern psychiatry, meanwhile, doesn't acknowledge causes and is only interested in the treatment of symptoms. In other words, the psychiatric establishment has severed cause and effect. These psychiatrists apparently are not interested in the possible underlying causes for the hundreds of disorders and dysfunctions, along with the subtypes and differential diagnoses they list in the diagnostic index of the 943-page 2000 edition of the Diagnostic and Statistical Manual of Mental Disorders (known as the DSM, it is the Bible of psychiatry and a publication of the American Psychiatric Association). It's as if these disorders exist in a vacuum. There is no interest or curiosity expressed in this manual about the origins of these debilitating conditions.

The writer L.J. Davis, in a 1997 article in *Harper's*, describes how, beginning in the 1960s, psychiatry dispensed with reality:

> Following World War II, the U.S. Army and the Veterans Administration revisited the timeless discovery that the experiences of battle did unpleasant things to the minds of its luckless participants. As a result, the number of known mental disturbances grew to a still reasonable twenty-six. The DSM-I appeared in 1952; it was the first professional manual that attempted to describe, in a single concise volume, the disorders a clinician might encounter in the course of daily practice. The DSM-I also described the disorders as actual, discernible reactions to something—an event, a situation, and a biological condition. But when the DSM-II was published in 1968, the word 'reaction' had vanished, never to reappear. Unobserved by the larger world, a revolution had taken place. By severing cause and effect, the psychiatric profession had privatized the entire world of mental illness, removed it from the marketplace of ideas, abandoned the rigorous proofs of the scientific

method, and adopted circular thinking as its central discipline. Henceforth, in the absence of cause and effect, a mental illness would be anything the psychiatric profession chose to call a mental illness.[xlii] The manual does not define the state of mental health nor provide guidance concerning therapy's goal.

The number of diagnoses grows each time a new edition of the manual is published. The previous edition, published in 1994, jumped to 886 pages from the 567-page earlier edition published in 1987. This "Encyclopedia of Insanity," as the Harper's article refers to the manual, has, in drifting away from the moorings of underlying causes, become an absurdity in itself.

The influence of this manual is considerable: psychologists, psychotherapists, and mental-health counselors are required to refer to its diagnostic and procedural codes when filing for health-insurance payment. Clients have told me that other therapists had conferred upon them various diagnoses from this manual—favorites being "bipolar" and other depressive disorders—that had no meaning for them because these diagnoses came with no satisfactory knowledge for a cure or treatment other than choice of drugs. Without the knowledge or tools to secure their own freedom, these people are left feeling helpless and dependent.

Davis writes:

> Not content with the merely weird, the DSM- IV also attempts to claim dominion over the mundane. Current among the many symptoms of the deranged mind are bad writing (315.2, and its associated symptom, poor handwriting); coffee drinking,

including coffee nerves (292.89), inability to sleep after drinking too much coffee (292.89), and something that probably has something to do with coffee, though the therapist can't put his finger on it (292.9); shyness (299.80, also known as Asperger's Disorder); sleepwalking (307.46); jet lag (307.45); snobbery (301.7, a subset of Antisocial Personality Disorder); and insomnia (307.42); to say nothing of tobacco smoking, which includes both getting hooked (305.10) and going cold turkey (292.0). You were out of your mind the last time you had a nightmare (307.47). Clumsiness is now a mental illness (315.4). So is playing video games (Malingering, V65.2). So is doing anything 'vigorously.' So, under certain circumstances, is falling asleep at night.[xliii]

The only reference to passivity in the current edition of the manual is a two-page entry for Passive Aggressive Personality Disorder, a disorder that, in my opinion, can only be treated effectively as a symptom of an underlying emotional attachment to inner passivity. As I have been saying, inner passivity can be treated directly with depth psychology. When passivity is successfully treated in this manner, its symptoms disappear.

Focusing on symptoms is like chasing rats down the street and ignoring their nest in the garbage-filled empty lot next door. Like conventional medical doctors, psychiatrists are trying to fight emotional challenges and disturbances from the outside, through the symptoms, while the inner causes, hidden in the psyche, are left untouched. This approach makes psychiatry easier in one sense—there's less hard work involved for the practitioners, who can therefore see more patients and make more money—and harder in another sense—psychiatrists commit suicide at a rate above the national average, probably because their inability to help themselves and others emotionally creates such inner misery. All this intellectual disarray in the profession is a symptom of our ineptitude and cowardice in mustering the effort to discover truth through our own psyche. Economic and establishment forces are obviously skewing this debate. The insurance payout for drugs is cheaper than for ongoing therapy. The establishment, as a reflection of our own repression and resistance, is willing to support and profit from a process that keeps people drugged and passive. It is not willing to support or pay for a process that creates inner revolutions in individuals and liberates them from fear, guilt, and passivity. As long as we don't know ourself, we are no threat either to society's oppressive forces or to the self-aggression, passivity, and egotism in our own psyche.

I believe the situation that psychiatry has created for itself is a collective effect of our individual passivity. It requires the best of us to penetrate effectively into our own psyche and, for mental-health professionals, to penetrate into the psyche of others. The path of least resistance is to refuse the call and to retreat behind diagnostic pronouncements that are essentially hollow and without enough meaning, while looking for answers in magic pills.

Various sleep and dream disorders are mentioned in the current diagnostic manual. Insomnia is another serious emotional problem facing millions of us. It is the experience of lying in bed in the middle of the night, our mind churning in speculation and consideration, in a feeling of total helplessness. We feel at the mercy of physical and emotional forces within us, as we desperately hope that time will pull us under into oblivion. Undoubtedly insomnia has causes other than passivity, but the experience of it is certainly passive. The following is a lyrical description of insomnia by the Argentine writer, Jorge Luis Borges, titled "Two Forms of Insomnia":

> It is attempting with ineffectual magic to breathe smoothly. It is the burden of a body that abruptly shifts sides . . . It is a state like fever and is assuredly not watchfulness. . . It is trying to sink into slumber and being unable to sink into slumber . . . It is the horror of existing in a human body whose faculties are in decline. . . It is being well aware that I am bound to my flesh, to a voice I detest, to my name, to routinely remembering, to Castilian, over which I have no control, to feeling nostalgic for the Latin I do not know. It is trying to sink into death, and being unable to sink into death.[xliv]

With passivity diminished, we are able when awake at night to enter an inner silence. This produces a sense of power and self-mastery. The silence offers a feeling of repose. We are not at the mercy of mental and emotional considerations and speculations, and are likely to fall back to sleep more easily.

Chapter 7
The Self-Regulation Battle

So why is it so hard to regulate ourselves? Why do we get in trouble with alcohol, drugs, smoking, food, and a wide range of negative emotions, and fail to act in our best interests? Deep in our psyche, shrouded in mystery, a secret agenda is operating that creates symptoms such as restlessness, tension, distress, anxiety, cravings, and desires. Through persistent, heroic effort, and aided by psychological insight, we are able to expose this agenda and neutralize its influence.

That inner agenda, when it remains unconscious, compels us to go through life in and out of painful emotions, in opposition to ourself, while convinced that something is missing in our lives and that we're somehow threatened and at risk. Often we feel emptiness inside, a void, a longing, and a separation—a disturbing sense of self-repudiation—that leads us on a desperate search for recognition and validation. Not knowing how to approach the inner problem, and feeling vague trepidation at the thought of doing so, we project our unease into the environment and attribute our distress to the "fact" that we don't have enough success, money, support, substances, recognition, and love. We become more frantic than ever for external pursuits, distractions, or some numbing effect to solve our inner problem.

In addition, we can feel chilled by the indifference of others and swamped by their negativity. In the workplace and in our schools, communities, and families, we are surrounded by a lack of civility, as well as insensitivity and suspiciousness. Negativity is flying all over because we don't understand how, unconsciously, we produce it internally and then spew it out at each other. Without this understanding, self-regulation is elusive.

The art of self-regulation involves the ability to live in a way that minimizes suffering and self-defeat and generates happiness, fulfillment, and creativity. It is not so much a matter of controlling our behaviors and emotions as it is the experience of witnessing or observing our thoughts, desires, and impulses, and then, after applying understanding of their origins, choosing whether or not to act on any particular option. It is certainly not mind-control or willpower. It is the expression of inner power, which increasingly is discovered within us as we dislodge and eliminate our psychic bedevilments. This art of self-regulation is a benefit of our efforts to gain self-knowledge and to overcome the conflicting and limiting elements of our psyche.

Self-regulation isn't limited to mastery over addictions and compulsions. It also involves the prevention of depression, anxiety, boredom, fear, jealousy, envy, apathy, anger, and hatred. It is a benefit of growing self-responsibility, through which we learn to become responsible not just for our daily duties and moral obligations but also for our negative emotions and self-defeating behaviors. To do this we need to penetrate and then make sense of the irrational side of our nature. The biggest obstacle is our hesitation in approaching our unconscious because of irrational fears of what we will find there. As well, our identification with our mind creates a stubborn arrogance. When our mind is befuddled by the paradox and complexity that we encounter in our unconscious, we are quick to ignore, dismiss, or even condemn that which humbles us.

Writing in *The Village Voice*, Mark Schoofs says:

> But denying the unconscious has profound consequences. It can blind us to the true emotional sources of authority, sap our personal power, and ultimately make us more vulnerable to political coercion and collective hysteria." He adds, "The chemical view of mental illness renders the patient passive, whereas Freud insisted that individuals engage society and make an accommodation with it.[xlv]

We are torn between two major impulses. One is to progress, to evolve, and to become self-empowering and self-authorizing, thereby fulfilling our potential. The other impulse, however, is just as compelling: we are lured into remaining stagnant, or regressing into security, safety, and dependence—emotionally returning to the protection of the womb. The first of these drives or impulses represents belief in ourself and the fulfillment of our destiny, while the latter represents passive acceptance of our fate.

Our lack of self-regulation is expressed in many ways. It is the basis for self-sabotage, the process whereby, despite our intelligence, good intentions, and skills, we manage to ruin opportunities for success and happiness. Irrational fears—of spiders, snakes, and mice, for instance—are another expression of our lack of self-regulation. Some among us are afraid of heights, darkness, and closed spaces, of losing control in public places or at the wheel of an automobile. Panic and stress disorders are common, and those of us with social phobias can be afraid of open spaces and each other. We can also be inordinately afraid of being attacked and violated. Our inner, irrational fears are projected onto the environment, to which we then look to account for our fear, thus creating an anxious if not paranoid perspective.

Obsessive-compulsive disorders have a basis, if not their root, in passivity. Behind compulsions such as chronic hand washing and housekeeping, or rigid orderliness and punctuality, is an inner voice of a nagging, harping nature, and inner finger-wagging, that holds us accountable for minor, trivial concerns. Examples include, "How come you haven't taken care of that?"; "You never get it right!"; "Look at that mess!"; "Did you forget again!"; "You had better be on time!" These inner dictates caricature a fussy, controlling parent. The directives have the authority to disapprove of us at will, while we run around trying to appease their demands or allegations. We don't have the inner authority to let things be and attend to our own equanimity.

Passivity is a factor in obsessive-compulsiveness in other ways, as well. For instance, an individual's obsessive cleanliness stems from his fear that germs will get the best of him, do him in, overrun his immunity, and render him helpless. "I'm not wanting to feel as if I'm going to be overcome and overwhelmed," goes his unconscious defense. "See how hard I try to eliminate all these germs with my cleanliness." A parallel situation involves environmental illness. People with this condition become convinced they are not able to withstand allegedly toxic conditions. Through the body-emotion connection, their physical or medical complaints or ailments do become a real problem. Obviously, some of these people have legitimate ailments. In many instances, however, inner passivity would appear to exacerbate the impression of being undermined or disabled. Similar are people who constantly feel "under the weather" or hindered by some minor ailment. They live in a chronic state of distress, under the negative influence of some external condition. In a sense, the condition or ailment "nags" at them, holding them back, keeping them down, and they live through the feeling of being impaired.

Our lack of self-regulation often revolves around shame and includes feelings connected with sexual, digestive, and eliminatory functions. It also includes shame about looking ridiculous or making a fool of oneself, feeling like a phony or a fake (though no objective assessment necessarily supports this feeling), forgetting names, and having secret wishes or fearing that some secret behavior will become public knowledge. Shame is associated with physical appearance and loss or mismanagement of money. It is also strongly associated with alcohol problems, eating disorders, memories of sexual or physical assault, suicide attempts, self-inflicted injuries, phobias, and sexually transmitted diseases.

A comparable range of irrational feelings revolves around guilt, through which people suffer inordinately for minor or even imagined transgressions. Problems of self-regulation are readily apparent in addictive and compulsive behaviors. These behaviors can have their roots in the individual's underlying conviction that he is the helpless, passive victim of others. We lose control of our behaviors when, emotionally, we are hungry, demanding infants who are fixated on the feeling of being refused, "not getting," and "missing out." We are thus often compelled to go after things or people that we can't have, that are out of reach, or that will harm us. Often we feel that we're not going to receive what we want or need from life or someone else, and so to compensate we give to ourself in an unbalanced manner. This kind of self-giving—in the form of excesses of sex, food, material objects, financial security, or other sensations—is compulsive and narcissistic. At its root is a variation of passivity that involves our secret inner willingness to experience ourself through a sense of deprivation and refusal, through separation and duality, as well as through feelings of loss, dissatisfaction, and neglect. The result is that people experience themselves desperately in need of fulfillment and salvation from sources and powers external to their own being.

This variation of passivity blocks us from accessing our inner powers and from self-realization. We live only through our ego, light-years away from contact with our authentic self. We are unable to make affirmations and decisions that we can live by.

In an earlier book of mine, *Secret Attachments: Exposing the Roots of Addictions and Compulsions*, I wrote that unconscious, emotional attachments to unresolved negativity produce self-defeating reactions and out-of-control behaviors. Here, in this passivity book, I refine this understanding by describing emotional or secret attachments as variations of inner passivity. The concept is now presented less intellectually and more on the level of feelings, allowing for deeper penetration of the required understanding and easier access to the meaning of our inner condition. In seeing the problem as passivity, we can also sense or imagine the experience of ourself on the other side of this passivity—our connection with inner power and resources that enable us to practice self-regulation. By way of example, one client's sugar cravings and another's compulsive shopping dissipated as they began to expose their inner passivity.

194

Our passivity descends into very deep levels of our psyche, often beyond the reach of our ability to trace it mentally and logically. Grasping a sense of these emotional attachments is difficult, in part because their existence defies common sense. We wonder, "How could I secretly be willing and even eager to experience what is painful and self-defeating?" We have to feel our way in. We're trying to uncover and dislodge our attachments to limited and painful ways of knowing ourself and to establish our inner authority. One way for us to achieve this is to sense how these emotional attachments, as variations of inner passivity, block us from accessing our birthright—the ability to function in the world in a high state of conscious being.

In the "low state" caused by inner passivity, "the buzz," as some substance imbibers call it, is especially alluring. The buzz is so important because we feel flat or dead without it. Our passivity creates an inner numbness, an emotional "disconnect" from others and ourself, which makes the buzz so desirable.

To attribute to passivity so many of our behavioral and emotional issues and struggles is a controversial position, one that is strongly (though indirectly) opposed by scientific and psychological orthodoxy. A fierce, hostile battle is underway among American intellectuals, particularly in our universities, concerning the influences of biology versus culture on our emotions and behaviors. There is a trend in anthropology, sociology, cultural studies, and psychology to dismiss the notion that innate biology has a significant effect on how humans think, act, or create their cultures. Culture is held up as the primary influence upon our feelings, attitudes, and perceptions. I can only say that if these intellectuals were to take the hero's journey and plunge into their own psyche, they would discover a great deal of universality in the human psyche, including the fact that passivity is a common emotional element—biologically induced, socially reinforced, and politically sustained—throughout the whole of humanity.

The intention of these social theorists is to attribute human behavioral and emotional problems to the failures of child raising and the negative influences of culture. This point of view is apparent in a comment made in a *Harper's* article titled "Let them eat fat: The heavy truths about American obesity." The article focuses on the American underclass and quotes an academic as saying, "Becoming obese is a normal response to the American environment."[xlvi] Here the culture is wrongly blamed for the problem. It would be much more accurate to say, "Becoming obese is a *passive* reaction to the American environment." Another passive reaction to the American environment is, through consumerism, to go broke and remain in debt. The passive element is imbedded in our psyche and is elaborated upon in our experiences of childhood and society.

Some scientists do want to establish a biological basis for addictions, but the basis they seek is genetic, biochemical, or neurological rather than psychological. These scientists need private and government funding for their research, and in promoting the value of their work, they convincingly present a claim that brain research will reveal all that is significant about being human. Consciousness, if it is considered relevant at all, is approached as a phenomenon to be explained through deeper penetration of matter. I believe this approach is superficial because matter is not intrinsic in itself but is a product of the consciousness and spirit behind it. Not a single atom exists on the basis of its own nature. Holistic theory contends that consciousness—formless, dynamic, aware, eternal energy and light—is the bedrock of existence. It sustains matter and determines its form, shape, and properties.

Through science we do indeed become more powerful in the manipulation of matter. But doing so—as in human cloning—becomes hazardous if we remain backward in spiritual awareness and self-understanding. Scientists are not more evolved psychologically and spiritually than other members of society. They can highly neurotic, emotionally attached to their belief system, and ready to proclaim that their vision of reality represents the highest truth. When that emotional shortcoming is combined with egotism, their work is more likely to be sterile, of marginal value, and potentially dangerous. Without deference to mystery in all things, the pursuit of truth through matter represents the irrationality of science.

Still, our physical, genetic, and chemical properties are a part of our physical reality. Using PET scans and other technology, neuroscientists have studied the brains of drug addicts and alcoholics, and have determined that an addicted person's brain is physically and chemically different from a normal person's. Drug and alcohol abuse does indeed "reset" the brain's dopamine system and other critical configurations, and these changes can persist even after long abstinence. Once this point of addiction is reached, some individuals may be psychologically too impaired to recover through the process of working out inner passivity and may need external crutches such as behavioral patterning or medicines. Many others who might benefit from psychological intervention simply refuse it.

Like scientists, many addicts also want to believe that genes or biochemical imbalances are responsible for their out-of-control behaviors. In believing this, they can let themselves off the hook, at least partially. Their self-aggression bombards them with accusations of their secret wish for the experience of passivity. Unknown to themselves, they make this inner defense: "I am not looking for the passive experience, nor I am under the influence of passivity. My addictions have nothing to do with passivity. I am blameless. My addiction is the result of a disease." To make this defense stick, they have to believe in the disease model of addiction, which involves the extraordinarily limited credo that they are addicted for life. I wish to repeat the point made earlier. Genetics, the environment, nutrition, and maybe even karma can affect our behaviors and emotions. But we don't want to be helpless victims of our genes, biochemistry, or whatever. We have to believe in our inner powers. Those powers are available if we believe in ourself and make the effort to access them. With them, we can free ourselves from addictions, compulsions, phobias, and negativity. However, if we don't make an effort to evolve, we can lose access to these powers.

Struggles With Overeating

The example of Tanya, a 37-year-old client, presents what is perhaps the most elementary way to approach and understand the passivity model for addictions. A professional woman talented in her field and comfortable with herself around others, Tanya did, however, binge on food once or twice a week. She was forty pounds overweight and unhappy about her difficulty in losing this weight.

I encouraged Tanya to become aware of her experience of herself in the time preceding one of her binges. For months as I worked with her, this pre-binge period was vague and unclear in her mind. "It's hard to say just what I feel at that moment," she related. "Sometimes, hardly anything registers. All I know is that I suddenly find myself eating something sweet that I know I'll regret. The time leading up to that moment is unclear to me. I guess I could say it's a general anxiety and a sense of weakening." I had Tanya try to make more effort to register her experience of herself in those crucial moments before bingeing. She described being "spaced-out and in a fog," considerably disconnected from herself, as if she were in a trance or under the influence of hypnosis.

"That's the passivity and that is you under the influence of it," I told her. "You have to connect with yourself and access the inner powers that will awaken you from that enfeebled state of being." After once-a-week sessions for several months, she began to describe this period before bingeing in terms of specific feelings and thoughts. One underlying feeling, previously unconscious, was: "I'm going to get what I want. No one is going to stop me. Nobody is going to tell me what I can or can't eat." Now she understood that she was reacting to the feeling of being forced (by the expectations of others and by her own catalog of "shoulds") to curtail her food intake. Through this statement, she was also reacting to her own deep passivity of the moment, saying in effect, "I'm not passive; I have power; I'm deciding what I want." This is how a child claims power when told, for instance, not to touch Daddy's stereo: "I am the one who has decided not to touch it."

Tanya's bingeing began to subside. When she now proceeded into the kitchen to snack inappropriately, she had more awareness of being under the influence of her passivity. Instead of being "spaced out, in a fog" and mindlessly going through the motions, she was more conscious of the process of preparing and eating her food, while simultaneously observing, in as non-judgmental a way as possible, her continuing acquiescence to whatever passivity was still being played out.

"I'm starting to see this passivity more clearly," she said. "I can see how pervasive it is. I can also feel I'm holding on for dear life to this sense of being powerless. Before I used to feel, 'Who will I be if I'm thin?' Now the feeling is, 'Who will I be without this coercive force over me?' That's even scarier. It's almost overwhelming to see it."

In the ensuing months, this closely held monitoring of her experience, while it initially didn't stop her from overeating nor prevent the ensuing guilt for doing so, reduced the frequency of bingeing and lessened her guilt. Tanya could still feel how willing she was to come under the influence of inner passivity. Before long, however, she began to enjoy the feeling of acting with power and strength. This feeling took hold and began to be a more attractive option, one that produced a genuine pleasure that she was eager to register and extend. She realized that the greatest pain of overeating was emotional—the feeling of knowing herself through her passivity and enduring the inner recriminations for it—and she experienced a new determination to avoid slipping into that passivity.

Tanya also began to feel that she was being more present to herself, more alert in the moment, as if she were standing guard or advocating for herself. "I know I can be there for myself to keep the passivity out," she said. "It's a new skill, a new ability, like being a wise parent who is watching over her child."

Whenever she succeeded for a time in curtailing her binges, the passivity would be felt in other areas. Several times it happened with shopping. "I go into Wal-Mart to buy a bottle of aspirin and come out with $200 worth of merchandise," she said. "I have a great time going down the aisles, getting this and that, but the pleasure is short-lived. I get home, look at some of the stuff I bought, and say to myself, 'What was that about?' I've got a bag in the porch of stuff I'm going to take back. And it's all the same feeling while I'm there: I can get what I want. Isn't this fun!"

Through her process of self-liberation, Tanya could feel and identify her resistance. It manifested as the sense that something precious was going to be taken away. "I know that I'm holding on for dear life," she said. "I still can't fathom who I will be if I am not this person I've been all my life."

We swing back and forth between wise and unwise behaviors, unable to live a consistent, healthy lifestyle. For instance, when we're doing something that's good for us, such as eating well and exercising regularly, we say after a while, "Hey, this is too tough on me—I'm going to lighten up at bit!" Because of our passivity, we have begun to feel controlled by the regimen that has produced beneficial results. We swing back to the old, indulgent self that is lacking in self-regulation: "I can do what I want, and nobody's going to tell me what to do." Many months and many pounds later, full of remorse and guilt as we realize that our health is suffering, we reverse course and revert to a healthy program that, because of our passivity, soon feels enforced and unnatural.

Much of the time, it is helpful to identify some particular event or experience that sets off a bout of substance abuse, whether it be with food, alcohol, or drugs. One client, Laura, always got triggered when she saw another woman, whether a stranger or an acquaintance, who Laura was prepared to feel at that moment was better or prettier than herself. In her youth, Laura had often reacted at such times with self-mutilation, cutting her arms or punching herself on her arms and legs. Later, she substituted bingeing as her form of self-abuse, thereby replacing one self-destructive reaction with another. Laura, in seeing the "more attractive" other woman, got "hit up" with her attachment to the feeling of self-rejection. Her attachment is revealed in the fact that, visually, she sought out other people who she believed (unconsciously, who she *wanted* to believe) were better than her. Her resulting feeling of self-rejection was familiar from her childhood, and she was still prepared to experience herself through it. She succeeded in dropping this attachment by first focusing her awareness on the understanding that her compulsion to peep (in this case, to look for what she could use as "evidence" to compare herself disparagingly against another person) was based on her secret willingness to experience herself through rejection.

Secondly, Laura realized and contemplated that her feeling of self-rejection did not represent the truth about the quality or essence of her being. This awareness—that we are secretly willing to experience ourself through an old, negative feeling that seems real but does not represent the truth about ourself—is very powerful. Anytime we expose such an attachment to the light of this awareness, we are marching toward inner freedom.

Laura, by the way, didn't need to see an actual living person to generate her reaction. One time her son described to her the qualities of his "beautiful" new girlfriend, someone Laura had never seen, even in a photograph. Within minutes of listening to her son, Laura felt a reaction begin to build in her, and soon she was aware of a temptation to binge. Our emotional imagination, as I call it, can provide us with all the images and feelings we need to compare ourselves unfavorably to others, as well as to feel deprived, refused, and controlled.

Sweets, Fears, and Desires

Here is an example of how unconscious, irrational forces override our conscious desire for health and longevity. Joyce, a 50-year-old freelance writer, was eating chocolate and other sweets on a regular basis despite being overweight and diabetic. She was sneaking the sweets, hiding this consumption from her husband, who was increasingly unhappy about her recent weight gain. "I can't deal with this," she said, referring to the growing hostility between them. "I feel so tired, sad, and worn-out. I haven't been feeling this bad for ages."

She and Ted, a computer programmer, had moved twice in the past four years. They were settled in one Midwestern city when, as she said, "even though I liked it where we were, he yanked me out of there" to move to the East Coast. Joyce managed to get settled in the new location with her work when "he yanked me out again to go to the West Coast."

"I gather you have some resentment about these moves," I said. We were speaking on the telephone about three months after their second move.

"I do. I feel I had no choice or say in the matter. I feel as if I'm being blown about by events, like a victim of fate. Since I've gotten here, I can't put anything together. There's been no work for me, and now I can't even bring myself to go out looking for it. And I can't see it getting better. Anything I've ever had to do, I've had to work at it. Now I can barely get out of bed during the day."

"Didn't you say your husband wants to get you a gym membership?"

"Yes, and he said he could bring me to the gym this afternoon."

"Are you going to take him up on it?"

"I could try to do it."

"What does that mean? Do you plan to go this afternoon or not?

"I don't want to."

"It looks like you are really angry at him. Is that right?"

"I try not to be. He's really a good person. But since I got here, and nothing's been going right, I can barely bring myself to talk to him. But I'm also just mad at the world. I've been trying to think, 'Well, he makes more money than me and I have to consider his needs for career advancement.' Then I say to myself, 'I'm supposed to be here; we're closer to the children; fate has me here for some reason.' But that mindset hasn't helped very much either."

When Joyce was two years old, her parents had moved from Baltimore to southern California. Four years later, they moved back. "That was my first plunge into the darkness of depression," she said. "It was winter when we got to Baltimore, where we lived in a smelly, old apartment. I kept remembering the sun and grass of California, where I had been able to run around in my underwear."

Joyce had gotten herself into a very tight squeeze with passivity. First of all, she was feeling dragged around by her spouse and forced, as she experienced it, to accommodate his career aspirations. Secondly, because she was already feeling passive to her husband, she was inclined to experience the passivity in other areas, and thereby to have less ability to resist the impulse or desire to eat sweets. Also, by choosing to binge on sweets, at great risk to her health, she was expressing some of her self-loathing, an aspect of how, through the passivity, she experienced herself (seldom in passivity do we like who we are). Thirdly, her use of forbidden food created an inner impression of thwarting her husband. This pseudo or passive-aggressive reaction gave her a sense of power. However, because she felt guilty about her consumption of sweets, she determined to keep her behavior secret from him. Understanding these and other elements of her passivity made a dramatic improvement in Joyce's life. For one thing, she began to talk to her husband more directly about her feelings, while he opened up to her more and showed more sensitivity for her position. Consequently, she felt much of her anger toward him drain away.

Jed, a highly intelligent young student with serious depression, was unable to regulate his marijuana consumption and compulsive overeating. He had fantasies of driving off on vacation, having his car break down, and becoming hopelessly lost as he trekked across the desert looking for help. Jed complained of insomnia, frequent feelings of total hopelessness, an inability to launch into projects and complete them (except in his imagination), laziness, and occasional attacks of nihilism and despair. As a youngster, he used to scream in his sleep, and recently he had been diagnosed with a bipolar disorder. His father, "an old hippy," had been extremely passive and addicted to marijuana.

After disclosing the above information in our first session, he told me, "I want to reveal everything that might be relevant, even if some of this sounds silly. I often like to think that I am a messiah, and that I have come forward at this time to bring peace to the world."

"How does that feel when you imagine yourself as a messiah?"

"It feels good. I have power. I feel like the big cheese."

"You are unconsciously attached to experiencing yourself through inner passivity," I told him. "That's why you create the messiah fantasy. Either you are in situations where you feel you have no power or, as a defense against your attachment to that feeling, you create fantasies through which you feel powerful."

"Does that tie in with my rape fantasies? I haven't had those so much since I'm back with my girlfriend. But I used to have them a lot."

"Yes, it does. The rape fantasy does give you a sense of power over the person you imagine you are attacking. But what's really happening in the fantasy is that you're identifying with the submissiveness and helpless of your imagined victim. This way, you're back into the passivity, and that feeling is made especially alluring when it is sexualized, as it is with sexual masochists."

"I often imagine doing harm to myself and going crazy if I don't get help soon," he said.

"Can you see what you're doing with that feeling? Emotionally, you go to a place inside yourself where you feel helpless to control or regulate your experience. It's the feeling that you're going to be overpowered by impressions, sensations, desires, and thoughts, even to the point of going mad. The more you imagine you might go crazy, the more you take on feelings of helplessness, impending doom, and a sense of your inability to support yourself and thrive through your own powers. All of this means you are sinking into the mire of passivity. I will teach you to see passivity for what it is, an emotional attachment, meaning a secret temptation to know yourself through an old, limited feeling. When you isolate this passivity and work your way free of it, you can escape your fate, which is to be like your father and fail to realize your potential."

"There's an overall feeling that I get, as if I'm no longer who I am."

"Because of your passivity, Jed, you can't get a genuine feeling for who you are. It feels as if your passivity is you. It is not you. Who you are is absolutely great. You will start to know and express yourself on that basis as your passivity is worked out."

Another client, Nancy, a 40-year-old housewife, illustrated how fear of starvation was a factor in her struggle with food. This fear had been unconscious until we brought it to light. Though she felt she wanted more attention and love from her husband, she unconsciously discouraged it, saying she felt anxious with male aggression. It felt to her that such male energy, especially when coupled with sexual intent, "will swallow me up." Whenever she felt threatened by it, she binged on food (she was thirty pounds over her ideal weight). She even felt that, at times, she attacked her food, swallowing it voraciously. Meanwhile, her husband was expressing unhappiness with her weight and becoming more insistent that she lose it. She commented: "I ask myself, how aggressive is he going to get? I know I'll feel overwhelmed and controlled."

Nancy had been raised by an aggressive, often angry father and a passive, compliant mother. She was slightly overweight at that time, and her father would assertively insist that she needed to lose weight in order "to look pretty" and please him. "His mission in life, it seemed to me, was to change how I looked," Nancy said. "He didn't even know me, but he wanted to change me. I felt I had to be nice to survive." Her mother, meanwhile, was herself fearful of weight gain and "would panic if she put on a pound or two," Nancy recalled. "Mother was fearful all her life, and it felt as if her fears endangered me."

Nancy's kitchen storage areas were heavily stocked with food. "There's enough there to make it through the winter," she laughed. She had a preoccupation with being safe and secure and was fearful of taking long trips. "I've always said that when I lose all my weight, then I'll travel more and be more interested in sex." She shuddered at the prospect of starting a diet and panicked at the idea, put forward by a friend, that a fast of several days might be a healthy option for her.

Nancy associated male aggression, originally her father's, with the idea that, in being so insistently encouraged to lose weight, her food would be taken from her. It felt that her mother couldn't protect her, and that the males in her family—father and brothers— ruled the household and imposed their will. If her father became more insistent, she would have to do as her mother did, submit passively to him and allow him to take away her food. Of course, her fear of starvation was irrational. No one was going to take away her food. But because this fear carried over prominently from infancy, she unconsciously interpreted the prospect of dieting or fasting through that lingering, passive feeling.

Nancy did overcome her fear of male aggression, and as part of that process she slimmed down as she lost her irrational fear of having to go without food.

With insight, we can regulate and subdue our irrational fears. One client said she frequently imagined that her husband might lose his job or that he would become ill and incapacitated. During such speculation, she exclaimed to herself, "Oh my God! What would happen then?" She also magnified challenging situations into life-threatening incidents. One time a house purchase fell through, and she seized on the belief that she would now be homeless. "It feels like the end of the world, like the end of life as I know it," she said of these occurrences. "It seems the situation is bigger than me and that I'll be defeated or obliterated by it."

"These reactions come out of your inner passivity," I told her. "You are peering into the future and creating worst-case scenarios solely for the purpose of experiencing yourself in a passive manner in the present moment. You feel overwhelmed or defeated by the circumstances that you imagine you will have to face. Since you are attached emotionally to inner passivity, you create a means through which to experience it. Notice that the situation you envisage is a product of your imagination, but imagination is all it takes to generate feelings of being helpless, overwhelmed, and defeated."

To repeat the essential point that confounds so many of us: the anxiety, fear, or panic that we feel is both a symptom of our passivity (the suffering we pay for it) and a defense covering up our attachment to the passive experience. The more acute our inner passivity, the more likely we will have phobias or panic attacks, because we have to construct a stronger defense, one which offers up more suffering, to persuade our self-aggression that our heightened suffering is proof we are not colluding in the passive experience: "Doesn't my fear (or panic) prove how much I hate to feel overwhelmed and helpless?" If we are suffering enough, if our defense is sufficiently self-defeating, the anti-hedonistic element in our self-aggression is satisfied and will back off, at least temporarily.

The past is just as toxic as the future when we are looking for ways to suffer. Another client felt continuing bitterness about the way, three years earlier, he had been treated and finally fired from a high-paying corporate job. His bitterness covered up (or defended against) his readiness to go on feeling what he had felt at the time—unappreciated in the eyes of four or five specific individuals who outranked him and helpless to counteract their maneuvers against him.

As he came to understand his secret determination to go on experiencing himself through these negative emotions and his use of bitterness as a defense, he began to break free into new realms of positive orientation. One of his biggest stumbling blocks in this process, as he acknowledged, was his feeling that, in dropping his bitterness, he would somehow be letting these individuals off the hook. I told him his resistance to letting go of his negative emotional attachments created this feeling.

Smoking and Other Addictions

Wise advice alone usually won't dissuade a 14-year-old who has started smoking cigarettes. The teenager already knows that smoking is unhealthy. The youth needs to be challenged to look at the underlying motivations. It's more than the pros and cons of smoking—it's much deeper than that.

Smoking masks underlying feelings that a youngster is aware of only in a vague way. He is beginning to feel the need to separate from parental control and establish a sense of autonomy. It is, of course, appropriate and necessary at this age to begin to express oneself as a maturing individual who can make his own life choices. The alternative is to remain in a place of increasing passivity. So choices have to be made, and when cunning marketers present smoking through the consumer culture as a glamorous adult-like activity, it becomes very attractive as an expression of grown-up freedom and choice.

Some children express their growing sense of freedom more wisely, making and affirming choices involving hobbies, activities, friends, and schoolwork. Individuals who are more challenged emotionally—particularly with passivity and feelings of being insignificant or unworthy—often make the choice to smoke. The weaker the child's sense of self, the more difficult it is to resist peer pressure and sustain independent thought and action. All that matters is to feel accepted by others, and actions that compensate for the underlying problem—an affinity for feeling unacceptable in oneself—are attractive. For insecure youngsters, smoking offers a chance to look "cool" without any of the effort that self-development entails. Young smokers don't have to change or grow to feel that their appeal has been enhanced. These individuals don't have a sense that their health is precious because they are not connecting with what is precious in themselves. Thus, they are less concerned about avoiding an alluring action that is self-defeating.

Often in addictive personalities an inner voice that represents a variant of self-aggression becomes the voice of authority. The voice says, for instance, "Yeah, let's do it! Just do it, do it!" Because of inner passivity, this voice displaces our sense of what is best for us. The popular aphorism meant to help regulate drug abuse, "Just say no," often doesn't have a chance against the compelling inner voice, "Just do it!"

Orality is also a factor in the desire to smoke. Smoking is used to fill an emptiness or hole inside of us and to suppress something that disturbs us in our relationship with others and with ourself. Smoking gives the appearance that we want some elusive satisfaction, but what we get is so inconsiderable—toxic, smelly, harsh, and sickening. Instead of deeply breathing fresh air that energizes us, the smoker inhales tobacco or marijuana smoke that generates only pseudo-energy and pseudo-wholeness. It's typical of passivity to accept a counterfeit experience.

Smokers rationalize that their habit has value and provides pleasure. It's true that occasional, ceremonial smoking has some delectation to offer. But in the case of chronic smoking—several cigarettes or more a day—one has to be under emotional distress to consider this a source of pleasure. Every cigarette represents this statement: "I'm not looking for the empty teat—look how much I want to get satisfaction, by sucking it right out of this weed."

An effective treatment, I believe, is group counseling, where young smokers are challenged to discuss their feelings about themselves, each other, and the ways in which they feel dissatisfied or unfulfilled. An exploration of the passive and widespread "I-don't-care feeling" could also be on their agenda.

Another effective treatment would offer a course in the history of cigarette marketing, showing how vested interests have used the passivity of the population to their advantage, sacrificing the health and well-being of others for power, security, and financial gain. Young smokers could reflect on what it says about them to allow themselves to be used and manipulated in this way.

The purveyors of unhealthy products are not feeling the essence or essential value in those they exploit. They can't feel that others are precious, since they are detached from what is precious in themselves. They can't see how they are cold and indifferent strangers to themselves, who worship the cold, indifferent gods of profit and security. Their values are materialistic, and so they feel that their comfort, security, and financial well-being are paramount. This perspective in itself is a form of passivity, blocking them as it does from the far greater values of wisdom, spirit, and Self. It hinders them from feeling the common spirit in all humanity. In passivity, they cling to the ego—the seat of the false self—that gives them an illusion of power and wealth but not the reality of it.

The following is a list of other self-defeating behaviors and chronic negative emotions, along with some of the psychological factors that underlie them. The clinical complexity of these behaviors and feelings is substantial, and what is offered here is only a sliver of insight into the problem:

Chronic overwork results from the feeling that one is inadequate or deficient in oneself and thus needs some external evidence in the form of more production to impress others and oneself. Beneath such productivity, the individual is negating himself or herself. Passivity is present in this person's lack of self-care and self-nurturing, as well as in his or her submission to the work ethic of those in authority.

Compulsive gambling involves the acting out of the feeling of being a loser. Consciously, the gambler feels he must win, that he needs to get more excitement and benefit from life, while unconsciously he is convinced that the world (initially mother and father) will refuse and deprive him and cause him loss. Passivity is present in the compulsive acting out of his dissatisfaction, as he feels hopelessly ensnared in this addiction and unable resist the appeal of it.

Alcoholics typically leave the early phase of childhood with the feeling that they are being deprived of maternal love. They are fighting an attachment to the subjective impression of a bad or refusing mother. According to psychoanalyst Edmund Bergler, they choose alcohol precisely for its injurious effect on them. They identify with the allegedly refusing image of their mother from their oral stage and, in revenge, fill her (themselves) with poison.[xlvii] Typically, alcoholics aggressively refuse the support of others or their acknowledgment and love, just as they feel unsupported by their life's circumstances and fail emotionally to support themselves. In an equally aggressive manner, they often refuse to admit they have a problem.

The *promiscuous individual* is "into" feeling unloved, unwanted, having no value—all expressions of self-rejection and self-hatred. It appears that he is desperate for love, but he is acting out an unconscious attachment to the experience and the feeling of not being able to find it. He also treats others the way he feels about himself—as having no value.

The *perfectionist* is entangled in a subpersonality created when he covers up his emotional attachments to feeling criticized, disapproved of, and, in more serious cases, condemned. In appearing to want perfection, he is covering up how much he experiences himself through criticism and disapproval. "I'm not looking for criticism," he contends in his unconscious defense. "Look at how perfectly I want to do everything." Often times a person with an attachment to criticism will act out with some painful addiction or compulsion, using the out-of-control behavior primarily for the secret purpose of condemning himself or herself. In other words, the real addiction is emotional—to the feeling of self-criticism.

Procrastination is a result of one's unconscious willingness to feel controlled and powerless. One feels helpless to take charge of some required action. The behavior is also a result of the willingness to criticize and condemn oneself for the procrastination itself.

The *jealous* individual is convinced he is going to be rejected or betrayed. Unconsciously, he is attached to the feeling associated with this expectation. In his defense against his attachment to this feeling, he claims through his jealousy: "I'm not looking to feel rejected; look how worried I am that it might be happening." Though his partner might be perfectly faithful, the jealous person can generate feelings of rejection and betrayal through his emotional imagination.

Envy is associated with orality and results from the feeling that one is being gypped, not given to, or missing out on some entitlement. Envious people are often negative peepers who use their visual drive or emotional imagination not for creative purposes but in order to see or to imagine events or situations in which they can generate feelings of being deprived or missing out.

Loneliness is the experience of feeling separation from oneself. It is produced by a willingness to indulge in feelings that "nobody loves me, nobody cares." The sense that we are unloved is a reflection of how we are rejecting ourself, of how we are failing to be there for ourself, supporting and validating our own existence rather than abandoning ourself and then feeling that self-alienation through loneliness. Attachments to passivity and to self-rejection underlie this painful emotion.

One of my own personal battles for self-regulation, and one of the dubious delights of my passivity, concerned the experience of being held up by traffic—the highway variety, most painfully, but also in bank lines and at supermarket checkout lines. I left Florida in 1993 after fourteen wonderful years there, yet I was pleased enough to be leaving behind the state's population explosion with its slowpoke senior drivers and crowded public places. "Spacey" and sparse New Mexico has given me room to zip around—physically and metaphysically.

Using slow traffic as my pretext, I created the inner impression that I was being acted upon by others and forced to submit to their pace and speed. I was determined to believe that these slow drivers were in charge of my experience and that I had no choice but to endure these unpleasant feelings. It could be a lazy Sunday afternoon—yet when I got in my car, I was in a hurry. Unconsciously, I wanted to create the impression that I was pressed for time. In doing so, I would invariably find myself on the back bumper of another poky driver. The faster I wanted to go—and couldn't—the more deeply I felt my passivity. I was using my former concept of time—as linear and limited—in order to "juice up" my attachment to passivity, specifically to the feeling I had to submit to the behavior of someone else.

My agitation at that point was a defense against this attachment. I was willing to "take on" or "get hit up with" that unresolved, familiar impression of being held up. My defense went like this: "I don't want to be held up—look at how upset I am that it's happening."

My emotional attachment to the feeling of being held up is now conscious, and my temptation to experience passivity in such manner has greatly diminished. The healthier we are, the more we inwardly accommodate the challenging circumstances in which we find ourself, and we accept as a naturally arising circumstance of life an annoying or difficult situation. If we can, we remain at ease for the duration, taking whatever pleasure is available even in an imperfect situation. This is possible even if we are being unjustly treated. We develop a growing ability to refrain from jumping into a negative reaction as we are more sensitive to the pleasure of our equanimity.

The goal is to respond rather than to react to a challenging experience, including an injustice. Sometimes, of course, we do have to speak up for ourself or risk being passive in our silence. Once we slip into feeling like victims, however, we become emotional and reactive, thus hindering our effectiveness and diminishing the quality of our experience.

For the sake of science, I must disclose another of my foibles. In my forties, when my nervous system first contemplated the serenity of the rocking chair, I began to become annoyed by neighborhood noises such as racing cars, blaring radios, honking horns, wailing alarms, barking dogs, and even wind chimes. Life is made noisy, I realized, not just as a consequence of technology but because silence, which causes our consciousness to turn inward, feels dangerous to many people. I would be a dissonant bird indeed out campaigning for bucolic serenity among people who need heavy metal to drown out their internal racket. I could just as well be selling books on fasting. Sidestepping an inspiration to become an acoustic-privacy activist, I had to look elsewhere for emotional serenity. Thank heavens—yes, what a surprise—I discovered inner passivity in this corner of my world as well.

Whenever I became annoyed by what I called "inevitable neighborhood noises" (somewhere under the 100-decibel level), I turned inward to monitor my experience. To this point, I hadn't been inwardly strong enough to maintain my equanimity in the face of such noises. My passivity invited the noise to intrude upon me, while my annoyance covered up my unconscious willingness to experience myself being imposed upon, forced to take notice, and obliged to react. For many years, I had persisted in feeling irritated at whatever din leaked into my den. I had wanted to feel at the mercy of insensitive neighbors, helpless to convert them to the pleasures of inner placidity. Meanwhile, I could feel that who I was didn't matter to them. Now that's all changed. The noise passes around and through me, and I use it to check in with myself and to bring me closer to myself. While not exactly the sound of silence, it's now the acceptable hustle-and-bustle of my town.

Into this mix of self-regulation issues we can now add money. Many of us lack regulation either in the gusto with which we accumulate money or the haste in which we spend it. On the surface, money issues often appear to be matters of insecurity and greed. Greed itself is a passive symptom, produced and acted out because we are anxious about the possibility of being deprived, missing out, not getting, as well as fearful of the prospect of being powerless and at the mercy of fate. We are fearful of letting go of the security associated with money because we don't trust life or ourself. So we allow ourself to be controlled, directed, and restricted by the notion of money as power, authority, and salvation. We give up our personal power to money, especially when we degrade ourself for the sake of it.

In the healthy approach to money, it is a means to an end, used for the purpose of acquiring items that one needs. If a person buys items based on desire rather than need, the healthy approach involves buying value commensurate with the price, buying what brings pleasure, and doing so without incurring unreasonable debt or financial risk. Impulse buying, however, is often generated by passivity. The impulse arises out of the need to get—to cover up the affinity for feeling deprived—and the individual feels powerless to resist the impulse. The impulse is based not on the desirability of the item itself, although we're convinced suddenly that it is essential, but on our willingness to experience ourself once again through the feeling that we have no choice but to submit to this impulse. In my book, *See Your Way to Self-Esteem,* I tell the story of walking into a rug store in Manhattan many years ago looking for a small Yoga mat for my wife Sandra and walking out thirty minutes later with a $3,000 silk rug, having been passively stupefied by an aggressive, verbally endowed salesman. I was "snookered," not so much by my passivity to a buying impulse but by my passivity to this man's "sales power." I commiserated with a man who told me later, "I'm afraid to go into a used-car showroom, even to look, because I know I'll be talked into a purchase."

Often people live in fear of being taken advantage of in money matters. They get angry and complain loudly about these possibilities, but invariably, in getting suckered or conned, they are acting out an unseen aspect of their passivity, the opportunity to end up feeling manipulated and cheated. Through their emotional imagination, these individuals create scenarios of being cheated that reflect their attachment to feeling controlled, coerced, and helpless.

A healthy individual does not sacrifice family, recreation, hobbies, or love to make as much money as he can. In contrast, an unhealthy individual devalues these aspects of his life in his desire to make and possess money. Such an individual might hoard money, spend it recklessly, speculate unwisely in a desperate bid to increase his hoard, be a penny-pincher, or become indignant or furious when others make financial requests of him. All of these behaviors indicate a lack of both emotional and behavioral self- regulation and create infinite possibilities for misery.

A Technique for Self-Regulation

When we wish to regulate an addictive or compulsive behavior, or to neutralize an emotion such as anger or the wish for revenge, we might consider taking the following three steps.

First Step. In order to create a distance, a separation, between our desire and ourself or between our negative emotion and ourself, we first need to create a pause before indulging. This pause brings our consciousness to our intention to self-regulate. We observe the power of our impulse or desire at the same time that we search for the key to resist it successfully.

Knowing in this context that behavioral impulses have an emotional basis, we ask ourself, "What's going on inside of me? Am I feeling deprived (or refused, controlled, rejected, criticized) in some way?" Even if there's justification for these feelings, in the sense that someone is indeed trying to deprive or control us, we still need to recognize our unconscious willingness to embellish on these feelings.

Are we feeling some inner emptiness and thus wanting to avoid ourself? Are we feeling powerless, having to surrender with no will to resist? Are we trying to love ourself with, say, food, because we feel so unloved in other areas of our life?

Ask yourself, "What role does the substance, feeling, or activity play in my life right now?" If, for instance, the substance is a brownie you are eager to eat, are you using it to secretly keep your weight up and thereby to act out your conviction that you're unattractive? Does the brownie represent how you secretly reject yourself, in the sense of making yourself sick or unattractive? Are you eating the brownie to fuel your self-aggression so that later you can feel condemned for having eaten it? Are you afraid of intimacy and love, and is this how you substitute for it? Are you simply an automaton that acts out all its desires and impulses? It helps to know precisely what you're feeling and where those feelings come from.

We look for our fears. Whatever we are afraid of, or very sensitive to, is what we are emotionally attached to. For instance, if we're afraid of being controlled or we're very sensitive to feeling controlled, that is our form of passivity, that's what we're willing to experience and put ourself through. Thus, we are likely to act out being controlled by some desire or impulse, generating a feeling that puts us into the heart of our passivity.

Second Step. Now, as you consider engaging in your preferred addiction or compulsion, you say to yourself: "I am choosing to submit (to this impulse). I am choosing to be passive (to such-and-such). I am willing to give in to this urge at this moment and allow it to control me. In this way, I know myself through what is old and familiar. I must want to feel this way, at the mercy of forces beyond my control. I do believe I can begin to know myself in a new, stronger way, but first I have to see how willing I am to stay here in my passivity because, even though it's painful, it's also familiar and, in a way, reassuring."

You might close your eyes in order to go deeply into this understanding. It helps to reflect on the experience of the child you once were, completely at the mercy of external events and situations, as well as your own body functions and emotions. In facing and owning this human predicament, you can begin to see and feel the strength of your being beyond this limiting passivity. Initially, all you may see is a profound emptiness, a great hollowness, a complete inability to represent your best interests. You tell yourself: "This is not who I am; this is not what I am."

For example, suppose you're very sensitive to feeling rejected. Now, as you're tempted to engage in an addiction or compulsion (or if you feel a negative emotion coming on), you say: "I am reacting to the feeling of being rejected. I am secretly willing to know myself through that old feeling. Eating (smoking, drinking, or feeling angry, jealous, or envious) right now is simply a reaction or a way to cope. If I overeat, I'm only trying to comfort or console myself to deal with the rejection. Food is my emotional substitute for love. And after eating inappropriately and neglecting my health, I'll probably reject and hate myself even more than I imagine others do, which is exactly the feeling that I'm so familiar with."

If you still want to engage in your addiction, or if you can't resist taking on a negative emotion such as disappointment or loneliness, go ahead and let it happen. Witness yourself in the process of doing or experiencing it. Become an objective observer of the experience. (See the section "Becoming an Observer" in Chapter 8 and the

223

section, "Becoming a Nonjudgmental Observer of Yourself," in the Appendix.)

In this process, you become nonjudgmental even as you are engaged in acting out an addiction or compulsion. You watch out for your self-aggression or inner critic to become activated, and you make the effort to stifle it. If you're consuming food, alcohol, or drugs, you are conscious of your every move. All the while you remain aware that underlying this behavior is some form of passivity. Whether it's food, alcohol, or smoke, you savor the aroma and the taste of it. You make it like a Zen tea ceremony, where you are meticulously aware of every movement and sensation. If you can, observe your feelings and actions with neutrality (not the inner critic or critical parent part in you), or even with tender compassion as you appreciate the degree to which you are making a brave effort to understand psychologically what is happening.

You can say, "Okay, this addiction is getting the best of me this time. But next time I will be stronger. My sincere intention is to break this pattern and become strong and free. I believe in myself, and I know I will succeed."

Usually we feel guilty after we have indulged our addiction or compulsion. The guilt, we believe, is for our "bad" or "naughty" behavior. This accounts in part for why many people see the acting-out of the addiction as the problem itself rather than just a symptom of a deeper issue. In fact, the guilt is produced because of our unconscious willingness to experience ourself through inner passivity and because our inner critic has become activated. When that guilt rises up to our awareness, we attribute it to something other than inner passivity, usually to a sense that punishment is appropriate for our failure in regulating

224

and controlling our behavior or for allegedly being such a defective person.

Third Step. Having practiced the second step for a while, you are ready to say to yourself (and act accordingly): "Engaging in this activity or this negative emotion is really going to hurt me. Now that I see and understand the passivity that has supported this behavior or emotion, I feel ready to move beyond this pattern." You are now more likely to succeed because you have exposed, more precisely than ever before, the underlying passivity behind your self-defeating behaviors and emotions.

Nonetheless, even as we practice this technique and assimilate the knowledge, we may still feel helpless to do anything but act out with our addiction or come under the influence of negative emotions. But with persistence, the liberating process will eventually take effect. The best we may be able to do initially is simply to observe ourself under the influence of our addiction or our negative emotion, and thereby get a glimmer of understanding its deeper roots. As mentioned, we try not to engage in self-criticism for our weakness, though doing so the day after a binge is often very tempting. Self-criticism leads to non-acceptance of ourself and intensifies our conflict. We also want to avoid identifying with any of the deadlocked parts of ourself that are debating whether or not to indulge. When we are simply observing the inner conflict like an impartial witness, and being aware of this witness position with both the knowledge of our passivity and the sincere intention to become able to regulate ourself, we are exercising strength and hovering close to our center. The more we practice this awareness, the sooner we will recognize a growing self-regulation.

In acquiring self-regulation, we honor ourself by overcoming what weakens us, and we carry this new sense of self-acceptance and self-care into our daily activities.

Chapter 8
Keys to Liberation

In my dream, I was waiting at a newsstand in a subway station when a police officer approached me and began to write out a ticket.

"What's that for?" I asked, taken aback. "Dawdling," he replied, passing me the ticket. "What's dawdling?"

He said I had taken a step or two in his direction, then awkwardly stumbled or backed away.

"I don't recall doing that," I told him. "And even if I had, it surely isn't illegal."

Ignoring my protest, the officer escorted me to a supervisor, a higher authority somewhere in the subway station, who confirmed in a stern, threatening manner that I did indeed warrant the ticket.

Reviewing the dream later, I remembered having a vague sense of guilt, an impression that, innocent though I might be, the police officer had a right to exercise his authority and to question my behavior. I had been standing around doing nothing, yet it felt in the dream that I wasn't supposed to be free to do that. Being held accountable, it seemed, was natural, and calling my behavior "dawdling," giving it that negative connotation, seemed to correspond with my lingering doubts about being an upstanding person.

We are free only in relative terms. We are under the influence of a parental model for experiencing ourself, through which we question, judge, censor, and inhibit the free flow and expression of our being. This part of us operates so subtly that we mistake its voice and influence as that of our own intention and judgment. It corresponds with the Commanding Self, the Sufi term described at the end of Chapter 1, and is a variant of our self-aggression, a kind of second cousin to it.

In psychoanalytic theory, this parental model begins to develop within us at the age of two, or two and a half, when a child discovers an ingenious device for maintaining a semblance of his infantile fantasy of egocentricity and omnipotence. The child at this age must contend with prohibitions from mother and father: "You can't touch that, you mustn't do that," and so on. The child, in effect to "save face," identifies with these prohibitions and incorporates them into himself. He still adheres to the admonition, "Don't do it!" but now feels that he, of his own volition, has chosen to follow these dictates. He believes: "I'm the one who has decided to do it or not do it, so it's not a problem." But later it does become a serious problem. Having thus incorporated and identified with parental admonitions, we begin to live through this parental model of authority, to which we now react either passively or passive-aggressively, meaning either to acquiesce or to defy. Either way, we maintain the inner conflict and miss the connection to ourself. An inner program of emotional attachments determines much of how we feel and act, while we naively believe that this is not so.

We also come strongly under the influence of our parents' impressions of us. Often the impressions they conveyed were completely subjective and based on their unresolved issues. They transferred and projected on to us all the blind spots in themselves. One client in his forties, struggling out of passivity and failure, said of his father's lack of support and condescension toward him, "My father wrote the script for my life and cast me as a fuck-up." Through passivity, an emotional impression such as this can feel like a life sentence in solitary confinement. When we live in the shadow of our parents' negative influence, it can seem that we will never access our own truth. Thus, we experience great difficulty in regulating our behaviors and emotions, supporting our own existence, and believing in ourself. This variation of passivity constitutes the feeling of having been forced by parents to be what they wanted us to be. We felt that, unless we complied, we would be bad or unloved. We are compelled to pass on this experience of our passive compliance to our children and similarly require them to submit to our sense of reality. Or in our passivity we go to the other extreme and fail to exercise enough strength to hold them accountable in an appropriate manner to higher standards and expectations.

Our parental oppressor is often more subtle and tactful than the policemen in my dream. Often the oppression takes the form of unwarranted allegations or insinuations. A common insinuation is the sense of *should*. Many of us have suspended over our heads a barrel full of "shoulds"—should have, would have, could have—tipped so that a steady stream of persuasion, coercion, and duress descends upon us. This was one client's inner refrain: "Maybe I should be doing something different from what I'm doing."

More than "shoulds" befalls us. Our parental inhibitor also usurps and clutters our mind and has us spinning in mental considerations and speculations that leave us feeling bewildered and unfocused. Instead of cavorting in the Zen of experience, we live under mental rules and inhibitions and emotional restraints. We end up feeling stuck in a bind, convinced that "everything I do is doubtful or wrong," and lost in the valley of ambivalence. Here we submit to random, senseless, negative musing, unable to find the integrated self who can bring order, coherence, and guidance to our existence. In desperation, we try through one limited function—our mind—to create order and make sense of the world. But all we create are speculations, beliefs, and rules—more confusion and blocks to our autonomy and integration. Now, instead of being ourself, we are artificial—compelled, contrived, cultivated, and cultured.

As a result, we feel tense and "under the gun" with respect to duties, chores, and responsibilities. One of my clients, a busy professional, was unable to relax at the end of the day until he had tidied up every last bit of his work. He had a knack for turning possible pleasure into chores. Calling friends, reading his professional journals, and even going through the newspaper came under the category of work. Often he was left with less than an hour of respite before going to bed.

In this form of oppression, we make ourself passive to a burdensome, often arbitrary agenda. We act as if the agenda is sacrosanct and must be duly honored. The agenda reigns over us, brought to our attention through an inner nagging that holds us accountable, while we naively believe that, rather than reacting to this inner authority, we have made a conscious choice to be active and busy. Our hidden intent is to create a situation in which we are under the influence of some schedule, program, or obligation, thereby feeling ourself to be accountable and compliant—the old passive self with which we are so familiar. It is a case of not knowing how to be truly free.

Invariably, we also recreate our inner oppressor as a living human being who hovers around us, blocking our spontaneity and our ability to be ourself. The more tyrannical our inner oppressor, the more likely it is that some petty tyrant, often a boss, co-worker, neurotic spouse, or other family member, will set his or her sights upon us and act out that oppressive role for us. Or we ourselves can be that petty tyrant or trifling terrorist. We become the oppressor, all the while identifying with the one feeling stifled (or whom we imagine feeling stifled) under our arbitrary authority.

We feel unable to operate independent of the influence—positive or negative—of others upon us. The world of others seems to overflow uncontrollably into our own, and their garbage and negativity seem to be ours, too; we feel we cannot be free to operate in our own sphere of influence, under our own stewardship. Through passivity, we are always reacting—by withdrawing or by being pseudo-aggressive (or most often somewhere in between)—to this feeling that we are being acted upon by others, even when all they may be doing is ignoring us.

Roger, an executive in his late thirties, went to a leadership conference in Florida and found himself being triggered by a colleague who was also in attendance. Roger knew this other man, Sebastian, through various associations in the city where he worked and had found him to be "pompous and arrogant." In fact, he was surprised to see Sebastian at the conference, and he was quite unhappy that he would "have to endure him for several days."

True to form, Sebastian made his presence felt. Halfway through the conference, he had commandeered the microphone on three occasions, more frequently than any other participant, and had spoken at length to the audience of several hundred. Roger was himself one of the stars of the conference and felt upstaged by Sebastian. Nevertheless, Roger could do nothing about it. He did acknowledge feeling intimidated and that he spent some time imagining himself "calling Sebastian's bluff and exposing his self-serving agenda" to other conference participants. Roger tried to justify his reaction by claiming that Sebastian "was trampling over everybody."

The conference was still going on when Roger, upset and angry, called me on his cell phone. I suggested to him that to work out his issue he needed to take the focus off Sebastian and start to become responsible for the effect Sebastian had on him. I told him how he could use the conflict with Sebastian to his benefit, while minimizing the unpleasantness he felt in Sebastian's presence. "Clearly, you are giving Sebastian a lot of power and experiencing him through your passivity. He is a reflection of how you relate to yourself, how you experience your own inner oppressor. The next time Sebastian speaks, tune in to yourself and what you are feeling. As you are listening to him, try to see your inner reaction, and through the reaction—probably annoyance or mounting anger—trace these emotions back deeper into yourself. You will see that they can only be coming from an impression deep within yourself that you are being forced to submit to his agenda and to endure his overbearing manner. That is what happens within you when your own oppressor pushes his way to the forefront and imposes his agenda.

"If you were not being passive," I continued, "you would first of all see Sebastian for what he is, a person struggling with his own insecurities and need to feel important, and therefore not someone to feel intimidated by. And you would listen to his words for any value in what he says, since, as you said, he does know his stuff. You would also trust that if he were to become inappropriate, conference participants would lose all respect for him and rein him in somehow.

"So," I concluded, "go inward when he is speaking, or for that matter whenever these feelings come up, and identify that part in you through which you are reacting to him. You are also likely feeling pushed aside by him, as if he is somehow better or more dynamic than you. Then you revert in yourself to feelings of being a lesser person or somehow unworthy. When you can see all this and take responsibility for it, something amazing happens—you no longer become triggered. Remember that inner conflict can't maintain itself for long when it is exposed to the light of your awareness."

Silvia's Enforced Passivity

In a mythical sense, our passivity can be understood as a component in the battle between the forces of good and those of the darkness. The good wants our evolvement and the development of our awareness as beings of light and love. From the dark side, however, we are subject to a range of negative intensity, from accusations of worthlessness to doubts and criticism about our decisions and conduct to an internal campaign designed to keep us ignorant and passive.

The more acute our passivity, the more danger the dark side will swallow us up. Our relationship with ourself is more antagonistic, and we find ourself living under an inner tyranny, in the cross-hairs of self-condemnation, self-rejection, self-hatred, and self-negation. The following example from a highly dysfunctional family illustrates the acute passivity and absence of a supportive, protective self that can result for a person subjected to such an abuse of parental authority.

Silvia was raised by a schizophrenic mother and was sexually abused by her older brother. She suspected that her father, a heavy drinker and compulsive gambler, also molested her. She does remember showering with him when she was eight or nine years old and being filled with shame as she tried to avert her gaze from his nudity. Silvia, now in her forties, is a married mother of two children with a career as a nurse. When she first contacted me, she'd had years of psychotherapy with various therapists and was still struggling with passivity issues.

"I always felt, from what I was told by my relatives, that my mother wanted me to die during her pregnancy," Silvia told me. "She didn't eat properly, she smoked, she drank, and she was so tiny while pregnant it was unbelievable. Then, after I was born, I know she didn't feed me enough or give me any warmth or love. Later, she would ignore me completely in the company of others. It was as if I didn't exist for her. When she talked to me, she would often call me by her sister's name. One time, many years later, I left my infant son with her, along with his bottle, and told her to make sure she held him when she fed him. She told me, quite matter-of-factly, that she had never held me and had always used one of those 'prop-up bottles' they used to sell back then.

"I know that I myself wanted very much to die. As a toddler, I often held my breath until I passed out. Doctors told my father, 'Leave her alone—she'll pass out and then her breathing will come back to normal.' I spent my childhood hiding from everyone and everything. When I was three years old, I went into the hospital to have my tonsils out. I wasn't eating or drinking much, and when I got back home I guess I stopped eating and drinking all together. They found me in my bed covered with blood and rushed me back to the hospital, where I was in a coma for a week. My brother told me years later that he believes my mother, enraged by all the care and attention I required, had tried at that time to choke me. As an adolescent I began to have epileptic seizures. These seizures would follow episodes in which I dreamed of going into a coma, of dying and losing myself, disappearing into an emptiness from which there was no return. I would fight to come out of it and wake up with my brain going crazy electrically and have those seizures. I wanted to shut down on myself, to disappear to myself. Now I can still feel like a non-person, as if everything exists outside of me. At eighteen, I got hysterical blindness that lasted on and off for four years. I dropped out of college and couldn't drive. It was like the end of all functioning.

"When I started to develop breasts, my mother was fascinated. Sometimes I would try to hide them from her because she would stare at me and look at them with anger. It was so horrible to have her look at me that way. I just wanted my breasts to stop growing. Every morning she checked to make sure I was wearing a bra. One time she made me wear a see-through blouse to school. It was so humiliating. A friend came up to me and said, 'Silvia, how can you wear that! Everyone can see your bra.' Other times she made me dress so that everything was all loose and covered up, as if I didn't have any breasts at all. She would smack me across the face if she didn't like the way I was dressed in the morning. On the street, she would always point to other women and tell me how bad I looked in comparison. As I talk about this now, pain shoots into my face and jaw, my teeth hurt, and my throat tightens up. That happens every time I talk about this.

"I had to endure all this. Only death would release me. Almost every day I spent hours in my room in a fetal position. I wanted to die so that I could get out. Whatever anybody did, I just had to take it. The pain is me holding back and holding back. I wanted to scream and I never did."

Silvia began therapy with me because she couldn't control her diet, and she was eating certain foods, especially sugar and carbohydrates, to which she had allergic reactions and which made her breasts sore. Both her parents had died in their fifties, her father of a rare male breast cancer. Silvia herself had cystic breasts. She felt certain that if she did not control her diet, she would also develop breast cancer. She also had recurring dreams of growths emerging from her breasts and breaking open with infection. Though Silvia's life was going well on several fronts, she was always apologizing for herself and was deeply mired in this struggle with food. At times of stress, she felt completely helpless to resist eating those foods that caused such painful physical and emotional reactions. All the while, she was acutely fearful of developing cancer and dying.

Several months into our therapy, Silvia described an incident that started at a restaurant. While there with a friend, she ate a serving of French fries. When she got home, her husband said to her, "You look really sick." She was pale and nauseated and missed work the next day.

"What were you thinking when you ordered French fries?" I asked her.

"I just thought it would be okay, that they wouldn't bother me."

"But you know you can't have carbohydrates."

"I always convince myself that this time it will be okay. Or else I just go ahead and eat that stuff without thinking about the danger. Sometimes I don't even know what I'm doing until I realize I've hurt myself again."

"Yes, you've told me how frequently you deceive yourself that way. It appears that you are trying to poison yourself. You are in danger every moment of trying to harm yourself, as you felt harmed as a child. You live through the feeling of not being safe, and you can't trust yourself to protect yourself. Just as you felt you were abandoned emotionally, you now abandon yourself at times of self-abuse."

"My mother didn't want me to exist," Silvia said, beginning to weep. "She obliterated me. I did everything to try to disappear. I can feel the message I got from her—she wanted me to destroy myself. And now I can feel that it's true—I am trying to destroy myself."

Moments later, Silvia clenched her fists and stomped her foot in anger. "The amount of anger I have for her is incredible. She tried to destroy me. Her whole life she tried to negate everything about me to everyone. She would tell others secrets about me and then, with her sly smile, get pleasure out of my pain."

237

Silvia composed herself and added, "Now I understand it better. Food is mother, that's what mothers stand for. And she was poison. She was so toxic that people couldn't stand to be around her. Now I do it to myself. I'm trying to poison myself. Do I hate myself that much?"

"The answer lies in the anger you just felt," I said. "It appears you are throwing the anger outward at the memory of your mother, but that anger, for the most part, is repressed and directed most severely at yourself. You absorbed your mother's angry look toward you, like the one you remember when she observed you dressing, and you turned it on yourself. Now you are emotionally attached to self-rejection and self-hatred. And through these attachments, you are carrying out your mother's wish—that you destroy yourself. That was your mother's wish for herself, at which she apparently succeeded, dying as she did at a relatively young age. Being as disturbed as she was, everything she felt about herself was replayed directly with you. Can you feel how passive it is to be acting out your mother's death wish for you? It is as if you were, and still are, under the spell of a witch.

"As well," I continued, "you lie to yourself about the dangers of certain foods when you say, 'It will be okay to eat this.' Lying to yourself keeps you in a passive condition, just as you were passive to your parents' lies."

"I recognize the anger," she said. "I often feel it toward others. And guess what—I was passive with these people to begin with. It all started with my passivity." It was a revelation to Silvia to realize that her anger was pseudo-aggression, not true power but a reaction to her passivity. "I always thought that anger was power," she said. "My mother would scream and curse at me—and I shuddered and quaked in my boots. But, of course, as I think about it, I see that she had no real power. She couldn't begin to stop all her addictions and her negativity."

A major symptom of passivity is the feeling of not being connected to oneself or to others. Silvia had related many instances in which she was extremely accommodating with others, to the point of overlooking her own needs and feelings. The result was to feel that she couldn't count on herself and had to rely on others. This corresponded with her emotional attachment to the feeling of being unrecognized or unappreciated. Silvia was highly sensitive to feelings that her husband's family didn't acknowledge or respect her. At the same time, as she said, "I am willing to submit to anybody."

One time she reacted with anger and inappropriate eating after listening to a woman tell of being abused as a child by the woman's father. Silvia told me a few days later, "I lost myself while listening to her story. I lost my hold on myself, and it felt as if I disappeared completely. That's what I did as a child, that's how I survived, by disappearing."

In many of our sessions, Silvia saw and felt her passivity very deeply. Her throat and jaw would tighten again when she acknowledged the times she had been unable to speak up for herself. One time as a young girl she had tried to tell her minister about her plight but had been unable to speak clearly. He was confused by her garbled communication and gave her a religious pamphlet. Silvia now realized, in many of the incidents she related, that she had become the one who shut down on herself.

Silvia was able to observe two parts of herself—first, her inner terrorist, her self-aggression, played by the impressions and memories of her parents and her brother,

239

and, second, the victim, her limited self, held in place by her own attachment to passivity. As she was able to step back from the clash of these two parts, she began to experience herself with a new sense of power. She told me one day, "It's been exhausting being inside this struggle, facing this ugly passivity day after day. Finally, the positive, life-affirming side of me is prevailing."

How We Experience Ourself

Seeing clearly how we impose a parental model of authority upon ourself is one key to inner liberation. Another key involves understanding how the nature and quality of our relationship with others and the world is a direct reflection of our relationship with ourself.

Few people understand in any depth that whatever we experience through our interactions with others or in situations in our life mirrors how we experience ourself. In other words, almost everything we do, say, and feel is affected by the quality of our relationship with ourself. To understand this concept, we need to appreciate that we not only have a self (an integrated sense of harmony, power, and oneness) but that we each have a relationship with our self (see Chapter 5). Because of self-aggression, many of us experience this relationship antagonistically, or at best we take ourself for granted. We are thus susceptible to self-doubt, self-criticism, self-rejection, and self-hatred. Whatever our relationship with ourself, that is how we act toward others, how we experience others, and how we experience the world. A person, for instance, who is stuck in a loveless relationship with his wife is invariably stuck in that kind of relationship with himself and others.

If he is going nowhere psychologically, then so is his marriage.

When we understand this concept, that our relationship with ourself mirrors our relationship to others and the world, we understand social phenomena and ourself much more clearly. For instance, high-school shootings and other expressions of hatred and violence are now comprehensible, even if no less horrifying. As I said, from the time of childhood some of our natural aggression is directed back at ourselves as self-aggression. A violent gunman isn't likely to be aware of the antagonistic relationship he has with himself. He convinces himself that somehow his targets are deserving of his hatred or that they count for nothing (as he feels about himself). He is projecting his own self-negation, self-rejection, and self-hatred onto others and thus imagines that others are worthy of his hatred or that they also reject and hate him, and he is completely convinced of the validity of this impression. If he assaults others, he is trying, in a sense, to throw off his own self-hatred—in fact, he is covering it up, refusing to see it. For him, the problem is their despicable nature and their hatred of him, not his own hatred of himself.

In the case of high-school shootings, students who have personality disorders can have a particularly difficult time regulating or moderating their negative reactions to feelings of being rejected or bullied by others. It starts with the negativity and hatred they feel coming at them from their own self-aggression. To cover up (or defend against) their attachment to that feeling, they create the impression the hatred is caused by the negative attitudes and behaviors of others towards them. Under this impression, these individuals now project their hatred outward to others. Sure enough, in a vicious cycle, this can cause some of those others to react negatively and hatefully toward them. One solution lies in improved teaching in our schools. Both emotionally stable and unstable students can benefit from a better understanding of psychology. However, as with other subjects, if the teacher doesn't thoroughly understand these deeper principles, he or she can't teach the ideas very well.

It is illuminating, for instance, for a schoolyard bully to come into the realization that his bullying of others is a reflection of his own hateful relationship with himself. Such deep insight can change his life forever. He is seeing that his aggression is a mirror of his self-aggression. When he understands this well, he recognizes inner passivity and self-aggression as a combo that produce and maintain his low self-regard or even self-hatred.

With such insight, he begins to understand (and detach from) the false and painful identity thus created, through which he has been experiencing himself. He can begin to recognize his lack of self-respect. The problem, he realizes, derives from his absorption of self-aggression, whereby he accepts punishment for allegedly being so flawed or bad. These negative feelings do not at all reflect the essential truth of his being. Seeing himself more objectively, he can now begin to release his self-rejection and self-hatred and, correspondingly, his rejection and hatred of others.

Such knowledge won't usually be assimilated immediately, of course. And an individual who is learning this knowledge can "forget it completely" when in the throes of acting out some painful drama. Such acting-out can also continue for some time, even as deep psychological knowledge is being assimilated. One client said, "It's not until later, when I'm in so much pain and so tortured and

242

feel the need to get out of it, that I begin to apply the insights I've been learning." It takes courage and consistent effort to release old patterning—"It's like coughing up hair-balls," another client said. But the reward of emotional independence and autonomy is worth the effort.

Many young people express and experience nihilism, the feeling that nothing is really important, that intrinsic value is nonexistent, and that no one can be trusted. So why should they care? Why should they worry about the consequences of drinking six sodas or beers a day or smoking cigarettes? Why should they try to be good and successful? This feeling of nihilism is a passive symptom that reveals an indifferent or antagonistic relationship with ourself. We feel nothing of value within our own being. The culture reinforces this conception, impressing upon us the notion that our value is dependent on money, knowledge, education, material objects, style, and status.

We are all up against our resistance to loving ourself. Such love represents the unknown, something unfamiliar. To move toward love is associated emotionally with the loss of our old, passive self. Despite its limitations, that old self is all we know. We fear letting go of our identification with it, in spite of the pain and suffering it evokes. As one client said, "I have to be in some pain to feel myself—that's how I know I exist!"

Who will we be without our old identity? We fear disappearing into nothingness. Can we trust enough in life to risk finding out?

We may also have guilt over the perception that loving ourself will hurt or betray others, since psychologically we may have to leave them behind. We may also feel vain and selfish for pursuing the forbidden pleasures of joy, health, and love, and that doing so violates parental and social injunctions against feeling and embracing such pleasure.

A particularly significant resistance involves the fear of letting go of our manner of rebelling against forms of power and authority in order to maintain the illusion of our own power and authority. In other words, we cling to our forms of rebellion, even though they are passive-aggressive and self-defeating, for to let go of them is to lose what sense of power we have— and thus, so it seems, to lose ourself. We must take the risk and enter deeply into trust in life. If we allow ourselves to "die" into the unknown, we can transcend our limited self to be reborn into harmony and unity.

Clearing Away the Debris

The experience of dislodging our passivity and clearing away our emotional debris can be quite intense. An increase in fearfulness at certain times, especially during the night, is a common symptom. We feel the fear as it is being cleared, and if we are too afraid or don't trust the process or ourself, we can shut down and block it all. One client going through the process was having dreams of seeing the political party he opposed come to power and impose new laws and restrictions on him. "It's very fearful," he said. "It feels as if I am losing me, losing control of my life. I wake up in a panic, and life and death seem to hang in the balance." Shock and dismay are other reactions. "Oh my God, I've gone there all my life," said one man suddenly realizing the extent of his passivity.

As our passivity begins to become dislodged and leave us, we can feel as if we are losing control, as if our defenses are falling away, leaving us exposed. We often have dreams with passive themes. These can, paradoxically, become more intense as passivity is being cleared out of our system. The scenarios include being chased; feeling helpless and unable to complete some undertaking or forced to submit to some individual, decree, or process; seeing people or animals in helpless situations; and seeing others being clumsy, weak, and ineffective.

A client in his thirties had a dream in which he was mowing a small yard. The older woman who owned the home didn't appear to be around when he finished. As he was leaving the yard, he noticed the patio was littered with grass clippings. He realized he hadn't finished the job properly but decided to leave anyway. As he was going out the gate, she came out of the house and called to him, carrying a pair of jeans that belonged to him. He had left them on a previous visit, when it was raining, and she had washed and mended them. He came back toward her, took them, and thanked her. As he turned to leave, he again saw the clippings on the patio. He knew he should sweep them up but decided not to. It felt as if he needed to get away without getting caught by her. He left feeling guilty about not finishing the job properly.

I believe inner passivity accounts for why he wouldn't take a minute to sweep the patio. He feels passive to the old woman, and passive-aggressively he declines to complete the job. His fear of getting caught is a defense: he is professing that he doesn't want to be called back by her and forced, in abject passivity and shame, to finish the job properly. In the dream, he attributes his guilt to his failure to complete the job. The guilt, however, is created because of his involvement in passivity. He comes under an inner accusation for his passivity, and his guilt provides his cover story in the defense of pleading guilty to the lesser crime: "I'm not passive—the problem is I'm negligent. And I feel guilty for that. I just want to get out of here before she catches me." Meanwhile, the old woman's generosity in cleaning and repairing his jeans deepens his guilt, giving more credence to that line of defense. It would seem that her possession of his jeans (she had the pants), as well as the fact that he was cutting her grass in the first place, represented his readiness to put himself in a position in which he could feel passive to her.

In the process of writing this book, I had dreams that exposed my lingering passivity. One was the loitering dream described at the beginning of this chapter. In another one, I was walking across a frozen lake when an adolescent girl nearby crashed through the ice and disappeared into the water. I ran over and plunged my arm into the hole in the ice, convinced I could grab her and pull her to safety. But she was gone. I circled my arm in the water to no avail, feeling horrified at her plight and at my inability to save her.

I awoke at that moment in a deep helplessness. As I lay in bed, I became aware of how much I was tempted to keep replaying the dream and to "take on" that helpless feeling. I kept replaying the dream sequence in my mind, bringing back the helpless feeling almost as intensely as my original experience of it during the dream. I was also identifying, I realized, with her helplessness in being unable to save herself. I saw my attachment clearly through the powerful temptation to remain in the feeling of helplessness. I fought off the temptation and bounced out of bed within a minute to begin my preparations for the day, feeling pleased about the power I had just exercised in throwing aside this experience of inner passivity.

Through technique and knowledge, we are capable of coming to our own rescue when faced with an emotional crisis. Often the main obstacle is our unwillingness to believe in our inner power. To rescue ourself, we often have to come face-to-face with our condemning part and neutralize its expressions of doubt and scornful accusation. We see the condemning part as the annihilating force that it indeed can be—unadulterated self-aggression—and we deflect its malevolent intent through our fortitude, awareness, and intelligence. We realize that we give credence to the accusations and insinuations of this inner energy if we are uneducated about its malevolent nature and our passivity to it. As I've said, we recognize that the feeling it evokes of self-rejection, self-condemnation, and self-hatred does not at all represent the truth about our being. We understand that when we fall under its spell and "buy into" its negative implications, we haven't yet cleared away our underlying issues.

In an emotional crisis, we have to struggle for rationality. We see through the smokescreen our defenses are erecting. Negative emotions such as anger, envy, greed, jealousy, and hate are themselves a cover-up for our willingness to take on old feelings of being deprived, refused, controlled, criticized, and rejected. With this knowledge, we pierce through our emotional turmoil to observe, with patience and impartiality, our willingness to experience ourself in old, familiar, painful ways. We recognize the power of the negative, emotional attachment, our readiness to experience ourself through it, and we affirm our intention to work our way free of it. As mentioned earlier, we can also be saying quietly to ourself, as we're feeling the negative effects of an activated emotional attachment, "Yes, I'm attached to this negative emotion. But it's not who I am. It's not my true self."

Often people don't take even the first step in self-rescue, let alone pursue the full process outlined above. Our passivity and our resistance block us from coming to our emotional rescue. One client told me, "The feelings just come up too strong for me to think about rescuing myself." The first and most important step is to try to spot the passivity and the resistance. We can talk to ourself in this process, staying connected to ourself: "Okay, Joe, do you want to try to pull yourself out of this emotional pickle barrel or do you want to sink into the brine? If you don't see your passivity, you'll be pickled for sure. Can you feel it in this situation? It's the feeling of being unwilling to make an attempt to help yourself, along with your willingness to stay mired in that feeling. Or, put another way, it's truly not caring enough about yourself and the quality of your experience, and being emotionally attached to that limited sense of yourself."

We can challenge ourself to rise to the occasion, as follows: "Why should I sit here and suffer when there's a chance I can extricate myself from these feelings? It doesn't make sense that I wouldn't try to help myself—unless indeed the passivity is in the way and unless, in my resistance and ignorance, I'm willing to continue to experience myself through it. Now that I see this, I can feel a stirring of motivation and determination. I feel I can move passivity out of the way, or at least move around it and do what I can for myself."

Lori, a client in her forties, was struggling to achieve more self-regulation, especially with overeating. She also felt unhappy that her relationship with her husband and children was remote and disconnected. In a session with me Lori described her unwillingness to tap into her strength: "I want to see myself as having none right now. I know it's a child-like feeling that goes back into my past, where everyone in my family was miserable. Nobody was happy, so I couldn't be happy. If I felt happy, I would be all alone, abandoned, an outcast. They were all so fragile. I felt I could align with their pain if I was fat. This was one way to reach them, to connect with their pain."

"Can you see," I said, "what a passive way that was to connect with them?"

"Yes, it is very passive to take on their pain like that."

"And as you know, you never really did connect with them, even as you sacrificed any connection with yourself in the attempt. That lack of connection with them was very painful. Now you're feeling it with your husband, children, and yourself."

"If feels as if who I am and what I am is of no consequence to any of them."

"Yes, and you feel that most acutely in regard to yourself. You are the first one to abandon yourself, to refuse to believe in your own power. As you said, you don't look inward for your strength. You are unwilling to do so. Your unconscious interest is to continue to experience yourself in that old way, without connection, without power. You are more interested in feeling that nobody is giving to you. Meanwhile, you are the one who is not giving to yourself, although you defend against that by giving too much food to yourself."

"This passivity is the most elusive, difficult thing to detect," she said in quiet wonder. "It can bring you to your knees—and yet it is so hard to see."

During a session shortly after I started working with Lori, I noticed that she was frequently ending her comments with the question, "Do you know what I'm saying?"

I pointed this out to her and asked, "Are you aware that you are doing this? What do you think it means?"

She thought for a few moments. "I guess what I'm saying is. . . I don't feel understood. I'm not being heard, not being effective, like I don't have the power to be understood. I'm not important enough for others to really pay attention to me, and I don't have the power to convey my meaning or my feelings."

"That's it! It also seems to me that in using that expression you cut yourself off and fail to elaborate more on what you want to express. In other words, it's part of how you block your own self-expression. Now, every time you make that comment, you will become aware of it, and you will know exactly what it signifies. It's a direct link to your passivity. Knowing so clearly what it means, you will sooner or later stop using it. And with that will come confidence that indeed you are making yourself understood. And you will also likely become better in communicating your ideas."

We uncovered another direct link to Lori's passivity. She would occasionally say, in reference to her inner growth, "I've sure got a long way to go," or "It's not going to happen anytime soon." I told her, "That is also your passivity speaking, under the influence of a linear sense of time. It's important to feel that your growth is happening right now—as indeed it is. Otherwise, you believe that, in this moment, you are still enfeebled and at a disadvantage. Thus you are more likely to overeat or act out in some other way since you've convinced yourself that inner strength is not available to you right now but is off in the distance."

Becoming an Observer

A client, Sam, was playing ball with his sons one weekend afternoon and felt very bad about himself when his athletic clumsiness became apparent to his children.

"Dad, can't you just throw the ball straight," one son protested after Sam chunked his third straight pitch into the dirt.

"You know your Dad isn't that great at sports," Sam replied. "We're just out here having fun, so don't expect too much."

Talking about the incident afterwards, Sam said he managed to laugh with his sons and play down the fact of his ineptness. But the incident rekindled the pain he remembered from his childhood, when his peers regarded him with disrespect if not scorn for being a klutz. Sam's main problem was not in being athletically inept but in using his limited athletic skills for self-criticism and self-condemnation.

"I know it's this critical part of me," he said. "I can even see it coming at me. But I can't get out of the way. I say to myself, 'Oh, I hate my kids to see me this way.' I get all hit up with it, and I'm left feeling so intensely imperfect."

After Sam had talked for a bit about his memories of self-criticism, I guided him through a visualization. "Imagine as your adult self that you are an observer. You are observing yourself as a child. You see yourself playing with other kids and being clumsy and inept as usual. What does that feel like?"

Sam closed his eyes and sat quietly for a few moments. "There is some shame as I observe myself. But I can feel also that I can be neutral."

"What are you feeling toward that clumsy child you see, and what would you want to say to him?"

"I guess I would say to him, 'Sam, you're doing the best you can. Try not to feel bad about yourself. You're a good kid. There's no need to beat up on yourself. Just hang in there and do your best. The other kids can accept you and like you for who you are. Try to believe in yourself.'"

"That's very good. And we can take it to another level if you would like to try to deepen the connection."

Sam said he didn't know where to go on his own with this suggestion. So I helped by saying, "Close your eyes. Go back into being the observer. You are watching young Sam. How are you feeling as you observe clumsy, young Sam? If the feelings are negative, go ahead and feel them. If the feelings are positive, feel them too. Communicate those feelings to Sam without any words. Let Sam know what you are feeling without your having to speak it aloud. Do that now for several minutes and try to generate that feeling."

I was silent as Sam experienced this exercise. After several minutes, I had him open his eyes and tell me what he experienced.

"At first I sensed my temptation to look at myself critically," he said. "Then I remembered that the purpose was to see myself from a higher, compassionate perspective. I could feel my attitude toward myself begin to soften. In a few moments, I was looking at myself with a rather neutral feeling. The kid I saw at that moment was neither good nor bad. He was just another kid on the block being who he was. As I watched him stumble around, I never felt sorry for him. Instead I began to feel a longing to get close to him, to get to know him, to understand what he was feeling, and to let him know that I could accept him fully even if he was the worst player on the field. His being a bad player didn't matter anymore. In a way it made him more lovable. I imagined reaching out and touching him with that feeling, to let him know that I liked him and accepted him just as he was."

I told Sam to practice this method, to see himself either as a boy or a man, to make the effort to observe himself from an objective perspective whenever he felt bad, and to cultivate the feeling that he understood, supported, and loved himself. Using this approach, rather than being entrenched in a negative self-impression, he could generate from within a feeling of support and com-passion for himself. However, for Sam to do this effectively he had to see and acknowledge his unconscious willingness to experience himself through familiar feelings of ineptness, criticism, and disapproval. "You are attached to that feeling and prepared to experience it repeatedly," I told him. "As you struggle to love yourself, you have to acknowledge this negative impression and your attachment to it." He had to "own" his continuing readiness to experience himself in that painful, limited way. Our limited self, I reminded him, is wedded to unlimited suffering.

Chapter 9
To Know Our Truth

Passivity for some of us takes the form of not knowing what we want in life. We lack a sense of mission for finding our truth or direction. People frequently say, "I don't know what I want, though I wish I did." In this situation, our first step is to decide if that's how we want to go on living. If we want an improved experience of ourself, we need to firm up our intention to find out just exactly what we do want.

We begin to observe that, when forgetting or forgoing our intention to discover what we want, we are in a passive state. We notice that our objective—to persist in looking within for our authentic self—is dissolved whenever we go off into the fog of our passivity. We keep bringing ourself back to our intention. In this way, we begin to become more clearly aware of the nature of our passivity. Soon we are able to observe our passivity creeping in, trying to dissolve our intention and impose its agenda, wanting us, in a sense, to live in the shadow of ourself.

Once past this hurdle and ready to discover truth in the world and in ourself, we are often confronted by a cultural bias that prefers crude irony and humor when approaching topics of substance. Many of us try to alleviate guilt for our complacency, and ultimately for our passivity, by convincing our conscience that everything is pointless and absurd, and that we shouldn't be held to higher standards, expectations, or responsibilities.

As we nonetheless move forward to dislodge our passivity, we begin to discover our truth and learn to speak it. Doing so can bring up discomfort, anxiety, and fear—but that soon abates as we become comfortable representing ourself. Wayne, a bachelor and advertising executive in his forties, had felt unhappy for years that his parents in Texas had never visited him at his home in the suburbs of a northern city. He certainly had plenty of room for them. Seven years earlier he had purchased a large, expensive house and furnished it in elegant style. But Wayne saw his parents and the rest of his family only when he flew down to Texas two or three times a year. He occasionally reminded them that they were always welcome to visit him, but he hadn't been particularly direct or compelling in persuading them to come.

"I don't want to have to beg them to visit," he said. "But it hurts me deeply that they haven't done so. They certainly don't mind traveling. They'll drive around Texas and adjoining states in their motor-home and be gone for ten days or more at a time."

With Thanksgiving a few weeks away, his parents told him they had decided to spend the holiday visiting his youngest sister and her children in Dallas, about a three-hour drive from their home. His parents asked him if he thought he'd be able to fly down, but they hadn't consulted him about his plans or preferences before making their decision.

"How do you feel about that?" I asked him.

"I think it sucks. Why shouldn't they ask me what my plans are and see if we can all arrange something that works for everybody? Now, as the situation is, if I want to participate, I have to scramble at the last minute to make plans that fit in with what they've already decided. It's just like it was when I was a kid. They made their decisions, and we were never consulted." Wayne was sensitive to the feeling of being excluded and overlooked, and we had been working on this issue for some time. Growing up, he had felt that his father had been consistently distant and insensitive to him. "My desires and opinions didn't count for a whole lot," he said.

"You can deal with this situation internally," I told him, "by recognizing and acknowledging how ready you are to feel excluded by your parents. You have to recognize how tempted you are to go on experiencing yourself through that old feeling. As you do that, you can start to feel how to be more supportive of yourself. In the meantime, however, it may also be appropriate at this point to be more direct and to let your parents know how you feel about their attitude and behavior. It probably wouldn't be wise to do this, however, until you feel you can be nonreactive, meaning you would speak to them sincerely, without negativity or blame."

As Wayne reported it to me, he called his parents a few days later. With some initial trepidation as they both got on the line, he told them, "Mom and Dad, there's something I want to say with respect to what's happening this Thanksgiving. It would be really helpful to me if you were to consider talking to me and getting my input whenever you're making holiday plans. It would mean a lot to me to be included that way. I know I haven't been perfect either about initiating things to find out what you're considering, but it would be nice if we could work together on this. In this way I think we would be more likely to get together on holidays, and at the least we would have good feelings for how much we would like that to happen."

Wayne continued saying to them, "I want to remind you that it's been seven years now and you haven't visited me here. Every time we get together, I've been the one who has hopped on a plane and flown down to see you. I do have some feelings about this. It feels unfair. I know you care about me, but this is not a good way to show it. It seems that you're not that interested in seeing me and that you don't appreciate and value what I can offer you."

As he spoke, his father remained silent, while his mother interjected several times, "Oh Wayne, I'm so glad you're saying this!" The next day his mother called and told him that she and his father wanted to fly up to visit him the week leading up to Christmas, and then to fly on Christmas day back to Dallas to visit with their grandchildren. "Will that work for you?" she asked.

"Absolutely, sounds wonderful!" Wayne replied, deeply pleased though dazed by the quick turnaround. "What made you decide to come?"

"Your father has always implied that I should be the one to organize a visit. Then he always found some reason why it wouldn't work. You know how uncomfortable he is in strange, new surroundings. But last night, when we hung up the phone, we looked at each other and we knew we had to do this."

As an aside, Wayne found out a few days later when speaking to his sister that his parents expressed their decision to visit him in passive terms. His mother had told his sister: "Yes, we're going because Wayne wants us to." That is a passive rendition of her experience. It would be more direct and self-responsible to say, "Your father and I have decided to visit Wayne this Christmas."

Wayne's experience illustrates how much our path in life hinges on what we are secretly willing to endure, despite our protests about how much better we want things to be. Passivity involves the feeling that we are at the mercy of circumstances. We feel that we have no choice but to endure some painful predicament or stalemate. Yet it is not a matter of what we have to endure, for that is so obviously passive, but rather the suffering we are unconsciously willing to indulge in, which is a deeper and more subtle issue. We find it difficult to see that deep down we are willing to endure such unpleasantness. On the surface of awareness, we think we hate our deadlocks, dilemmas, dissatisfactions, and disappointments. We say we want these old, painful feelings to go away. But they won't without our awareness of how emotionally attached we are to them and how determined we are to experience ourself through them.

When we can know and speak our truth, we have the sense that what we want, if it is realistic and worthwhile, is within our reach and can be attained through our effort and sincerity. In the example above, Wayne truly did want his parents to visit him, but at the same time he was secretly willing to indulge in, and to act out, the feeling of being excluded by them. He finally had to override that passive component, to speak up with power and sincerity, if he indeed wanted to get what he claimed he wanted. The statement he delivered to his parents was very powerful. To express it, he had to connect to himself and to speak on behalf of his higher intention, with sincerity, courage, and straightforwardness. The challenge is to learn to do this when not angry or otherwise reactive in order for our statement to be real rather than a protest or defense.

To know our truth, we have to begin to appreciate our own being, our essence. No one can do this for us.

We may feel that expressing our truth is selfish or egotistical, that it betrays our parents and their values and beliefs. From our childhood perspective, if our parents feel pain, so should we. Our being in pain validated their pain and in some ways helped take care of it or make it better. To win our parents' love, we supported their pain and tried to make it go away. We are not supposed to see into the dysfunction of our parents. To see the truth is a threat both to their survival and ours. Thus, we adopt and absorb as our own our parents' feelings, traits, attributes, limitations, beliefs, self-damaging behaviors, expectations, ideals, prejudices, fears, and self-rejection.

If we do not absorb and validate our parents' pain, we assume they feel we don't care about them. We feel cruel and heartless in holding to our truth. This assumption is the source of the unconscious belief, "If they ever knew the real me, they would discover how bad and worthless I am (or what a fake and fraud I am)." Despite the pain of living through our false self, that self becomes invested in its own survival and what is real for it.

We associate our truth with danger and the likelihood of rejection. We fear losing the love of those to whom our truth is addressed, and indeed we do run the risk of being disliked for speaking it. Children are convinced that their truth is unacceptable to their parents, as indeed for many parents it is. In expressing our truth even to someone close to us, we can feel very much alone. The feeling is, "If I choose me, then I'm alone, separate from everyone." Our experience of ourself, and thus our sense of what is true, has become emotionally associated with guilt, shame, rejection, abandonment, and worthlessness.

We can imagine the shocked expression when, for the first time, the other person hears us speak to him or her with our inner authority. One woman who was considering the need to make a direct statement to her narcissistic mother-in-law said, "It would be like taking a butcher knife and stabbing her fifty times in the chest." She decided that, since she saw her mother-in-law only once a year for a few days and seldom spoke to her on the telephone, she would refrain from speaking up. Instead, she inwardly maintained her poise and equanimity in the presence of the woman.

This choice is fine. Understand, however, that the feeling beneath it stems from a childhood impression. The child can feel, "Being me will annihilate them; they will die or self-destruct. I am thus responsible for their life, for their happiness." Thus many of us spend much of our time catering to others, trying to please or save them, and negating or annihilating ourself in the process. As one client put it: "Other people feel real to me, while I don't feel real to myself. If I'm with someone, I exist. If I'm by myself, I'm an empty shell. My existence hardly matters."

Another woman, who in childhood gave up her sense of self in the process of trying to win her father's love, now felt in her fifties that, to garner God's love, she should give up her life's aspirations involving romance and art and try to become a saint. As she struggled to recover her sense of self, she said of passivity: "I can see why people go through their whole lives without wanting to deal with this. I can see that, yes, I want to feel better, but then again this is all very familiar. I can feel how attached I am to this limited sense of myself."

For the sake of compassion, we don't necessarily have to speak our truth to our parents or others. They might not be so pleased to hear us saying what they were never able to say for themselves. What matters is that we feel it and know we can say it if the need arises. We learn that we can represent ourself through the quality of our inner experience without a need for proclamations or confrontation. However, confrontation or at least honest openness does often serve the best interests of all concerned.

With time, it doesn't matter so much to us how our truth is received. We feel so good in knowing it, and in having the power to express it, that this testimony to our strength and integrity is a great satisfaction in itself. Our new lightness of being and the positive feelings we enjoy from expressing ourself in this manner override the fears that stopped us in the past.

Another client, Don, faced a situation comparable to Wayne's, also involving parents and holidays. Don had always been passive to his father, but now, after several years of therapy, he had become stronger and more assertive. His father, however, seemed more determined than ever to maintain the status quo and to go on experiencing his son as submissive and compliant. Under these strained conditions, Don and his wife, Chelsea, had planned with his parents to drive the 50 miles to the parents' home for Thanksgiving. Three days before the holiday, Don's father called with an invitation to meet for lunch the following week, saying that he and Don's mother had made other plans for the holiday. Don questioned him, but his father said only, "We're going to spend time with some friends."

Don was stunned and didn't say much more to his father. Later he told me, "It certainly felt as if I was being manipulated and brushed off. I thought, 'He's lying to me, damn it!'" Don talked to his wife shortly after his father called and began to process his experience. He felt a lot of anger that evening and knew he would be petty and vindictive if he were to talk to his father at that point. Repeatedly he imagined saying to his father, "You're a vicious old bugger." Later that evening Don began to access sad, wounded feelings underneath his anger, and then, a few hours later, he felt renewed by a sense of strength and resolve. He knew he had to make a statement on his own behalf. Risking further estrangement, he sent his father an email the next day.

"Dad," he wrote, "I want to say something about what is happening. I feel you're being insensitive to Chelsea and me. It's not the right thing to do, calling me like this a few days before Thanksgiving and telling me that you've decided to exclude Chelsea and me from your plans. It may seem to you that I have no feelings about this. But in fact it hurts. I feel sad about it. I'm just stating what I see and what I feel. I would like it to be better, and for that to happen we have to respect each other and to care about each other. I would like our relationship to move forward, but I have to tell you that I don't need for that to happen. I'm feeling very good about who I am. Whether you care about that, or whether you can see it or acknowledge it, is up to you. I do care about you and I am reaching out. And so, if you have anything to say, I'd like to hear it. Otherwise, I'll wish you a happy Thanksgiving and maybe we'll talk next week or something."

"I felt good about writing that and sending it to him," Don told me a week later. "Chelsea and I had a great Thanksgiving with friends."

Don didn't talk to his parents for several weeks, but gradually, through his mother's intervention, he and his father resumed their relationship. This time, however, Don's father understood that his son was a stronger man and, initially somewhat begrudgingly and then with an air of pride, accepted him as such.

If our parents didn't want to hear from the "real me," nor even recognize the possibility of a "real me," then as adults we have an emotional association with feeling that the "real me" has no value. As one woman expressed her childhood experience, "I saw myself as a reflection of others. Without that, I didn't exist. I also felt that I had to have an impact on others. Unless they reacted to me somehow, I didn't exist. Now, recognition and validation don't count if they come from me. I'm struggling to break out of that impression of myself."

Thus we perceive ourself as wrong, deficient, or limited and assume emotionally that anything intrinsic coming from us is of limited value. To believe in ourself is thus unrealistic, childish, unnatural, and presumptuous.

One woman, Jean, realized she had been allowing her husband to scold and berate her repeatedly for minor or imagined offenses. Jean had experienced herself as a disappointment to her stern father, and now she was willing to replay the feeling with her husband. She had also wanted desperately to be "a good girl," believing that her job as a child was to make everybody feel good. If they didn't feel good, she was somehow responsible. Of course, since she was actually powerless to make them feel good, this conception of herself and her role was all a setup for her to feel helpless and passive. Now, it seemed to her that if her husband didn't feel good, he had a right to scold her for being inadequate. "It would be rude to walk away without letting him have his say," she rationalized. Of course, she felt dreadful after these verbal onslaughts, and she retaliated with passive-aggressive behaviors that led him to scold her even more.

After realizing her attachments to passivity and to the feeling of being a disappointment, Jean finally was able to tell her husband, "Talking to me in this harsh manner is no longer acceptable. It has been our pattern in the past, and I'm not blaming you for it. I have been a part of this. I have tolerated it; I have even invited it. But it is no longer possible to proceed this way. If you're having a feeling about something to do with me, I'll certainly listen to you. But blaming me or reprimanding me is no longer an option."

Jean was able to speak up for herself in this manner because she had seen and studied how she had relinquished her authority. She had uncovered the precise manner in which she allowed others to control and define her. Her husband soon realized from the new quality in her voice and demeanor that things were indeed different and that she meant business. A relationship of mutual respect was soon established.

The Problem of Indecision

Living through a false or limited self is like trying to skirt the shoals of life without a certified navigator. We struggle to make the simplest decisions, or we frequently make poor decisions. We can see our dilemma through the symptom of indecisiveness. A classic example is the man standing in a video-store with a movie selection in each hand, studying one possibility, then the other, reading the cover text over and over, pondering assiduously for ten minutes, and then putting both videos back on the racks and leaving the store empty-handed.

Mark, a middle-aged writer plagued with ambivalence, told me, "I am a walking democracy. Or, let me put it more accurately, I'm a gaggle of committees and ministries. There's the minister of finance, who has a lot to say about what something's going to cost. Then the minister of health butts in, worrying whether I'm getting enough sleep. The minister of social services wants to know if I'm making enough new friends and taking care of current ones. The minister of education sees the pros and cons of everything—and can't get past that point. On it goes. And, of course, if one of them vetoes some option, I'm left feeling stymied. Maybe what I need is a good fascist in there to settle matters *tout de suite*."

"What is your main fear about making a decision?" I asked.

"I'm not confident it will be the right decision. It might be a decision I'll regret."

"Then you do have a tyrant in there. He's the one that jumps all over you whenever you feel or imagine you've made a bad decision. That's your self-aggression or inner critic. You are ready to get hit up by that negative energy, even at the slightest suspicion that you might have made an inferior choice. That stops you in your tracks."

"Maybe so," Mark conceded. "It's true that I can be hard on myself afterwards. But I don't think that's the whole problem. Trying to make a decision is more painful, actually, than any feelings I have after making a decision. By the way, if not a fascist, how about a CEO?"

"Okay, how about a CEO. Who would that be?"

"My rational side? I like to think that all my decisions are well thought out and rational."

"I think this so-called rationality, as you exercise it, is a cover-up for passivity."

"How so? It feels to me that making a decision, or let's say the process of making a decision, is in fact active. It certainly feels active."

"Well, it's beneficial if you're making good decisions and getting results. But some activity is the product of disharmony and a profound state of indecision. Sometimes the activity is only mental; nothing is actually being done. Your mind is spinning a million miles an hour, creating the illusion of being active, but you're going nowhere."

"That's a hard one for me to see. I know what passive is. On the weekend I cooked for my daughters, and when I put the food on the table I said to myself, 'Okay, they know it's ready. They should come.' After a few minutes of waiting I realized I was being passive, and I called for them to come."

"Yes, that's a good example, simple and straightforward. Our passivity, however, in most of its guises, is complex and heavily defended. You have to see it on those levels in order to dislodge it completely."

Mark was having this trouble finding his voice or, as he put it, the authority of the CEO inside him, because his passivity blocked that access. Crystallization of his inner forces was impeded, and he couldn't regulate or orchestrate the diverging, competing voices that, as he said, considered to exhaustion all the pros and cons, incapacitating his decision-making powers.

The indecisive person feels that, "Whatever I do is wrong. I can't make a decision or commit to anything because it will be a mistake, and I will pay dearly (in self-aggressive reproach). Therefore, I won't make any decisions or commitments." This no-win situation of doing nothing becomes intolerably painful. When this individual finally does make himself do something (decorate the house, buy a car, commit to a relationship), it can turn out to be a "bad" choice or one that he regrets, and he is thrown back into the feeling, "No matter what I do, it always turns out wrong."

A woman plagued with indecision about whether to leave her job told me, "I don't know what decision is best for me." She had been agonizing for more than a year whether to seek other employment.

"It's not a matter of what decision is best," I said. "We can't always know for sure what is best. What we can do, though, is make an informed decision and stand by it. Then your agonizing will end. That is believing in yourself, believing in your truth. It is exercising your inner authority. And if it turns out not to be a good decision, you don't second-guess yourself. You block the self-aggressive reproach by exposing its irrationality and by understanding your attachment to it. You try to learn from your mistakes at the same time that you still believe in your inner authority, understanding that it is not infallible."

How Am I Today?

We can also have trouble finding our voice or our authority because of the emotional conviction that nothing significant exists beneath the surface of ourself. As mentioned earlier, we often feel when turning inward that, "I'm nothing, I don't exist." One woman put it this way: "The only thing that seems real about me is what I'm expressing, meaning the words that I think and say, not what I am." When she tried to slip into inner silence, beyond words and thoughts, it felt to her like death, "the final aloneness," and consequently she held back from venturing inward.

One helpful technique involves learning how to communicate with ourself. The final chapter in my wife Sandra's book, *Is Anyone Listening? Repairing Broken Lines in Couples Communication*, deals with this process. In brief, it describes how we can become our own best friend. Instead of taking ourself for granted, or being our own worst enemy, we begin regularly to check in with ourself. We care enough about ourself to actually address ourself and inquire about our feelings. Sandra writes: "Soon you see that you have a friend in yourself who understands your hurts, responds to your needs, and sustains your faith in yourself."[xlviii] It is through the emergence of this friend that you know your truth and are empowered to speak it.

Before this inner friend fully emerges, however, you have to begin to engage and then to integrate the parts of you that feel rejected, abandoned, neglected, isolated, victimized, and so on. So you start by owning and accepting whatever you are experiencing or feeling. You need to become a friend to yourself as you are and refrain from rejecting yourself because you're not who you think you should be. As you dialogue, you can experience yourself from either point of view, but remember that the two speaking parts of you are ultimately one. Your inner dialogue might go like this:

Caring self: How are you feeling?

Neglected, passive me: Do you really want to know?

Caring self: I'm asking, aren't I?

Neglected, passive me: Absolutely rotten.

Caring self: What's happening?

Neglected, passive me: It's a long story.

Caring self: Come on; tell me, I'm interested.

Neglected, passive me: Well, okay. (A story or explanation follows)

Caring self: Thanks for telling me what's happening. I'm sorry you're having a hard time. Remember I'm here for you. I really care about you. Let's check in later and see what's happening.

Neglected, passive me: Okay, thanks for listening.

This is a fairly light exchange. Our exchanges with ourself can be experienced on multiple levels. Deeper, more elaborate examples are provided in *Is Anyone Listening?*

The essential point is that this conscious, directed communication with ourself, at whatever level, begins and continues the process of uniting with ourself. It is also similar to the process of making a new friend. To do so, we have to engage that person, show interest in him, and, ideally, indicate that we honor his being.

To our rational mind, such dialoguing might seem silly. But it is a very powerful technique in self-acceptance. It is, incidentally, a model of the ideal relationship between a parent and a child, wherein the parent is interested in the child's experience, allows the child to express his or her true feelings, and thus supports the child's self-expression.

Learning to love ourself involves accepting our mistakes, negative traits, and weaknesses. Through this consciously directed inner dialogue, we can explore the reasons why we don't acknowledge or love ourself and begin to override our resistance to connecting with ourself. If we don't know ourself, how can we know our truth? And if we can't be honest with ourself and speak our truth, how can we hope to express it in the world? True happiness relies on such inner self-acceptance.

We can also dialogue with our self-aggression. If we let it, our inner critic or self-aggression will demean us and undermine our sense of truth and autonomy. Dialoguing with this part of us is like going eyeball-to-eyeball with a tyrant. The technique is effective and powerful. If we have a partner who harps at us and is constantly critical, we know we have to talk to this person and resolve this difficulty if we want to establish a harmonious relationship. In a similar way, we can turn toward our self-aggression and, advocating for ourself, challenge its nitpicking, authoritative, and often vicious stance.

Self as advocate: Hello there. Yes, you. You seem to be having a problem. Do I hear you saying that I'm stupid for locking myself out of my car?

Self-aggression: That's right! It is stupid! Any fool knows better than to do that.

Self as advocate: (Speaking calmly) Locking myself out is certainly a mistake, and perhaps it's even silly of me. But it's not stupid. I know who I am and I know I'm not stupid.

Self-aggression: I say it's stupid. And I don't expect to change that opinion anytime soon.

Self as advocate: Your opinion isn't based on reality. I understand that you're simply pure self-aggression looking for an excuse to let me have it. You can go ahead all you want and criticize me. But I'm becoming less passive. I'm not as attached to feeling abused by you. I can feel that your irrational accusations have less and less power over me.

Self-aggression: You're not getting off that easy. I'll sneak in when you're asleep.

Self as advocate: I'm not afraid of you. Let me know if you ever change your mind and want to come over to my side and join forces with me. You will have to submit to my guidance and power, but I will give you room to be part of who I am.

In this next example, an attempt is made to be more compassionate toward the self-aggression and to listen to its insinuations and complaints without being defensive.

Self as advocate: Did I just hear you being critical about my efforts to manage my business?

Self-aggression: Is someone talking to me?

Self as advocate: Yes. It's me.

Self-aggression: I do indeed have criticisms.

Self as advocate: Well, would you like to talk about that?

Self-aggression: Nobody has ever asked me to talk about what I think before.

Self as advocate: Here's your chance. Go ahead. I'm listening.

Self-aggression: Okay. (There follows a series of complaints concerning the previous year's efforts with the business.)

Self as advocate: Wow, you really had a lot to say. By chance do you have any good things to say about my work over the last year?

Self-aggression: (Hesitates) Well, yeah, a few.

Self as advocate: Please tell me.

Self-aggression: Compliments and praise are not my strong point.

Self as advocate: I understand that. You're being challenged to grow and expand.

Self-aggression: (Silence)

Self as advocate: I'll be happy to dialogue with you anytime you're willing to have a discussion with me that is not all negative and one-sided. Otherwise, I won't be able to take you seriously.

Self-aggression: You did indeed succeed in a few areas. You learned a lot and you were persistent. I suppose I have to admit that the business is supporting us. (There follows more details on the areas of success.)

Self as advocate: Thank you for those words. Don't hesitate to offer a kind word now and then.

Through this process, we begin to understand that there need not be a split or separation within us between right and wrong, good or bad. We are the author of our own interpretations. Once we are inwardly integrated, we shake off our old cocoon so that our experience of ourself becomes more objective and free of infantile impressions and negative beliefs. Now the unknown stretches before us as an adventure, not something to be feared.

Things now happen in front of you but not to you. You move through your life in a state of alert awareness and accept what life brings. There are no rules to follow, none to dispute. There's nothing to fight for, nothing to oppose. Pretense and performance are dropped. Your life is a reflection of inner truth that flows naturally from within. The natural expression of your inner truth, not necessarily activism or zeal, reforms the world.

With the discovery of our truth comes trust in ourself and trust that life will support our existence and encourage our progress. Trust grows as passivity recedes. With growing trust, inner fears subside and disappear. Desires and the lure of materialism diminish because nothing in the world of sensation or matter can equal what we have discovered in ourself. There is no need for hope or salvation or other bothers about the future. The future is secured in the quality of our present relationship with ourself.

As I was working on this book, I continued to have encounters with my passivity. One night I had two "passivity dreams," as I call them. In one I was playing golf badly, unable to hit a decent shot. In the other I was waiting around for another man (who in real life I know to be quite passive) to finish some work that was taking forever.

On awakening I began to reflect on where and how in my life I was being passive. I considered several possibilities and then realized what it was. I had been following very closely the Florida recount in the 2000 election, reading my newspaper, watching the evening news, and then tuning in to the evening television talk shows. I was feeding off the excitement, inserting myself emotionally into the drama and speculating along with the media hosts and guests about evidence, strategies, and outcome.

Following the developments in this exciting event was one thing, vesting myself so completely into it was another. As I sat before my television set into the evening, I had been allowing the verbal and visual excitement to override my equanimity. All the hoopla about great moments in history was overshadowing my own experience of my life and of myself. Expressed another way, I was mesmerized by, as the pundits put it, "the magnitude of the issue." I had, on entering this fray, checked my inner harmony at the door.

I continued to follow the news of the historic election and its aftermath, but at a more discreet distance.

The terrorist attack of September 11, 2001, and subsequent events are now churning up the collective unconscious. We now enter a wrinkle in time that I believe will expose truth and falsehood on many levels. Our collective destiny is to grow in consciousness and love, while our individual souls are enjoined to leave the world a better place. To turn our back on our destiny is to engender depression, disruption, disaster, and disease. Destiny is in our hands. With our truth in the vanguard, the evolutionary clock can jump ahead an hour or more to "human-saving" time. Consciousness, acting faster than a speeding computer chip, can shatter old configurations in the blink of an insight.

Epilogue
Now's the Time

Our problems and those of the world are due more to passivity and the roots of our psychology than to symptoms such as greed, hatred, and aggression. All the good and all the bad are reflections of our nature.[xlix]

When we break into a new level of awareness, we access more wisdom and power. Creative energy is released to beneficial use when no longer bound up in psychic defenses and repression. In freeing ourself from inner passivity, we greatly enhance our intelligence. In the darkness of our psyche, however, the maintenance of defenses and repression is more important than truth or objective understanding.

So much is at stake. Our world needs inspired intelligence and leadership—our leadership—to solve the enormous problems of war, civil rights abuses, terrorism, pollution, injustice, health care, wildlife protection, education, and resource allocation.

For each individual, the present is the best time to address inner passivity. Tomorrow it will be harder, the day after harder still. The hero accepts the call, plunging into mystery, darkness, even chaos—all elements of the unconscious.

It's time to discover who we truly are, to know we are extended beings of light and love. We have been experiencing ourselves in limited, painful ways as we search outside ourself for value, wisdom, and salvation. Everything is in place for a golden age of humankind, and each of us contributes to it when we are conscious of spirit supporting our existence and our purpose, as we connect to our being, our true Self. It's time to realize our destiny, to be one with ourself, each other, and all existence.

We have shut ourselves off from the divine source within, in part because we are enthralled with what is external and seduced by the pride we feel in our ability to understand, manipulate, and profit from the world around us. We go looking for sensation, value, and wisdom outside ourself when our own being is richness beyond our imagination, an eternal consciousness capable of the greatest pleasures, feats, and joys.

To know this, we need to see it, so that it is real for us and is known through our own experience, not just a figment of the intellect or a fanciful dream we wish to believe. The inner revolution starts with ourself, by engaging the specter of inner passivity, the ethereal phantom that mesmerizes us, leading us away from ourself into foolishness, doubt, and calamity.

All of us are stuck with unconscious patterns and expectations that are unresolved from childhood and that bind us to a narrow, fragmented, and often painful sense of who we are. Liberation requires that we explore the realms of unconscious patterns that rule our way of perceiving and interpreting the world, in order to discover insight into the desires, motives, and compulsions behind our surface feelings and behaviors. We also must contend with our great resistance to exposing our unconscious collusion in the negative outcomes of our lives.

With greater understanding of these inner dynamics, we can forge a new relationship with ourself, as we move away from playing victim and claiming entitlements, and begin at last to accept fully on an emotional level the premise that we are heroes, sovereign keepers of eternal kingdoms, here with our fellow loved ones to secure our own redemption, to manifest our collective glory, and to fulfill our destiny.

We are living in a time that places many challenges upon us. Society values and rewards us according to our talent, our abilities in the workplace, the image we project, and often for conformity, rather than for just being who we are and expressing the truth of ourselves. Many of our contributions as wife, husband, father, mother, student, and worker are not recognized or appreciated by society. Still, the stress of such external circumstances are minor compared with the power of internal or psychological factors to hold us back and to separate us from each other and from ourself.

So it's time to stop the futile exercise of restructuring the external in the attempt to solve our personal problems. It's time to stop blaming others and to face our secret willingness to feel that some outside force (whether a spouse, a supervisor, our children, the government, the majority, and so on) opposes our happiness and inhibits our self-expression.

It's time to transcend outdated notions of right and wrong, to see that greater understanding comes not from warring among ourselves over good and bad but from the support and compassion we have for ourself and each other. It's time to choose to make our life and relationships work, rather than passively waiting for things to be the way we want or hope.

It's time to expose the self-sabotaging patterns we have carried forward from childhood and to see these elements operating in the collective, so that we can understand and overcome the self-destructive tendencies that humanity has perpetuated for thousands of years. It's time to recognize the extent of our self-doubt, self-rejection, and self-hatred, and to begin to appreciate the enormous resistance we have to slipping free of negativity to embrace the light within ourself.

We all can feel vulnerable, weak, negative, fearful, confused, and empty. Help is needed to deal with these emotions and challenges, and it is available when we connect to the deepest part of our being, where we feel and learn honor, respect, and love for ourself. In respecting the integrity of our being, we respect the integrity of others and all living things.

An inner conflict common to us all is the battle between feelings of having power and being powerless. We struggle often to make something happen, to change others, to get our way and get what we want, and to feel in control. Then we turn around and in anguish feel passive, like failures, used or manipulated, under the influence of others and our desires, habits, and addictions. When we connect with ourself and embrace our being, we feel as if we have plugged into a cosmic power source. The duality between feeling power and feeling powerless falls away. We step forward just being ourself—loose, open, natural, and supported by all of life.

In discovering the great treasure in ourself, we now feel that all life has value, that every conscious action we take has value. We can throw out the old value scorecard, based on social and parental judgment and expectations, and see the value in doing even nothing, just in being alert and observing consciously, with no insistence that anyone or anything be different.

When Christine kisses the phantom at the end of the opera, redemption happens. In her gracious act of mercy and love, he is freed from further need to suffer. Now he can depart the scene, bow out of the heroine's life, and retire into the void.

So too with inner passivity: it needs to be embraced. It will haunt our lives and thwart our love until we turn and face it, recognize it flittering in the shadows, and call out to it both a warning and a supplication.

The warning call sings out, "We will not live in the shadow of our false self; we will not be less than who we are; we will find ourself and secure our freedom."

Our supplication to the phantom follows: "Yes, you are real. You are more than just an outline in the gloom. I honor your presence as I begin to see you more clearly. You too are me. You are not my enemy. I must ask, however, as you come fully into focus and I break free of your alluring spell, that you be so kind as to take your bow and retire to the wings."

Now, should I hesitate before the radiance of who I truly am, it is I, not the phantom, who stands in my way.

Appendix

How to Identify Your Form of Passivity

As a reader of this book, you have likely recognized elements of your passivity. Passivity is an emotional attachment. That means that you are unconsciously compelled in various circumstances to experience yourself through passivity and to pay the price by limiting yourself, defeating yourself, and making yourself miserable.

Passivity has many variations or flavors. It is important for your sake to understand your versions and expressions of it as precisely as possible. Does your passivity take the form of being tempted to feel deprived or refused? Or is it related to feeling controlled and helpless? Does it consist of your attachment to feeling excluded or dismissed? Your passivity can encompass some or all of these attachments and more.

First Step. Write a list of what you feel is missing in your life right now. State what you want as specifically as possible. Elaborate on any concerns or fears.

For example, "I want more money and a more successful career. Money and success will give me security and a feeling of having enough. Right now, I feel I don't have enough and worry that what I have I'll lose." (This statement reveals an emotional attachment to the feeling of being deprived, missing out, and expecting loss.) Once you have identified such an attachment, you need to begin to take responsibility for your secret willingness to experience yourself and life through that passive feeling.

282

Second Step. Write why you want each item on this list. Example: "I would like a million dollars because then I could do what I want. I would be free, independent, and not have to take orders from anyone." (This reveals a secret attachment to feeling restricted and controlled.)

Third Step. Write out excuses for each item on the list. Why have you not manifested these wishes in your life? Example: "I was lazy and didn't do chores well enough. Now I feel I'm not good enough to go ahead and be successful." (This reveals an attachment to feeling criticized, by others and by yourself, and to experiencing yourself through doubt and uncertainty.)

Fourth Step. Now write out how you are responsible for not having what you want in your life. Example: "I take jobs that are beneath my abilities and that don't pay enough." (This can reveal an attachment to various feelings—being deprived, helpless, or criticized.) You may have to do this exercise a few times to be confident that you have clearly identified one or more emotional attachments.

Fifth Step. Having identified your forms of passivity, be alert to them. Be wary of situations in which they are likely to be felt. Watch for how you slip into the negative feeling and react defensively. Look inward past your defensiveness to see clearly the negative emotion with which you are willing to get "hit up." Pay attention to how your passivity interferes with your goals and aspirations. When you see your passivity kicking in, you have a chance to avoid becoming entangled emotionally in it.

The Breath of Life

Sometimes passivity sits very heavily upon us. Psychological insight is the best remedy to push it away. At times, however, we may need additional help, such as deep breathing that charges up our body with energy.

Stand with your feet shoulder width apart in front of a chair. Arch your back slightly and lean your head back as you draw in a breath through your nostrils.

Quickly bend forward at your waist at least 45 degrees and, as your stomach contracts, expel the air through your mouth. (As you become more comfortable with this exercise, you can begin to expel the air through your nostrils.) Immediately lift your upper body and repeat the in-breath through your nostrils. Then exhale again through your mouth, bending forward.

The complete motion—inhaling and exhaling—can take three or four seconds.

Do three or four motions and stop. Monitor how you feel. You may feel dizzy and have slight pressure in your head. Sit on the chair and place the tip of your tongue on the roof of your mouth. This will circulate the energy in your head down through the front of your body. (Don't do this exercise in the evening unless you want to stay awake later at night.)

Observe any variance in your energy as a result of doing this exercise. On the side of caution, decide how often you want to do it and how many repetitions are right for you. Be conscious also of what difference it makes for you in creativity and alertness. If you feel that you benefit from this procedure and yet stop doing it after several days, your resistance to growth and empowerment may be intruding.

Standing Room Only

One way to practice freeing yourself of passivity is to imagine you are standing in a room where one side represents being in your passivity and the other side represents being free of it. In any experience, you want to be conscious of whether you are stranded in your passivity or standing clear of it.

Suppose through some experience or situation you feel you are slipping into passivity. For the purpose of this exercise, this corresponds to sliding or stepping into the passive side of the room. As you stand there, don't fight what is happening. Monitor yourself. Be aware of being in passivity. This awareness alone can help you from slipping further into it (or stepping deeper into the passive side of the room) and can make it possible for you to take a step or two toward the other liberated side of the room.

As you stand there you can say to yourself something to the effect of, "I am experiencing myself and this situation through my passivity. I can feel the unpleasantness of it. I would like to be able to move out of it and step into the clear side of the room."

This declaration represents intention. You are indicating you want to be free of passivity, and this act of positive intent can help you take a step or two in the right direction.

You go on to say (or to realize), "I am secretly willing to experience myself through my passivity. I am emotionally attached to this way of knowing myself. I am tempted to go on knowing myself through this familiar old feeling."

This awareness, you may feel, gives you the ability to move a few more steps toward the clear side of the room.

Now you say to yourself, "This passive feeling does not represent the truth of who I am. I am not this passive experience. I am not this passivity. I may not know as yet who I truly am—but I know I am not this passivity. I wish to throw it off."

Try now to feel that, in this state of inner awareness, you are able to tap into inner strength. Look to yourself, believe in yourself, as a source of inner strength. Imagine this strength beginning to expand from within you.

This final phase may get you, figuratively, into the clear side of the room. And if it doesn't, that is okay. It will stabilize you nonetheless. Keep practicing this exercise. The deeper you realize the truth of your being, as you are exposing on a feeling level the fact of your attachment to passivity, the sooner you will feel new power.

Discriminating Against Negative Feelings

Many of us repress what is dark and negative about ourselves because we associate goodness and spirituality with what is positive and light. We attempt the spiritual bypass when we overlook or spurn the need to work out our negative attitudes, beliefs, and feelings. If negative emotions do come up, we feel contaminated by them. We try frantically to fix them, banish them, or pretend they are nonexistent or not a real problem.

When we censor our negative emotions and try to act good, our underlying negativity does not go away. We feel anxious that these "bad" feelings or thoughts will resurface, and consequently we live in fear of our feelings. We create a greater division within ourself, a division between the "right" part and the "wrong" part, and these parts are perpetually in conflict with each other.

When we act and sound spiritual according to someone else's specifications, we hand over our power to others in the same manner we adopted our parents' conditioning as our own. We thereby squelch the truth of our feelings and abort the prospect of becoming more aware. The negative elements inside us can be understood as our growing edge, the underworld through which we must journey to get to our true Self. Rather than running from our negative feelings and self-defeating behaviors, we need to acknowledge them, discover where they come from, and learn the meaning behind them.

Becoming a Nonjudgmental Observer of Yourself

Spiritual and psychological growth is an emotional experience (not an intellectual exercise) in which you come to know yourself intimately—your positive and negative traits, thoughts, and feelings. It requires a spontaneous, nonjudgmental way of relating to yourself and the world.[1]

Notice how much time you spend on feeling disappointment in others, feeling bad about yourself, bemoaning what you are not getting, feeling controlled or trapped, experiencing rejection and criticism, wallowing in past grievances or emotional injuries, fantasizing about the future, worrying and imagining catastrophes, and feeling overwhelmed by to-do lists and chores.

Whenever we are in the "observer mode," we are less reactive, more powerful, and more able to see ourself slipping into the above behaviors. It is important to learn how to observe our reactions, to know what we feel, and to understand where our feelings come from within ourself. Admit what you feel. If you're feeling hurt or used, acknowledge it to yourself. Observe what you're feeling in a neutral, curious manner.

The purpose of nonjudgmental observing is to break the barrier between the conscious and the unconscious mind. When we observe, we create a distance or "breathing room" between other people, our reactions, and ourself. We can be more aware of what happens inside us, without blindly reacting to others or outside events.

So try to observe with neutrality your fears, fantasies, frustrations, thoughts, judgments, criticisms, complaints, and other emotional reactions. In doing so, you are enacting your intention to understand the origins of these feelings within yourself. Usually, we're making someone or something else responsible for these feelings, or we're trying to get rid of them because "they're bad." Start by watching how your awareness is drawn outside of yourself. Let's look at an example. Your husband leaves his clothes all over the floor. You become angry and upset. All you can think about is how sloppy and inconsiderate he is. You are so wrapped up in his behavior that you forget yourself. You are taken away from yourself by your reaction.

Using the observer technique, you watch yourself reacting and getting caught up in his behavior. Notice the feelings that you have created inside yourself as a result of his behavior. Why are these feelings there? Does his behavior really justify such powerful negative feelings in you? Why are you taking things so personally?

As you observe your reaction, perhaps you can say to yourself, "Hey, I really have a strong reaction to this. This is interesting. I must be taking his behavior as a slight against me, as if he does it to ruin my day. Or, I feel that he is discounting me and my needs, and I am sensitive to that feeling from childhood and still resonate with it, and deep down I discount myself and my own existence."

See the other person's behavior and your reaction. You will experience the observer when you can bring both into your awareness at the same time. You can also calmly and objectively decide what you might say to your partner to help him become more sensitive to your experience and the difficulty you are having with his inconsiderate behavior.

If you care to, take time each day for one week to observe and write down your thoughts and feelings about others and yourself; any preoccupation with past or present emotional grievances or hurts; reflections on future scenarios, whether positive or negative; concerns about chores that have to be done; creative ideas; any peeping at what others have attained or accumulated and comparing yourself with them; distress about what you feel you're not getting; fears and worries; emotional ups and downs; and likes and dislikes.

Notice how much time you spend on each of the above categories. Watch how your feelings come and go and how they may build up into powerful emotional reactions that overwhelm you, perhaps resulting in your saying things you later regret. The observer makes no judgment against us. It is the viewpoint of detached compassion, so different from the self-aggressive energy we are often experiencing and absorbing. The observer is also interested in understanding and truth, so much unlike the inner tyrant, who values secrecy and opposes our well-being.

Just this one powerful exercise can help you move away from your preoccupation with what others are doing or not doing and how much the outer world is either supporting you or against you. You will be able to see that your reactions come from inside yourself, that your feelings and thoughts are self-generated and have more to do with your own relationship with yourself than with anyone or anything else.

Learning to observe without judgment gives us a neutral perspective from which to learn about ourself and how we interact with others and the world. It takes practice to become aware of your feelings and reactions as they occur and to watch yourself react. The trick is simply to watch. Don't try to change anything. Just observe how it happens. Statements such as "I shouldn't be feeling this way" or "Stop thinking like this" can be judgmental and have the effect of repressing what we're feeling.

Soon you will be able to discern the motivations behind your feelings and actions. This ability will result in enhanced feelings of empowerment, of being in charge of yourself and your life. You will learn to befriend yourself and connect with yourself in ways you never thought possible.

Benefits of Reclaiming Our Self

Acknowledging our resistance to letting go of self-negating patterns, attitudes, doubts, and fears through the process of inner dialoguing takes us to a whole new way of relating to ourself. The following is a list of qualities and characteristics that are brought forth as we discover ourself:

1 - We engage in life and our relationships with joy, humor, and compassionate detachment.

2 - We adopt a non-judgmental, curious attitude toward our feelings, thoughts, motives, and behaviors, without fear or shame for acknowledging our deepest quirks, flaws, and truths. We accept ourself completely with compassion and humor, with the understanding that failure and "badness" do not matter so much as lessons, learning, intentions, and insights.

3 - We move beyond personal, parental, social, and planetary boundaries, beyond beliefs, norms, roles, rules, approval, group identifications, gender identifications, and self-image, into the full expression of ourself, not with fear or shame but with confidence, contentment, honor, and reverence for who we are.

4 - We reach out without fear or shame to express our love, compassion, and joy outwardly, sharing of ourself spontaneously from our heart, letting others see and experience the true beauty of who we are.

5 - We realize our ability to create and manifest our own original ideas, feelings, aspirations, and visions. We express compassionate detachment in our interactions with others, allowing others to work through their own problems and take responsibility for their emotional issues, while exuding a loving concern for their predicament with no investment in the outcome.

6 - We express and manifest the principle of co-creative cooperation in all aspects of our lives, inner as well as outer, working together with ourself and with others, contributing equally, participating equally, in our own personal as well as planetary evolvement.

7 - We rest in security, belief, trust, and confidence in ourself, trusting explicitly in a positive and beneficial future, as opposed to emotional dependence on external, imagined security or reliance on outside authorities.

8 - We are open to and curious about the nature of other realities. We accept knowledge and insight into our Self with a loving heart and eager mind. We have reverence for all life and regard other life as equal to our own, including animal and plant life forms.

9 - We are willing to explore and manifest our powers and abilities, our limitlessness, our love and compassion, our creativity, our intellectual abilities and knowledge, and our bliss and joy in service of others. We pursue our aspirations, visions, and life's purpose, and aligning with our Self we freely acknowledge the need for assistance and guidance, while co-creatively fulfilling our mission for this lifetime.

Bibliography

Assagioli, Roberto, M.D. *The Act of Will*. Penguin Books Inc., New York, NY. 1973.

Bentov, Itzhak. *Stalking the Wild Pendulum: On the Mechanics of Consciousness*. Destiny Books, Rochester, VT. 1988.

Bergler, Edmund. *Principles of Self-Damage*. International Universities Press, Madison, CT. 1992. (Originally published by Philosophical Library Inc. 1959. Republished by Intercontinental Medical Book Corp, 1974.)

Bergler, Edmund. *The Psychology of Gambling*. International Universities Press, Madison, CT. 1974.

Bergler, Edmund. *The Superego*. International Universities Press, Madison, CT. 1952.

Bergler, Edmund. T*he Talent for Stupidity: The Psychology of the Bungler, the Incompetent, and the Ineffectual*. International Universities Press, Madison, CT. 1998.

Conroy, John. *Unspeakable Acts, Ordinary People: The Dynamics of Torture*. Alfred A. Knopf, New York, NY. 2000.

Davis, Russell H., *Freud's Concept of Passivity*. International Universities Press, Madison, CT. 1993.

Dossey, Larry, M.D. *Space, Time & Medicine*. Shambhala, London and New York, NY. 1982.

Fromm, Erich. *For the Love of Life*. The Free Press, New York, NY. 1986.

Gay, Peter, ed. *The Freud Reader*. W.W. Norton & Co., New York, NY. 1989.

Hixon, Lex. *Great Swan: Meetings with Ramakrishna*. Shambhala. London and New York, NY. 1992.

Malcolm, Janet. *Psychoanalysis: The Impossible Profession*. Alfred A. Knopf, New York, NY. 1981.

Marvin W. Meyer, trans. *The Secret Teachings of Jesus: Four Gnostic Gospels*. Vintage Books, New York, NY. 1986.

Osho. *Returning to the Source*. Element Books, Shaftesbury, England. 1995.

Purdy, Jedediah. *For Common Things: Irony, Trust, And Commitment in America Today*. Vintage Books, New York, NY. 1999, 2000.

Roheim, Geza. *Psychoanalysis and Anthropology: Culture, Personality, and the Unconscious*. International Universities Press, New York, NY. 1950.

Shah, Idries. *The Sufis*. W.H. Allen & Co, London. 1964.

Spence, Gerry. *Give Me Liberty: Freeing Ourselves in the Twenty-First Century*. St. Martin's Press, New York, NY. 1998.

The Upanishads. Penguin Books, New York, NY. 1965.

Yogananda, Paramahansa. *Wine of the Mystic*. Self-Realization Fellowship, Los Angeles, CA. 1994.

Notes

---

[i] Roberto Assagioli, M.D. *The Act of Will*, Penguin Books Inc., New York, NY. 1973.

[ii] Paper by Nordic Winch, of Naples, Florida, distributed for the purpose of psychotherapeutic training.

[iii] Ibid.

[iv] Laurie Hays. "Computers: PCs may be teaching kids the wrong lessons." *The Wall Street Journal*. April 24, 1995. p. B1.

[v] Arthur Krystal. "Who speaks for the lazy? Skirting success is harder than it looks." *The New Yorker*. April 26, 1999. p. 106.

[vi] Gerry Spence. *Give Me Liberty: Freeing Ourselves in the Twenty-First Century*. St. Martin's Press, New York, NY. 1998. p. 8.

[vii] Ibid, p. 12.

[viii] Ibid, pp. 76—77.

[ix] Peter Gay, ed., *The Freud Reader*. W.W. Norton & Co., New York, NY. 1989. p. 760.

[x] Edmund Bergler. *The Superego*. International Universities Press, Madison, CT. 1952, 1989. p. 7.

[xi] Russell H. Davis. *Freud's Concept of Passivity*. International Universities Press, Madison, CT. 1993. p. 4.

[xii] Gay, *The Freud Reader*, pp. 703—704.

[xiii] Lionel Trilling. *The Experience of Literature: Poetry.* Holt, Rinehart, and Winston. New York, NY. 1967. pp. 143—144.

[xiv] Ibid, p. 144.

[xv] Edmund Bergler. *The Talent for Stupidity: The Psychology of the Bungler, the Incompetent, and the Ineffectual.* International Universities Press, Madison, CT. 1998. pp. 30—31. This book was published under the auspices of the Edmund and Marianne Bergler Psychiatric Foundation, forty-six years after Bergler completed writing it in 1952.

[xvi] Geza Roheim. *Psychoanalysis and Anthropology: Culture, Personality, and the Unconscious.* International Universities Press, New York. NY. 1950. p. 409.

[xvii] Bergler, *The Superego*, p. 38.

[xviii] This is perhaps the most contentious and challenging theory in psychoanalysis. Just as many doctrines have their secret knowledge, this is the equivalent in psychoanalysis. This knowledge is based on the work of Edmund Bergler (1899—1962), author of twenty-four books and almost three hundred articles published in medical and psychiatric journals. Up to now we have been too defended against a more open-minded appraisal of his work.

[xix] Nicola Gavey, Kathryn McPhillips. "Subject to romance: Heterosexual passivity as an obstacle to women initiating condom use." *Psychology of Women Quarterly*, Cambridge, MA. June 1999. pp. 349—367.

[xx] Sandra Michaelson. *LoveSmart: Transforming the Emotional Patterns That Sabotage Relationships.* Prospect

Books, Santa Fe, NM. 1999. pp. 102—105.

[xxi] Spence, *Give Me Liberty*, p. 152.

[xxii] John Conroy. *Unspeakable Acts, Ordinary People: The Dynamics of Torture.* Alfred A. Knopf, New York, NY. 2000.

[xxiii] Marvin W. Meyer, trans. *The Secret Teachings of Jesus: Four Gnostic Gospels.* Vintage Books, New York, NY. 1986. p. 19.

[xxiv] Ibid, p. 41.

[xxv] *The Upanishads.* Penguin Books, New York, NY. p. 49.

[xxvi] David L. Wheeler. "Stress is found to hasten the onset of AIDS in men infected with the virus." *The Chronicle of Higher Education.* June 4, 1999. p. A18.

[xxvii] Erica Goode. "Ideas & Trends: Your mind may ease what's ailing you." *The New York Times*, Week in Review section. April 18, 1999.

[xxviii] Kim A. McDonald. "Atherosclerosis linked to sense of hopelessness." *The Chronicle of Higher Education.* Sept. 5, 1997. p. A26.

[xxix] This material under the subhead, "Emotional Resistance to Physical Health," is taken, in some places verbatim, from an article written by Sandra Michaelson.

[xxx] Alexander Lowen, M.D. "Breathing, Movement, and Feeling." Institute for Bioenergetic Analysis lectures given at the Hotel Biltmore, New York City. Fall 1965. p. 2.

[xxxi] Ibid, p. 3.

[xxxii] Jane E. Brody. "Personal Health: Detecting colon cancer

when it is curable." *The New York Times*. September 28, 1999.

xxxiii Larry Dossey, M.D. *Space, Time & Medicine*. Shambhala, London and New York, NY. 1982. p. 21.

xxxiv Ibid, p. 25.

xxxv Ibid, p. 54.

xxxvi Erich Fromm. *For the Love of Life*. The Free Press, New York, NY. 1986. p. 35.

xxxvii Dossey, *Space, Time & Medicine*, pp. 54—55.

xxxviii Dr. David G. Williams. *Alternatives*. Vol. 8, No. 7. Mountain Home Publishing, Ingram, TX. January 2000. p. 1.

xxxix Kathleen Fackelmann. "Stress, unhealthy habits costing USA: Estimated annual tab is $250 billion." *USA Today*. October 3, 2000. p. 5A.

xl Mary Ellen Lerner. "Facing your fear." *USA Weekend*. September 29—October1, 2000. p. 8.

xli Ibid.

xlii L.J. Davis. "The Encyclopedia of Insanity." *Harper's*. February 1997. p. 64.

xliii Ibid, p. 62.

xliv "Insomnia: Six poems by Jorge Luis Borges." *Harper's*. February 1999. p. 50.

xlv Mark Schoofs. "Freud vs. Prozac: The architect of the unconscious faces his greatest challenge." *The Village Voice*. October 20, 1998. p. 40.

[xlvi] Greg Critser. "Let them eat fat: The heavy truths about American obesity." *Harper's*. March 2000. p. 41.

[xlvii] Edmund Bergler. *The Psychology of Gambling*. International Universities Press, Madison, CT. 1974. pp. 106—107.

[xlviii] Sandra Michaelson. *Is Anyone Listening? Repairing Broken Lines in Couples Communication*. Prospect Books, Santa Fe, NM, 1999. p.149.

[xlix] Notes by Sandra Michaeslon contributed to the writing of this Epilogue.

[l] Sandra Michaelson wrote "Becoming a Nonjudgmental Observer of Yourself ", as well as the section in the Appendix, "Benefits of Reclaiming Our Self."

Made in the USA
Columbia, SC
18 August 2020

16687992R00181